China from the Inside

Liam Brunt

China from the Inside

Letters from an Economist

palgrave
macmillan

Liam Brunt
Norwegian School of Economics
Bergen, Norway

ISBN 978-3-319-65671-7   ISBN 978-3-319-65672-4 (eBook)
https://doi.org/10.1007/978-3-319-65672-4

Library of Congress Control Number: 2017952100

© The Editor(s) (if applicable) and The Author(s) 2017
This work is subject to copyright. All rights are solely and exclusively licensed by the Publisher, whether the whole or part of the material is concerned, specifically the rights of translation, reprinting, reuse of illustrations, recitation, broadcasting, reproduction on microfilms or in any other physical way, and transmission or information storage and retrieval, electronic adaptation, computer software, or by similar or dissimilar methodology now known or hereafter developed.
The use of general descriptive names, registered names, trademarks, service marks, etc. in this publication does not imply, even in the absence of a specific statement, that such names are exempt from the relevant protective laws and regulations and therefore free for general use.
The publisher, the authors and the editors are safe to assume that the advice and information in this book are believed to be true and accurate at the date of publication. Neither the publisher nor the authors or the editors give a warranty, express or implied, with respect to the material contained herein or for any errors or omissions that may have been made. The publisher remains neutral with regard to jurisdictional claims in published maps and institutional affiliations.

Cover Image © Bernhard Schmid / Alamy Stock Photo
Cover design by Samantha Johnson

Printed on acid-free paper

This Palgrave Macmillan imprint is published by Springer Nature
The registered company is Springer International Publishing AG
The registered company address is: Gewerbestrasse 11, 6330 Cham, Switzerland

*To Mum and Dad,
who taught me that
there is more than one way
to skin a cat.*

Preface

These letters offer an unusual perspective on China. We are a Western family who went to live and work in China for seven months more-or-less off our own bat (i.e. not sponsored by a foreign company). This means that we lived entirely outside the expat "bubble". My wife and I are university professors who decided to take a sabbatical at a university in Beijing. So we had some help with visas and accommodation from our Chinese hosts (which is essential—otherwise I don't see how you can even get a visa) but not nearly as much as someone on an expat "package". Hence, we had to do a lot of the administration ourselves; we lived in a Chinese part of Beijing; we sent our children to the local Chinese school; we used the local hospital. We cannot claim that we experienced China in the same way as a Chinese person: that would clearly be impossible, even if we spoke perfect Mandarin, because we are obviously Western (Caucasian) and people would react to us differently. But I do believe that we experienced life in China much closer to the way that Chinese people experience it, compared to the vast majority of westerners.

I have always preferred to go and live in a foreign country than visit as a tourist. This invariably involves far more hassle (opening a bank account, getting a telephone, sorting out schooling and so on). But you learn a lot about the people and the culture and the politics and the economy by tackling all those issues. We certainly learnt a lot from our time in China.

Some of it was reminiscent of my childhood (England in the 1970s); some of it sounds like the Soviet Bloc (judging by stories told to me by Eastern European friends from before the fall of Communism); and some of it was simply unique. Some things turned out to be much easier than I had feared, such as settling the children into school. But a thousand other things—which it never even occurred to me would even be an issue—turned out to be problematic or impossible to solve. Life in China is very different to life in the West, but in the most unexpected ways. As a business school professor, I am staggered that China manages to be so successful on the world stage and I really wonder how much longer it can continue.

Dramatis personae

Liam Brunt. Husband and father. Economics Professor at the Norwegian School of Economics.

Lucy White. Wife and mother. Finance Professor at Boston University. Attended high school in Hong Kong. Has some grasp of Mandarin.

Annabelle Brunt. Eldest daughter (aged 8). Started attending the French school in Boston aged four, and began learning Mandarin around the same time. Known as Bai Xiang An ("Bye Shang An") (白湘安) in China. Bai means "white"; An means "peaceful".

Catherine Brunt. Middle daughter (aged 7). Started attending the French school in Boston aged three, and began learning Mandarin around the same time. Known as Bai Xiang Yu (白湘玉) in China. Yu means "jade".

Elizabeth Brunt. Youngest daughter (aged 5). Started attending the French school in Boston aged three, and began learning Mandarin around the same time. Known as Bai Xiang Lan (白湘兰) in China. Lan means "orchid".

Lily. Young Chinese person who lived with the family for a while in Boston to help teach the girls Mandarin. Also helped the family during their time in Beijing.

Fig. 1. Map of China, showing important places visited.

Fig. 2. Elizabeth at school on a smoggy day.

Fig. 3. Catherine climbing on the exercise equipment for old people, watching the retirees playing mahjong at our local park.

Fig. 4. Annabelle helping with the cooking on our military expedition.

Acknowledgements

I must first thank my children for inspiring us to undertake this adventure: without their dedication to studying Chinese language and culture, this trip would never have been conceived and certainly never borne such interesting fruit. I must then thank our university and school hosts in Beijing for making the whole thing possible. I hope that we will be able to enjoy their welcome again in the future to deepen our understanding.

We are eternally grateful to the many Chinese friends who helped us adapt and thrive, and took us into their homes and their trust. The most unique experiences and insights come from the amazing times that we shared with them in Beijing and all across China. They know who they are—many of their stories are retold in these pages—and it would be impolite to name them.

For valuable discussion, and feedback on the manuscript, I am very grateful to Dan Friel, Oliver Grant, Ken Marden, Olivia Milbourn and Will Pack.

Contents

Letter 1	Life on Mars	1
Letter 2	Getting There	7
Letter 3	A Poison Pen Letter	17
Letter 4	The Temple of Heaven	23
Letter 5	When the Chips Are Down	27
Letter 6	Building Sights	31
Letter 7	Xi'an	37
Letter 8	A Week of Firsts	55

Letter 9	Safety and Security	71
Letter 10	A Cup of Tea and a Nice Sit Down	87
Letter 11	"You're in the Army, Now"	123
Letter 12	Inner Mongolia	139
Letter 13	"School's Out for Summer, School's Out for…"	161
Letter 14	Journey to the West, Part 1	175
Letter 15	The Journey to the West, Part 2	207
Letter 16	Huaguoshan and Guizhou	241
Letter 17	*The Art of the Steal*	263
Letter 18	Hukou's There?	275
Letter 19	China's "Japan Moment"	295
Index		313

Letter 1

Life on Mars
4 March 2016

Dear Alan,

You probably know that we have now arrived in Beijing. We spent the month of January travelling, since it was Chinese school holidays before the New Year arrived on 8th February. So we actually touched down in Beijing on 20th February, having had to go back to London to change visa status (more on which later!). I have been writing down my first impressions for the amusement of my friends—and to vent my spleen. (You are really just a cheap form of therapy—unless you start sending me invoices, at which point I shall stop emailing.)

We have a nice apartment arranged by our hosts—big by Beijing standards (three bedrooms), hardwood floors—although it was in a shocking state when we arrived. (It was very dirty—the kitchen was really foul—so I have been scraping and scrubbing like Cinderella. I don't think that my fingernails will ever be the same again.) When we arrived at the apartment, the comment of the person who saw us in was that it was "OK now that they had cleaned it and replaced the furniture". I don't think that she was joking; they just live in grime here on a daily basis. (Stir-fry has a lot to answer for—the kitchen was covered in a layer of emulsified grease. In fact, this is now recognized as such a problem in China that some cities are trying to ban street vendors from cooking food in order to cut down pollution!) I was somewhat prepared for this after our January travels (if people cannot clean a posh hotel properly, then what can be expected to clean?) but I sadly had to rectify this deficiency, since I just cannot stand to live in a dirty apartment.

Getting things done here is hard work. You go to register with the police; then you go to register with the police (again); then you go for a health check; then you go for a health check (again); then you take your child for a health check (at a different clinic); then you go to open a bank account; then you go to open a bank account (again).... Obviously, if you have to do every job three or four times, then you don't get much done in a day. The level of bureaucracy and inefficiency here is unbelievable. Maybe not for your colleague Peter, because he was born under Hungarian Communism, but for those of us who have a more rational benchmark. It even makes Oxford look progressive! Naturally, everything here is "Made in China"—which is not generally taken as a stamp of high quality and which can be hard to cope with on a daily basis. My sink started flooding the kitchen yesterday morning and I had to call two different plumbers to the apartment to fix it, which basically took the whole day and involved a lot of additional cleaning on my part, since they pumped slurry out the pipe and flooded the kitchen floor (twice—and didn't clean up after themselves once). Last week, I already had the water pipes changed on two toilets and the taps changed on the washbasin—not because I am fussy but because they were leaking all over the floor; and I had the drains in the bathroom floor rodded because they smelled so bad that it was difficult to sleep. So I am becoming firm friends with the plumber already.

In fact, living in China makes me feel like Matt Damon in "The Martian"—which is a good film, if you ever have time to see it. Life is a constant struggle for oxygen, potable water and edible food. I brought a ceramic water filter with us to purify the tap water and have then been boiling it. Obviously, you cannot eat the skin of anything (because you cannot be sure that it is not covered in excrement or pesticides), so we are peeling everything. And I have had the facemasks in operation against the pollution. We were very lucky with the pollution in the first week; it was sunny and very windy—which takes the pollution out to sea—so the city seemed no more polluted than London or Paris. Now it is pretty bad (400, on a scale of 0–500) and you cannot see the end of the street.

I bought big air filtration units for the house and we are wearing face-masks to walk the children to school. I have an app on the phone that updates me constantly on the pollution outside (so that I know whether to wear the mask) and inside (so that I can make sure the air filters are turned up enough). So it is really like living in a space station, with a hostile environment outside. Fun, isn't it?

The girls have started school and are amazingly happy with it. Indeed, I am quite proud of them for the way that they have adapted. The Chinese is no problem (actually, Elizabeth seems to know more characters than anyone else in kindergarten and complains that it is rather easy). The main stress has been getting into a new routine. In particular, there is much more homework here than in Boston and it took them some time to realize that the smart approach is to do as much as possible in class, so that there is not so much to finish at night. Even then, there is still a lot to do every night and they have been going to bed about 10 p.m.—much later than in Boston—and still getting up at 6:30 a.m. to get to school on time, which leaves them exhausted. I have taken to waking them up by blasting them with upbeat pop songs with crazy videos because it is the only way to get them to "voluntarily" open their eyes! The 1980s are a useful resource and we have been through Madness ("I like driving in my car"), the Bangles ("Walk like an Egyptian") and many others. Lily helps them with their Chinese homework several nights per week (we can help with the maths), and a couple of nights per week they have "homework play dates" with some of their classmates (i.e. they go to someone else's house and are supervised by the parents of another child who is doing the same homework). This seems to make it much more fun and gives better incentives to be efficient, so as not to be disgraced by having a mountain of homework. Obviously, the other parents are able to help with the Chinese in a way that we are not. Then on Fridays we have these children to our house for an English play date, which is a good trade because most parents think it's great if their child can spend several hours per week interacting with native English speakers.

I must say that the parents here have been very welcoming—more than you could hope—and the school, too. The school is attached to the university that we are visiting and reputed to be the second best primary school in China. It would be called "progressive" in education parlance and teaches more in the US style. The school day is exactly the same length as Boston, and I think that the atmosphere is relatively similar—not so much of a hothouse as you might expect, trying to be open to the world and so on. And it does not give as much homework as other Chinese schools, even if it is still about four times what they get in Boston! Most families have at least one parent who is an academic, since you need a link to the university to get your child admitted to the school. The non-academic parents have a wide variety of occupations (homemaker, real estate manager, fund manager, oil engineer, to name just a few). Their personal circumstances seem correspondingly varied. One family—two children, parents and grandparents—lives in a small apartment, as you might imagine, given property prices in the centre of Beijing. (Having said that, I believe that they also have a place further out—maybe an hour's drive away in the countryside—where they go at weekends.) And then there are families at the other end of the scale. When Annabelle went for a homework play date recently, she and her friend were picked up in a chauffeur-driven car and whisked off to a large apartment ("big enough to ride a scooter round the living room!") where the cook kindly went out of her way to make them European-style food for dinner. (I didn't quite get what this dish was. When Lucy had the "European option" in the university cafeteria, it turned out to be a plate of rice with melted cheese and tomato on top. When she expressed surprise—since she had never seen such a thing in Europe—her Chinese companion replied: "Really? We [the Chinese students] always ate that when I was a student in England." I think that European food in China is a bit like Chinese food in Europe—heavily adapted to local tastes and bearing only a passing resemblance to the original. The classic in the US is chop suey, which is supposedly Chinese but I believe was invented in San Francisco, and which most Chinese natives seem to think is a weird concoction.)

Our apartment is close to Peking and Tsinghua Universities (with Renmin University also nearby) and next to Beijing's "tech hub" (which is located on the Tsinghua University Science Park). We walk past Google, and so on, on the way to school—they are all in the street next to our house. Bizarrely, therefore, there are more fancy pastry shops within 500 m of our house than I have experienced in any other town where I have lived, including Lausanne and Paris—although "Paris Baguette" turns out to be a Korean chain, rather than a French one. (Nonetheless, their baguettes are excellent and they produce a fine selection of *pains* and *pâtisseries*, and the staff are far more attentive than any you would find in France, that is for sure. Everything comes daintily wrapped in tiny boxes with gold ribbon; watching the checkout girls knot them at lightning speed reminds me of little girls lace-making for 12 hours a day during the Industrial Revolution, but that is another story.) You are probably unaware that Korea is a cultural icon in East Asia: the people are perceived to be sophisticated, super-polite and—at the same time—a little bit edgy. In a sense, Korea is to China what the UK is to the US. Korean TV programmes are incredibly popular and have a câché that Chinese programmes simply cannot match, I think in part because they can push boundaries that would be frowned upon in a Chinese setting with Chinese characters. And K-pop (i.e. Korean pop music) is a phenomenon all over East Asia. The impact of Psy was felt in the West with "Gangnam Style" but we then heard nothing more. Why? Because he has been too busy cashing in on the East Asian market and the West is just small beer to him. But these other bands (or should that be "brands"?) of teenagers are also a smash hit all across the region. It is a funny set-up, if you are used to the Western idea of bands. Each K-pop band has an entire stable of performers (say, 50 teenage girls) and maybe five to eight of them perform at any one gig—but there are another 42 in reserve! So they rotate them and can thereby constantly perform concerts and make public appearances. It is really like bringing factory production to the music business. I thought that it was interesting when one of the K-pop bands showed up at Los Angeles Airport recently and got immediately deported. Apparently, they had the wrong kind of visas and their suitcases contained only sexy underwear, so the immigration officials assumed that they were in some other line of business! Maybe that is what happens if you try to compete head-to-head with Lady Gaga.

Our other local pastry shops are less swanky than Paris Baguette but have the advantage that you can actually sit and eat there. "Tous les jours" is pretty good and sufficiently cheap that you can actually afford to eat there *tous les jours*—at least, if you are on a Western salary. They also play edgier music (Oasis and other English stuff), whereas Paris Baguette is mostly classic French (wall-to-wall Charles Aznavour). On our first morning—when had no food in the house and woke up very early from jet lag—we found the "Golden Phoenix" just around the corner from the apartment. As you might guess from the name, this chain has a more Chinese appeal—less expensive, weaker coffee, but still pretty good (and it has another café right next to the girls' school, which is handy). And then there is "Bunnydrop". As the name suggests, this one has a strong bunny theme—beloved of my daughters and unmarried Chinese women in their late 20s (of which there are an increasing number). This is more expensive, has better Wi-Fi (since all those single women spend their time stuck to their phones, surfing their social networks) and softer music. I saw a pink Hello Kitty sports car parked outside, which I think sums it up.

Other eateries also abound—the six subway sandwich shops within walking distance, the Pizza Hut, KFC and McDonalds. If my children get their way, then think that I shall end up eating more junk food in China that I ever had to endure in the US. So, although we are not in the "foreign" part of Beijing (i.e. the east), we feel perfectly located here. There is even a Carrefour within walking distance! We see a few foreigners each day (mostly students, I think—there is a language university just along the street) but have never seen a Western child, so our kids are rather unique.

It has been a very tough first few weeks—dealing with children and chores by day, and apartment and admin by night. Having done a gut-busting amount of effort of the last couple of months to get this show on the road, I now feel that we are finally on the verge of… a gut-busting amount of effort over the next several months. Wow, I was so smart to volunteer for this! Since I am too old for the army, this was probably the next best thing!

I am now going to send this via my incredibly useful Express VPN (which everyone uses here to get around the China's Great Firewall—so that we can access illicit sites such as Google and YouTube). Then I am going to cook my dinner! I hope that you are all well. Please enjoy the Green and Pleasant Land for us. I will drop you another line when I get time.

Very best wishes,

Liam.

Letter 2

Getting There
10 March, 2016

Dear Alan,

I didn't tell you what a trial it has been getting into China (let's just hope that it does not require an equally difficult trial to get out!). Since my sabbatical started in January, it seemed sensible to plan to arrive then. Also, there are essentially no breaks in the school calendar—no half term, no teacher training days—so once the girls' school starts there will be few holidays in which we can travel. So the obvious solution is to travel around China as much as possible before the school semester starts and after it finishes. This turns out to be a logistical nightmare. The university had to get us visas as visiting scholars. Now, I have lived and worked in numerous countries, and applied for various visas and work permits, but never have I had so much difficulty with paperwork. I have even extended my English vocabulary, having been required to complete processes that I never knew existed in any country.

In order to get our visas, we first needed to provide copies of all our *bôna fides* (certificates for Bachelor's degrees, Master's degrees and doctorates). This may sound entirely reasonable to the average Joe, but I will confess that no one has ever asked me for them before. If I apply for a job as a professor at a university, then they assume that I have a PhD because I have already been working as a professor at another university. As long as your first employer is happy with your *bôna fides*, the others take them on trust. Since my first employer was the university where I got my PhD, there was never really a question as to whether I had actually been awarded all the qualifications that I was claiming. So when we found out that we needed this stuff, we didn't even possess the requisite material. We desperately contacted the university offices in Oxford and spoke to a very helpful person who was able to send out copies of all the certificates very promptly. We were quite impressed. (Oxford has many fine attributes but "efficient" is not an adjective that is generally bandied about in the university administration. In fact, you are supposed to pay for duplicate copies of your university certificates. We confessed that, although we thought that we had never claimed them, we could not be totally sure and could they please check and bill us accordingly. Amusingly, the answer came back that—although the university is 800 years old—their records system does not go back to the year 2000, so they had no idea whether we had been issued certificates or not. So they just decided to send them for free—although they might not thank me for sharing that particular gem....)

But the academic *bôna fides* were only the tip of the iceberg. We also needed birth certificates for ourselves and the children—just to show that we were not trying to stealthily sneak someone else's children into China for seven months—and our marriage certificate. All these documents had to be notarized and apostilled. I avow that "apostilled" was a new one on me. The notary looks at each document and signs off on it to say that it is indeed an official document (this is being "notarized"). The government of the territory in which the notary is located then has to stamp the document to say that this person is an officially registered notary (this is being "apostilled"). Where does it all end? Should I then get the UN to stamp everything to say that the government is the officially recognized sovereign power in that location? This whole process seems very Chinese: everything has to pass through many offices and be stamped by ever higher-up officials—and come with ever-larger gold seals and ribbons (literally)—to make it more official and acceptable. I am told that this approach is general in East Asia and friends who live there find it odd that I find it bizarre. I may be coming at this too much from the point of view of an economist, expecting efficiency and effectiveness, but it seems to me that we are taking a sledgehammer to crack a nut—and it is not even clear that this is an effective nutcracker. Let me explain.

First, is there a problem that needs to be fixed here? Personally, I have never heard of a case in Europe or the US where an academic has been hired and subsequently found to have a fake PhD. I have heard of cases in which the PhD was plagiarized, but the guilty party then was a German defence minister rather than a professor (so no students were harmed in the making of this scandal). I am told that academic fraud is real problem in East Asia; if this is true, then it is an interesting question as to how and why. In my experience, subject areas are sufficiently narrow that people who interview you for a job would know whether or not you had a PhD—they are likely to have seen you at conferences and they would have reference letters from members of your thesis committee (whom they would probably also know personally). So it would take a real conspiracy to cover up the fact that a candidate had no PhD. Who would take the risk? Why would they want to? Maybe I am just too parochial in relying on the fact that people in an academic area know each other; as the world becomes more globalized and anonymous, perhaps this will become a more serious and evident problem. Second, can this sledgehammer crack this nut? I don't think so. If you wanted to corrupt the system, then you would obviously just start at the bottom. You would find a dodgy notary who was willing to sign off on something for a bribe; then, once it has entered the system, the next steps follow automatically and you can create any paper trail that you want. So the higher-up offices basically just absorb more time and money without adding any security. In fact, in Massachusetts *anyone* can become a notary—as long as they are over 18, can read and write English and pay a $50 registration fee—so you can save yourself the trouble of finding a corrupt notary by becoming one yourself. Fundamentally, verification can only occur at the lowest level. My PhD examiners are in a position to verify that I have written a PhD; Oxford University then has to take their word on trust and issue its imprimatur; and everything else follows automatically. If higher authority cannot trust the person at the bottom, then the system is doomed to fail, no matter how many additional layers of authentication you add.

In fact, we did not go via the Massachusetts route, for several reasons. The first dilemma is: do you apply for your Chinese visa through London (bearing in mind that we are UK citizens) or through New York (since Lucy and the children were US residents)? Unfortunately, I was not resident in the US and therefore ineligible to use the US branch of the China visa machine. So it was unclear that they would process my application with the others. But it seemed risky for me to apply through London, whilst the rest of the family applied through New York: it might look suspicious, and we would certainly need twice as many documents (Lucy and I would both need an entire set of marriage and birth certificates). And it would take more time because all the documents would have to be sent from the UK. So instead we defaulted to London—the Capital of the World. I should say that I have never been a great fan of London because it is too big, too busy and too pricey. But I see its attractions ever more as I get older. In particular, people in London need to be able to do business—right now, anywhere in the world. So if you are willing to write a big enough cheque, then someone in London will get it done for you today, whatever it is. A minor matter that I did not mention is that, in addition to having all these documents notarized and apostilled, you have to get Mandarin translations—which then have to be notarized and apostilled. So you need a notary who can read and write Chinese. Two days before Christmas. (Government offices in the West are shut between Christmas and New Year, but not in China. So if the documents arrived in Beijing on Christmas Day, then university could still submit them to the appropriate government office and there might actually be progress in the following fortnight. So time was really of the essence, given that we wanted to fly to China in January.) In this situation, London is the way to go. You contact a big London law firm and have the documents sent directly to them—from Oxford University, from the County Registrar and so on. They get them all notarized, translated and re-notarized, and then send someone to Chancery Lane to get them all apostilled by the Foreign and Commonwealth Office. Job done. For about £2000.

Well, actually not—only one-third of the job done. China must pay close attention so that no afflicted foreigners pitch up on their shores, since China is such a healthy country and the rest of the world is so woefully sickly. I was a little surprised by this, having successfully been granted work permits for the US, Switzerland and Norway and never having needed a medical before. Moreover, working in those countries involves a health insurance package, so falling sick or being diseased would have burdened my Western hosts with healthcare costs (since they would be picking up the tab for my treatment); by contrast, my Chinese hosts would not be burdened because they were not providing any health coverage (I would be paying any bills myself). Anyway, before you can be granted a Chinese work visa, strict new rules mean that you need to have a full medical in an approved hospital before you travel. The problem is that there are no approved hospitals. The ministry that dishes out visas can, of course, set any rules that they like; but they do not necessarily have the machinery to implement them. So they can command you go to an approved hospital, despite the fact that they have no competence to approve hospitals themselves or any ability to get the health ministry to do it for them. Obviously, this leaves the applicant in a tricky situation—but the visa ministry does not give a hoot. (In fact, so much the better because that means fewer applications to process.) We were told to phone the Chinese Consulate in New York to get the approved hospital list and they happily assured us that there was no approved list and they could not help us. Now, I would not like you to think that this is a purely Chinese phenomenon: my brother-in-law visited a university in Singapore around the same time and had exactly the same problem. Eventually, someone from the university phoned the Singaporean Health Ministry and got them to agree that he and his wife could have their medical checks at an approved Singaporean hospital after they arrived, in the absence of any approved hospitals overseas. After chasing our tails for several days, the university kindly provided us with a list of things that had to be checked in the medical examination and we simply went to our own doctor to get it done, in the hope that this would create a ream of paperwork sufficiently voluminous that the visa ministry in Beijing would be overawed and not want to read it. It seemed to work.

Now, the third part of the job was actually applying for the visa. All the preceding paraphernalia was a *sine qua non* of the process. But all it got you was permission to apply. Once you were approved to apply, you would get a wodge of documents that you could take to the China visa office in London to actually make the application. At this point, a serious spanner was thrown into the works. First, we did not know how long it would take to get the approval from Beijing—but we were told that it was unlikely to arrive in January. (Generally speaking, no one knows how long the bureaucracy in China is going to take to do anything—it is not like there is a federally mandated timescale, as in the US—so it is all just guesswork based on recent experience.) Chinese New Year was starting around 7 February so, if the visa approval did not arrive by then, then it would certainly not arrive until the end of February (since China is essentially shut for two weeks at Chinese New Year). Second, we discovered (from the internet, not from any liaison officer in the university or bureaucracy) just how Chinese work visas work. You enter China on your visa. You immediately (i.e. within 24 hours) register at the local police station. You must then exchange your work visa for a residence permit. This exchange must be completed within 30 days. But the process can take four to six weeks, so essentially you have to go to the Foreign Police Office immediately and hand in your passport and other documents so that they can be sent away and your residence permit issued. (The eagle-eyed amongst you will have noticed that the timings in the previous two sentences do not add up—specifically, six weeks is longer than 30 days—but let's gloss over that and move on.) Now, you cannot travel without a passport. But if you recall your passport—suppose that you needed to go home unexpectedly for a funeral, for example—then the process is cancelled and you have to start all over again. I mean, you have to start by applying for a work visa whilst in your home country, and submitting all the paperwork to the ministry in Beijing to be approved and so on and so forth. So you definitely don't want to leave China whilst your residence permit is being issued. And you cannot delay applying for it, once you have entered the country, because the clock is ticking.

This was a problem for us because we had already arranged to spend Chinese New Year in Hong Kong. Whilst Hong Kong is, of course, indubitably and inexorably part of One China, it nonetheless has its own visa arrangements and you need a passport to move between the Chinese mainland and Hong Kong. So, even if we got our work visas by the end of January, we would not want to enter the Chinese mainland and trigger those visas because we would then not be able to travel to Hong Kong. Why were we so determined to visit Hong Kong? It was partly because Lucy was brought up there and she wanted to show the children where she had spent her own childhood. And it was partly because Hong Kong would be open for business—because Hong Kong is always open for business! Everything on the mainland would be shut and public transport would be an absolute nightmare (Chinese New Year is famously the greatest migration on earth, as all the migrant workers head home for their one opportunity in the year to see their families) so we wanted to steer well clear of it. By contrast, on New Year's Day in Hong Kong we were able to go to Hong Kong Disneyland—which obviously had the girls in raptures (we have never been to any Disneyland before) and it was a day on which it was not too crowded because most Chinese were spending the day with their families. In fact, there were plenty of things to do in Hong Kong for ten days. I had booked rooms in the Bishop Lei Hotel, which is a little up towards the Peak in Mid-Levels—so we were able to watch the New Year fireworks over the harbour from the convenience of our bedroom window. It was beautiful, and a lot less stressful than taking three small children down to the harbour! In fact, the children were enchanted by Hong Kong and on day three asked if we could move there permanently. (They seem to be under the impression that you go to Disney, see wild dolphins and watch grand firework displays every day in Hong Kong; I think they might be in for a disappointment later in life.)

How to square this particular circle? We decided that we would go to China on tourist visas in January. Having got all the documents from the university in Beijing, we would then fly from Hong Kong to London to submit the work visa applications after Chinese New Year. We could then finally fly London-Beijing and start work. (Why not just submit the work visa application through the China visa service in Hong Kong and fly to Beijing from there directly? Because you *must* apply through your home country or country of residence. So dragging a family of five from Hong Kong to London, and then immediately back to Beijing, was just all part of the fun—and expense—of the whole China experience.) I am constantly amazed at how difficult governments make it for normal people to be lawful and upstanding citizens. I am really not trying to be clever. I am really not trying to bend any rules. I am only trying to go to work. And pay taxes. Why does it have to be so hard? In case accountancy is not your strong suit, I can tell you that this is starting to add up fast: we are talking thousands of pounds for two sets of visa fees, visa service fees and plane tickets. China is not alone in this: the US is no easier, and I am told that the UK is equally difficult.

The tourist visas enabled us to travel around China from the beginning of January until we went to Hong Kong. And it was a good choice because we were able to see some amazing things in that period, which would otherwise have been impossible. This is most obvious in the case of the Harbin Ice Festival—even though it is in the far north, there is not much point in going there in March because it has all disappeared! The Ice Festival is a unique and beautiful event. There are massive sculptures—such as entire palaces 30 m tall and 100 m square—made from blocks of clear water ice (i.e. they are transparent). They put coloured strip lights *inside* the ice, which gives a really nice effect as it shines through the walls. You can walk through these palaces and stand on the balconies. There is a theme each year and for us it was "The Silk Road"—which was particularly appropriate (since we were planning to go there later in the year) and peculiarly surreal (since the Silk Road runs through the desert and you will definitely never see an ice palace there). So there were mosques with minarets, desert fortresses and other images from China's far west. The theme the previous year had been… *Frozen*, which was perhaps more apposite and which I am sure that girls would have adored. The festival is also like a fairground—you can pay to shoot down the luge, or take a ride in a horse and carriage, or have your photo taken with an arctic fox (tick, tick and tick—I was spending money like a man with three arms). We did at least get a good deal on the arctic fox: not that we got to wear it, but that Lucy insisted on one photo with three girls—as opposed to one photo each—so we effectively got it at a two-third discount. We had to use our "walking-away power" to get that: the owner of the arctic fox was refusing to budge until we started to walk away, whereupon he wisely decided that 50 RMB was better than none. (The girls assure me that arctic fox fur is exceptionally soft, by the way—just in case you are ever tempted to wear one….) Lily negotiated a decent deal on the horse and carriage. We wisely did this when we first arrived, on the basis that we were still warm at that point—so it would be more fun, and it would help us to keep warm (being bundled up together in a carriage, with heavy blankets over our knees, was less cold that walking around the festival).

It is fair to say that it was quite cold. Lucy and I are used to the cold: in ancient times (I call it B.C.—Before Children) we liked to go backcountry skiing and winter mountaineering in Quebec, where the daily high is often −20°C. But you could actually feel the body heat being sucked out through your boots as you walked around the Ice Festival. I had taken the precaution of putting chemical warming sachets in the girls' gloves and boots, but it did not seem to offer a noticeable degree of comfort. We left the ice festival earlier than Lucy and I would have chosen, since the children complained bitterly about the bitter cold. Partly for that reason, we actually had more fun at the Harbin Snow Festival, which is the less flashy younger brother of the ice festival. The Snow Festival takes place in a large park outside town. Huge blocks of snow are created by compacting snow inside squares of wooden shuttering (thus creating cubes that are maybe three or four metres long on each side). Each block is then carved into a unique design by a different team or artist. Some of these are local—such as a team of students from the Harbin Institute of Technology—whilst others are created by professional artists. Some of the concepts are striking and the execution is stunning. There are scores of snow sculptures in the park: some are "standard" statues (a recreation of Buddha, or some animals, or whatever) and some are more abstract (such as a steam train that was deforming, as you moved from front to back, that was supposed to represent the transformation of technology through history).

We spent hours running around the park with the children, on a lovely sunny day, admiring and trying to understand the transient creations. Our understanding was not limited only by the abstract nature of some of the work but also by our ignorance of Chinese culture. So it was useful to have Lily there to explain to us what various motifs signify in Chinese. For example, the Chinese words for "bat" 蝠 and "blessing" 福 have similar characters with identical pronunciation—"fu"—so things are often decorated with bats in order to bring good fortune. Fish are also considered to bring good fortune and are always eaten as part of the feast for Chinese New Year. Since the sculptures would last through to New Year, there were frequently fish effigies incorporated into the designs. This practice would have been a little puzzling if we had not known how lucky fish are in China—we might have thought that Birds Eye had sponsored the event. (This is not an entirely stupid comment: a massive fish ice sculpture in town was sponsored by Golden Dragon Fish cooking oil, whose logo is obviously a golden fish. The fish sculpture was rather handsome, untainted by the transgenic beans scandal—unlike the oil itself, which has seen a subsequent large decline in its market share.)

Unlike the Ice Festival, the Snow Festival Park was not at all crowded. On one side is a large lake that was, naturally, completely frozen over. We stopped for lunch in a lovely café with picture windows looking out over the lake. At one end of the lake was the impressive façade of an ice palace; in the middle was an ice ship, tipping to one side as if trapped in the pack ice (the ship was so tall that even I could not reach up to touch the gunnel, so there was no chance that the girls could climb onto it and cause trouble). After lunch we hired "ice bikes" to ride around on the lake and the children later went up and down a luge multiple times. Lily collected her skates from the car and did some skating—the lake surface was beautifully smooth. It is relatively unusual to find a natural lake that is in good condition for skating: either the surface is very uneven (e.g. due to melting and refreezing) or it is covered in snow. But Harbin is actually quite dry, even though it is cold. They bring in the snow for the sculptures from outside the city and the park had enough snow to be pretty (i.e. the ground was white) but not enough to be troublesome to walk around. (This might prove more troublesome when the Winter Olympics come to "Beijing"—actually, a venue quite some distance north of Beijing—where it is also cold but very dry in the winter. Snow for skiing and boarding might be in rather short supply.) In any case, Harbin ends up as a fairytale winter venue and I would recommend the Snow Festival even more strongly than the Ice Festival, despite its lack of celebrity.

OK, I think that you are now up to speed with Chinese visa applications. The word "Byzantine" springs immediately to mind, but that might be doing the Chinese a disservice: the Chinese Empire clearly surpassed Byzantium, and I fully believe that its bureaucracy expanded to match its greatness. I am going to take an aspirin and lie down; I'll write again when I recover.

Very best wishes,

Liam.

Letter 3

A Poison Pen Letter
18 March 2016

Dear Alan,

Well, if Emily is going to laugh at my cleaning efforts [sniff, point nose in the air], then I am going to start sending you poison pen letters. (And what could be more Inspector Wexford than that? Seems appropriate for your life in rural Northamptonshire.) Actually, the main poison at this end is the pollution, which has cranked up a notch or two recently. On Friday, I put on my spacesuit to collect the children and braved the hazardous pollution levels outside (360/500—purple, on a scale of yellow to black, where I think the colour coding refers to the colour of the inside of your lungs).

Something that is strange is that they do not have playtime ("recreation") in school. The Chinese government realized a few years ago that their children were getting overweight and very unhealthy, since they spend all day with their nose to the grindstone and getting no exercise, and that this is a public health time bomb. So, in a suitably centrally planned fashion, they decreed that all schools should have a certain amount of exercise each day (whether or not they have any outdoor space, for example—which obviously they do not, in the middle of Beijing). So, twice per day, the children are marched outside and lined up, hundreds at a time, and they have to do stretching and star jumps and such like for

15 minutes, in time with the teacher. They are then marched back indoors to continue with classes. (On days when it is too polluted to go outside, they jump up and down in the classrooms in time to an exercise video. In Elizabeth's school, they have hopscotch taped onto the floors so that they have something to do.) I am not exactly sure when children are supposed to make friends or relax during the day—but maybe neither of those things is necessary for building a Socialist Utopia.

A general upshot of this lifestyle is that every evening the children are either very tired or completely wired (i.e. have spent so many hours in school or doing homework that they just want to run around and be silly). Although they are not doing that much extra homework each day, it is a relatively large chunk of their normal allocation of free time, and you do notice the difference—especially since most physical activities that they might typically do in the week are currently absent (taekwondo, soccer, ice skating, gymnastics, dancing…). Obviously, Catherine is particularly affected by this, since she is a Perpetual Motion Machine. We must try to arrange some more physical activities for them, but the mismatches of location and transportation make it a bit tricky to fit much in (especially given the homework load). We are rather spoilt in Boston, since everything is readily available within a few streets of the school or our house. They have started dancing for 90 minutes one evening per week—but that is less than they were doing in Boston, and a lot of it seems to be stretching. (In suitably Chinese style, there are a lot of students in a small classroom—I think that they barely have the space to dance!).

In our constant search for Child Hamster Wheels, we went to see the Great Wall on the Sunday before last. Parts of it are near Beijing (90-minute drive) and we chose a particularly vertiginous part at Juyongguan. Since "guan" means "pass", the wall swoops down from one crest, crosses the valley floor and then sweeps up another crest on the other side; a big fort guards the valley floor, where the road from the north runs down towards Beijing. We ascended to one of the crests to admire the view, so the children had thousands of steps to charge up and down and tire themselves out in the process. The weather was lovely (sunny, no pollution!) and it was extremely picturesque and atmospheric. Of course, it is a bit "Disney": the Great Wall is basically a bunch of ruins, since no one maintained it for hundreds of years and bits were stolen to make local housing, so the "restored" bits are essentially modern re-imaginings of what the wall was like. It is a bit like Carcassonne in the south of France: it looks spectacular but people might question how historically accurate it is.

So far, we have been lucky to find various picturesque places to tire out the children on our Chinese travels. In Kunming in January we visited the Shilin Natural Park, which is a karst landscape that has been very largely eroded. There seem to be a lot of karst areas in China. The early stages of erosion create marvellous canyons and caves of the kind that you see in Guilin (the place that features in all those old-fashioned paintings of China—boatmen in straw hats pushing sampans along with poles, with crazy mountains in the background). Now play the story forward a few million years and, instead of having lots of rock with funny holes in it (canyons and caves), you end up with having lots of holes with funny rocks in it (crazy stone spires): this is the "stone forest" (i.e. "shi lin"). The children loved it because they could run wild and climb over everything, which would obviously not be permitted in a comparable US or European National Park, and crawl through all the small caves. Since our children climb anything and everything, it was ideal for them and burnt off plenty of energy. The park itself is very nice, both well appointed and well maintained: it could just as well be in Switzerland as China (with entry prices to match!). There is a pretty lake near the entrance—complete with a musical show by the local ethnic minority—and pedestrianized roads around the large park; there is nicely mown grass in the clearings and a great viewing platform in the middle of the main area. Even the lavatories could grace a five-star hotel—floor to ceiling marble and hand soap!

Another wonderful resource in Kunming for adults and children is the very large lake on the edge of the city. I am told is very pretty in the spring—although we were there in January—and on the far side is a mountain covered in small temples. You ascend the mountain by an amazing trail that is hacked out of the sheer rock face; at one point you climb a long staircase inside a tunnel that is hewn entirely through the rock. Presumably, there was originally a natural fault in the rock that created a faint track up and across the face. This was then widened by a crazy monk with a hammer and chisel, who spent a decade or more working on it in the late 1700s. The monk wanted to create a place to contemplate the meaning of life, so he also carved several grottos in the rock along the path and sculpted patterns all around to decorate them. Then he built temples in the grottos, with statues of Buddha and so on, all highly decorated—painted with vivid colours and covered in gold leaf. The whole thing is really beautiful and spectacular. These days, in addition to the "extreme" sections of the path, there are various flights of steps that take easier ground up to small platforms and temples and benches and so on. It is very pleasant to sit and eat a snack and enjoy the ambience. On top of the mountain, there is a big viewing platform that offers a tremendous vista over the lake and city. The whole mountain is now a park and the smart thing to do—which we did—is take a taxi from the main gate around the back of the mountain to the other entrance. Then you can walk right through the park without retracing your steps, and always be heading downhill!

Anyway, back to the present. Having bought ourselves some time by tiring out the children on the Great Wall, we drove to the Ming Tombs (or the "Valley of the Mings", as I like to call it) in the afternoon. It is a valley halfway between Beijing and the Great Wall where the Ming emperors decided to be buried, so there are 13 enormous tombs (*de facto* empty, duplicate palaces with the same layout as you find in the palaces in Beijing) where they were buried with their treasures. It is now a UNESCO World Heritage Site. We saw two of the tombs: the first, largest and best preserved one, called Changling; and the one where the excavated burial chamber is open to the public, called Dingling. It was very impressive—a huge underground vault for the richly decorated sarcophagus of the Emperor and his wife, with various tunnels and massive doors controlling access to the complex. Amazingly, most of the other burial chambers have not even been excavated, as far as I can understand, except as far as they have been "accidentally" uncovered and then excavated in order to safeguard the artefacts and keep the tomb sound. The guidebook says that Dingling was found after some Indian Jones-esque detective work (deciphering ancient runes and so on), although knowledgeable friends assure me that this is not true—on the contrary, the site of the tomb was well known and it was even used as an air raid shelter in the war. There were some nice artefacts on show, although not as many as I had hoped and the presentation/explanation was rather limited (in both Chinese and English). My understanding is that there was more stuff in evidence before the Cultural Revolution but no one likes to talk about that (ahem). We really enjoyed ourselves and hope to visit the Valley of the Qings (which is northeast of Beijing, rather than northwest) on a future weekend.

We are making good use of all the Parisian bakeries to be found between our apartment and the school. I might finally live up to my traditional New Year's Resolution of visiting more pastry shops. (I always think that it is rather stupid to make a New Year's Resolution that will make you unhappy if you seriously pursue it—such as to lose some weight; or unhappy if you fail to achieve it—such as to lose some weight. So I like to make a New Year's Resolution, the pursuit of which will make me happy—such as visiting more pastry shops. Sadly, like everyone else, I have been failing to live up to my New Year's Resolution for the last 20 years. But I think that I might actually achieve it this year. Indeed, I think that I have already done so.) Frequenting pastry shops may be the only way to avoid losing weight while I am here. Walking the children to school each morning is a 45-minute round trip (minimum) and frequently the same to collect them in the afternoon (although I do not need to do that every day). But last Friday I had to make two afternoon trips because Annabelle and Catherine get out of school at 12:50 on Fridays, whereas poor old Elizabeth is stuck there until 5 p.m.! (It is a little odd that the youngest children spend the most hours in school; we would obviously do the exact opposite in the West.) Anyway, that was at least two hours of walking for me. If I am not careful, then I will be wasting away.

Of course, we are all very safe here, and have the peace of mind that comes with living in a police state. Still, the traffic manages to be rather Parisian. That is, people park wherever they want (typically double-parked, blocking driveways and pedestrian crossings) and they drive wherever they want (often the wrong way up a divided highway or through a red light). Despite the presence of police and security guards everywhere, there is a remarkable lack of law enforcement! Hence the traffic chaos. My personal hypothesis is that this helpfully leaves more opportunities for corruption and the arbitrary exercise of power. In any case, walking to school is therefore an exercise for the mind (and moral fibre) as well as the legs. "Mens sana, in corpore sano", as they say.

I hope that this all makes Emily snigger. I love Sniggers—they are one of my favourite chocolate bars (and my eldest daughter knows how to ask for them in Mandarin, which is handy).

Very best wishes,

Liam.

Letter 4

The Temple of Heaven
23 March 2016

Dear Tim,

I hesitate to give you all your treats at once—lest the rest of your week seem to stretch ahead of you in a dreary dual carriageway of budget cuts and Brexits—but I was feeling inspired to write an account of this weekend's activities. On Saturday, we visited the Temple of Heaven—attracted partly by the forecast of good weather and low pollution, and partly by the fact that BBC News featured it in their article "The 10 most beautiful ceilings in the world" (check out the magnificent photos on their website). I must confess, you cannot really see the ceiling when you visit the temple (at least, in the main building, which is the Hall of Prayer for Good Harvests). As with most Chinese places and temples, there are barriers across the doorway and the best you can do is peer in from outside (having elbowed your way through the perpetual crowds, who are waving their arms and selfie sticks in the air and taking photos on their phones). Then, if it is bright outside and dark inside—and especially if the ceiling is very high—you cannot really see much. The BBC photo is much better.

The temple complex is nonetheless quite interesting. The Hall is unusual because it is round (basically all other Chinese temples and palaces are a series of rectangular halls). It also has an innovative colour scheme. Instead of being red outside with a green tiled roof, it is red outside with a blue tiled roof (to represent Heaven). The beams are a standard blue and green pattern with gold dragons and so on. As you might have noticed from my description thus far, there is a certain homogeneity (aka sameness) to Chinese temples and palaces. There is much more heterogeneity across (even) English cathedrals and palaces, let alone European cathedrals and palaces. Other interesting parts of the complex include the Divine Warehouse—which we thought would be the place for storing the Divine Bicycle and the Divine Roof Rack and so on. But this actually turns out to be the place where the sacrificial offerings were kept the night before the Emperor offered them at the spring ceremony to bring good harvests. These offerings were prepared in the Divine Kitchens (presumably by Divine Cooks who turned out cuisine that was simply Divine). The animals (calves, pigs, deer, rabbits) had previously been through the Pavilion of Sacrifice—otherwise known as the Animal Beating Room, since they all had their heads bashed in with wooden hammers before having their fur scalded off in huge vats of boiling water, their blood let out and their bones removed (Evelyn Rawski is good on this in her book *The Last Emperors*). We all know, of course, that China has been a fantastically advanced society for millennia—well ahead of the West—so it was a little surprising to me that they were still ceremonially extracting animal innards in 1912 to guarantee good harvests.

There were some other interesting areas in the complex. The Imperial Vault of Heaven is a smaller version of the Hall of Prayer, with fewer crowds, which means that you can actually see the ceiling. It also has a circular enclosing wall (the "Echo Wall") that is rumoured to have interesting acoustics: you can whisper on one side of compound and someone can hear you clearly across the other side (except that they are so many tourists trying to do this at the same time that, of course, you cannot hear anything). There are also some grand quadrangles around the temples to accommodate endless processions of flunkies. Some of the buildings contain beautiful artefacts. For example, the Emperor's carved wooden dragon chair is magnificent—multiple twisting, intertwined dragons where the carving goes all the way through the arms to create a kind of lattice effect. And there is a small, blossoming tree where each of the blossoms is actually carved from jade—but they are so realistic that it is hard to tell with the naked eye. It would have been nice to be able to read more about them, but Speaking In Tongues seems to be strictly confined to the Judeo-Christian tradition of heavenly communication; the Temple of Heaven in the Middle Kingdom sadly offers only Chinese explanation.

On Sunday we took the children to the theatre—a stage performance of a cartoon that they have seen on television called "Da Tou Erzi, Xiao Tou Baba" ("Big Head Son, Little Head Dad"). I am not convinced it was great art (although I am not strictly qualified to comment, since I do not speak Mandarin and I slept through almost all of it), but it seemed to establish a good precedent—that is, that the children understand enough Mandarin that it might be enjoyable to go to the theatre. Next week they have an all-singing, all-dancing, all-kung fuing version of the Monkey King (which is Catherine's favourite, and particularly suitable for the Year of Monkey), so I guess that we will also go to see that. I might even stay awake for that one.

OK, it is now 9:30 p.m. here (and, as usual, it feels like at least 11:30 p.m.) so I am going to call a halt to this email and follow Lucy to bed.

Bonne nuit (or "Wa an", as they say here),

Liam.

References

Glancey, Jonathan, "The 10 Most Beautiful Ceilings in the World", BBC News, 17 March 2016.

Rawski, Evelyn S., *The Last Emperors: A Social History of the Qing Imperial Institutions*, Berkeley: University of California Press, 1998.

Letter 5

When the Chips Are Down
25 March 2016

Dear Tim,

Time for your weekly update from the Dark Side of the Earth. Or, at least, the Dark Side of Humour.

I attach a photo of Chinese potatoes. Did you ever see such a sad sack of scabby excuses for tremendously tasty tubers? You see them in the draining rack because I scrub them with detergent and a Brillo pad, then rinse them in boiling water, before I even consider cooking them (and then reconsider my initial ambition…). I should point out that all the root vegetables in the supermarket are completely covered in a thick, clay soil—so it is unclear what you are buying at the point of sale, and half your money goes on soil (since everything is sold by weight). Obviously, these potatoes have been scrubbed up for their photo op. In fact, even if you saw the state of the potatoes before sale, it is not clear that you could do much about it. There is only one potato choice in the supermarket on any given day, so it is that or nothing. In a way, it is nice because I am a historian and supermarkets in China remind of supermarkets in England in the 1970s—rows of unappetizing produce displayed in an unattractive way in narrow aisles, and trolleys that don't work. It makes Lidl look like the food hall at Harrods. Carrefour is better, but nonetheless clearly geared towards the Chinese market (i.e. it is not like a Carrefour that you would find in France or elsewhere). Chinese shoppers obviously expect to be operating in very cramped conditions, so all the aisles are narrow and laid out irregularly; it is quite an obstacle course to get round with a trolley. If Carrefour supermarkets looked like this in Europe, then no one would shop there. Of course, Carrefour is the most successful Western supermarket to enter the Chinese market (in stark contrast to Tesco, for example) and it is presumably because they have correctly adapted to local tastes and expectations.

In fact, I am being a little unfair on Chinese supermarkets. There are lots of nice biscuits and pastries in the supermarkets here. They have many foreign products (from Danish butter biscuits to Dove chocolate), and there are also quite a lot of nice Chinese products in the bakery section (a kind of shortbread biscuit covered in peanuts is my particular favourite). So if you need a sugar boost, then you have many good options. They also have a fairly wide range of fresh fruits and vegetables. The main problem with the fresh produce is that it does not keep very well. They obviously have slow supply chains—so the mushrooms are already starting to get brown spots before you buy them, and the tomatoes start to go off after a day or two at home (despite the exhortation of my local Lotus Supermarket to "Fresh your life!"). You tend to end up shopping several times per week, therefore, if you want to eat fresh produce. On the other hand, there are no frozen vegetables at all, so that is not a good substitute.

We heard a rumour that M&S had opened in east Beijing last December, so yesterday we made our Pilgrimage to Marks. Normally, we just face that way to pray, but we anyway had to leave our Western haunts and head over there to collect our passports (another story) so we thought that we should push on to pay homage and purify ourselves (our bowels, at least) with some English food. The food part of the store turns out to be rather limited—mostly biscuits and chocolates and tea, and other things that you might give as twee gifts. I was rather hoping for some steak and ale pies or salmon en croûte, but they were entirely absent. They did, at least, have frozen pastry, so we bought about ten packets and Lucy has promised to make some pies and Cornish pasties (yum!). And they had oven chips—unheard of in China because most apartments do not have an oven. We also timed our visit to precede Easter, on the basis that they might have hot cross buns (we emptied the shelf—tee-hee-hee!) and Easter eggs. The regular Easter eggs were ferociously expensive (about £15 each!) so we skipped that and bought numerous teeny ones that the children could eat themselves and also give away at school. (You see—we are adapting to local custom. Constantly buttering up anyone who might be useful to you is a good way to get things done here—including help with your homework!)

The non-food items in M&S are breathtakingly expensive. They are clearly positioning themselves as a luxury foreign brand. True, the quality of the children's clothing was better than you find in the typical Chinese shop. But the price was about ten times higher—£23 for two pairs of pyjamas for a six-year-old! Of course, we were in the international east of Beijing (equivalent to the West End of London). Hence we passed the EtonKids day care and the Ivy Academy ("The multiple intelligences pre-school"—never knowingly undersold—which I guess is what you get for being in partnership with the Harvard Institute of Education). That area of town is rather more upmarket and clean (and impersonal) than our area of town. In truth, I experienced no desire to be living in the illustrious east; I did not have the impression that the expensive expat lifestyle would be a good fit for me, any more than I felt that South Kensington was a good fit for me when a friend asked me to buy something for them in Harrods. I feel rather more at home in gritty, working west Beijing. I realized recently that I haven't actually spoken to another Westerner since we arrived.

Well, I will shortly be taking my children to our second kung fu lesson. The first one was extremely interesting. The particular style of kung fu is called "wing chun", made famous by Bruce Lee. It is quite particular and places great emphasis on standing close to your opponent (always within touching distance) and punching from your centre line (so as to generate the most force) to your opponent's centre line (where he is forced to absorb the whole of the shock). I have read about this, but to see it in action and start to understand how it works is quite something. The *shifu* (kung fu master who runs the school) is not a big man—fairly muscular, but nothing like a bodybuilder—but he is incredibly quick with his hands and generates amazing power with very short punches. One exercise was for me to try to punch him while he blocked me (just by slapping my arms down with his hands). Although he seemed to be expending no more effort than if swatting flies, it *hurt*. It was one of those "OK, don't let the tears come to your eyes lest he realizes that you are a complete wimp" moments. That night, I had trouble getting to sleep because my brain was so active, reliving the new experiences of the day (never having done any kind of martial arts before). When lab rats have to find the cheese in a new maze, they apparently have more dreams that night. I may not be any good at kung fu by the time we leave here, but I think I will be excellent at finding cheese.

Enjoy a nice big pie for me,

Liam.

Letter 6

Building Sights
31 March 2016

Dear Tim,

As a dedicated DIY dad, I thought that you would be interested to see some of the challenges that await you in China, in the (increasingly) unlikely event that you should ever be attracted to moving here. Your mission—should you choose to accept it—is to create a habitable and functional home in the face of Chinese plumbing. In fact, if you know any decent plumbers in London who can also speak Mandarin, then I think I could find a lot of work for them out here….

Exhibit 1 is the ceramic water filter that we have been using—the kind that you take camping when you go into the wilds. It basically drains the water through a piece of tile, which has holes so small that even bacteria cannot work their way through. This technological breakthrough does not seem to be widely adopted China—people are more likely to have huge water bottles delivered—even though Henry Doulton has been selling them in England since 1827 (check out "Ceramic water filter" on Wikipedia). The Chinese are so up with new technology…. I noticed after three weeks that the inflow pipe was turning a suspicious shade of brown (rather like an unflushed toilet, in fact, with a Sinker that has been lurking in the bottom for a week). Compare the inflow pipe to the outflow pipe in the photo; obviously, they were both the colour of the outflow pipe when I received the filter in the post! You can see why people don't drink the tap water in China. I wouldn't even fancy it after boiling, quite honestly. But I have now got the Mother of All Filters working. It is like a huge stainless steel tea urn with multiple ceramic "candles" inside (each of which has an activated charcoal core—the kind of thing that they use to absorb the noxious substances released in a chemical or biological attack). This has the advantage of not only catching the crud (including tiny crud, such as bacteria) but also absorbing poisons (such as lead) that might be dissolved in the water. Thank goodness for those ingenious Georgians back in the nineteenth century.

Exhibit 2 is the plumbing in the kitchen and bathrooms. Did you ever see such a display of Heath Robinson pipework? I think that the fellow who fitted it used to work in the noodle shop. Actually, that is an insult to people who work in noodle shops—drawing out noodles from a slab of dough is very skilful and a joy to watch. There is *nothing* about Chinese pipework that is skilful or a joy. Remember that this is a "high end" apartment. In regular apartments, they just run two water pipes from one end of the kitchen to the other and add faucets randomly along the wall (sometimes above a sink, but often not); it is like living in a factory. This is very handy if you need to fit some unexpected new machinery in your kitchen (maybe a power washer, or a milking machine…) but a little unnecessary and unattractive for regular living. The bath tub actually has a regular tap (i.e. it is marked hot and cold)—but that is just for the look, as it runs only cold water in reality. The hot water comes through the rubber hose that you see hanging from the electric water heater. Obviously, the water is scalding hot when it comes directly out of the tank. So when we run the bath we hook the end of the hose through the faucet handle in the bath, make sure that the children are locked safely in another room and then let rip with the water heater faucet. As long as you don't like your baths too hot, the tank contains just about enough water to run one whole bath, which is very considerate.

Exhibit 3 is some public toilets that we came across on our visit to the Ming Tombs. (WARNING: viewer discretion is advised. People who have eaten in the last 24–48 hours may wish to have a bucket handy. You may also be able to smell the photos through the internet.) I went into the male toilet and Annabelle went into the female toilet.

I heard: "Er, daddy…?" To which I replied: "Yes, I think that we should find somewhere else." Sanitation like this seems to me to reduce hygiene levels, rather than improve them. But probably it looks good on the map of the local city officials—they have got public toilets, roads, everything that a modern society needs.

Exhibit 4 is the view from our living room window early in the morning—on a pollution-free day and a polluted day. As they say in Apocalypse Now, "God, I love the smell of napalm in the morning!" Breathing the air in Beijing without a facemask over the course of a year is supposed to be the equivalent of smoking 20 cigarettes a day. Apparently, that is not enough for the average Chinese male, since they typically decline to wear facemasks *and* smoke 20 cigarettes a day. I think that their lungs are the main source of tar for resurfacing the roads. Obviously, I am a complete sissy and wear a mask whenever the scale goes over 150/500 (which is considered "Unhealthy" by the WHO) because I find it more comfortable to wear the mask than end the day with a sore throat.

Exhibit 5 is the view from our bedroom window—on a good day. The quality of the window glass here is absolute rubbish. It is all milky and full of air bubbles, like frosted glass with an added fizzy drink effect. As a historian, I should be pleased: I only expected to see that kind of thing in mediaeval cathedrals. I didn't realize that you could find people who still made that stuff (and managed to sell it). They should put them in a museum. I tried cleaning all the windows, but it makes little difference. (Obviously, the windows are filthy inside and out due to the pollution. But all that I achieved by scrubbing them was to change the colour of the glass from grey to milky white. I suppose it is an improvement, but hardly what I was expecting.) Our apartment is not unique in this respect. The next photo shows the view from the local underground station, out over the bike racks. Although it looks like a rainy day, it was actually perfectly fine: the droplets that you see are in the glass, not water running down the window.

Happily, we do not have this problem with the "glass doors" at the entrance to the building—because they have no glass in them! (Honest—I give you Exhibit 6!) At least I never have to worry about losing my entry key. High-end apartment buildings in other cities have different solutions to this particular problem; for example, a friend of mine who lives in the

Whitehouse Apartments in London has a concierge who knows everyone in the building by name. But Beijing is more liberated and simply has doors with no glass. Other buildings in Beijing do have a complete quota of glass: there are numerous swanky, gleaming office blocks, especially in the east—Chaoyang—where the financial centre is located. The thing that strikes me when I look at them, though, is how irregular the surface is. When you see a glass tower in bright light in London or New York, it reflects the landscape around it like a mirror. But you do not get a clear image when you look at a Chinese glass tower because the panes are so irregular that the reflection is extremely distorted. It is not attractive to look at and hardly an advert for the quality of construction. One great benefit of the doors in our apartment block, though, is that I can get through them without needing to duck; this is contrary to my experience at a local university, where I went to give a seminar and had to be careful not to knock myself out multiple times on the way to the lecture theatre. My host commented that they are not used to people of my size in China (although I am really not that tall—6'2"—and I certainly see Chinese men of that height on a fairly regular basis).

The other interesting thing in the lobby of our apartment building is the lifts. There are two lifts and it used to be fun to have lift races with the children—and a good way to get them out the door as fast as possible when we were in danger of being late for school. Unfortunately, we soon realized that one lift is always slower than the other, no matter how hard you flog it. This is partly because it always stops on floor 7, need it or not (actually, I wonder if it is pining for its owner, who happens to live on floor 7). I have also had the nasty experience of going into the lift, pressing the button, watching the doors close and… nothing. Shit. That was scary—especially because it was just after the story came out about the 40-year-old woman who was trapped in a lift in China for a month over New Year and died of dehydration. Apparently, she was the only resident left in the building and the maintenance workers shut down the lift because they needed a spare part. Unfortunately, no one checked if there was anyone in it before they flipped the switch and went on holiday. Happily, Lucy had the presence of mind to push the button for the floor that we were already on and the doors popped open and we jumped out as if we'd been standing on a hotplate. I tend to avoid using that lift now, although it is not much of a loss because the other one is so much faster.

Just for fun, I also added a picture of the kitchen wall. You may recall that I complained that the kitchen was filthy when we arrived. In the photo, half the wall has been cleaned and half has not. Can you tell which half is which? Now imagine the whole kitchen being the colour of the dirty half. The floor was much, much worse…. Mind you, in all fairness, the floors in Chinese apartment blocks do have a hard life. For example, when people bring their scooters home—or when deliverymen arrive— they do not waste time parking outside. Oh no, they just ride them up the disabled ramps and into the building. You have to be a little careful when waiting for the lift because, when the door opens, someone might ride out on a moped and head off along the corridor. (I think it is the modern equivalent of riding your horse into an eighteenth-century inn.) Of course, being out and about all day in the pollution generates a lot of phlegm and it is socially perfectly acceptable to spit everywhere and anywhere in China—including inside apartment buildings. I frequently see people spitting on the floor as I enter or exit our apartment block. So, with the phlegm and tyre marks, you can easily see how a floor could get dirty.

We are fortunate that our apartment building has plain concrete entry steps. Many apartment buildings have entry steps made out of "structural tiling". That is, someone throws down a few blocks and a bit of cement so that it is roughly step-shaped. Then they cover it in tiles—often quite nice ones, such as marble or granite. Unfortunately, much of the tiling, especially along the edges and corners, is unsupported (i.e. it ends up being structural or load bearing, not just decorative). So the tiles break up in short order and you end up with a gleaming set of wrecked steps, which is neither attractive nor functional (as in Exhibit 7).

But there are a few things that I really do appreciate about Chinese buildings. First is the ironwork. China is a bit like Spain or Italy, where everyone feels it is necessary to put bars over all the windows, and railings around every piece of ground. Much of it is quite nice, though—with decorative flowers or swirls or geometric shapes, as you see in Exhibit 8. It is much nicer than the ubiquitous chain link fence that you see in the US, which makes you feel that the entire country is one enormous open prison. Second is the stonework. There is stonework everywhere in China—on bridges and benches, in squares and shop doorways. Most of it is new but carved in traditional styles. There are many pedestrian bridges across rivers and lakes that are carved from white marble. Exhibit 9 shows a fairly simple carving near my office. But you have to realize that this balustrade runs for miles (literally). There is a river running between the Summer Palace (just north of Peking University) and the Forbidden City (in the centre of Beijing), up which the Emperors were carried by boat to get reach their summer haunt. The balustrade runs all the way between the two; and every time they add another bridge, they use the same style of balustrade. There are also many restaurants and temples with huge stone elephants either side of the doorway. And many banks have huge carved lions outside—some in traditional Chinese style (with the ball in the mouth and the cub under the foot) and some in the English style (more realistic and with flowing manes). You cannot imagine this in Europe or the US because the cost would be astronomical. Of course, Chinese stonework is not limited to architectural applications: everywhere you go, you can find sculptures made of jade and other stone in shops and temples and museums. You will also come across fine pieces of carved wooden furniture and fixtures. This can be movable furniture (chairs, benches and so on) or things like doors and shutters and screens. One of the most remarkable uses of wood—which I have never seen before—is the carving of tree roots. Take a huge tree that has been blown over in the wind; cut off the trunk and take it away; now completely clean the roots (imagine blasting off the soil with a power washer); then carve the roots. Obviously, the wood is twisted and tangled, so the artists fashion it into a flock of birds sitting in trees; or a shoal of fish leaping in a wild ocean; or dragons chasing each other across the sky. The carvings are truly magnificent: extraordinarily vibrant and very imaginative, as in Exhibit 10.

Well that is probably enough "building sights" for now.

Happy Easter!

Liam.

Letter 7

Xi'an
10 April 2016

Dear Kathy,

WOW! That was amazing. Genuinely amazing.

The first Monday in April was a public holiday for "Tomb Sweeping". This is a big deal if you are Chinese. You have to go to the cemetery to revere your ancestors and ensure that they have everything that they need in the afterlife. You do this by burning paper effigies—primarily of money, but also of cars, houses, whatever you think your dearly departed is desperate to receive. I used to think that this custom is really very silly—who would spend real money to buy paper money to burn at a graveside? Why not just cut out the middleman and burn the real money, which has surely got to be better value for both the giver and receiver? But then *Second Life* took the world by storm and Westerners also started spending real money to buy pretend money to buy things for themselves in their after(work)life. So maybe this taps into some underlying short circuit in the human mind.

Anyway, the girls get off school at lunchtime on Fridays. So we decided to skip school on Friday and take a long weekend (i.e. Friday to Monday) to travel somewhere in China. We took the plane to Xi'an on Thursday night and checked into a hotel around midnight. So—even allowing for getting up rather later than usual—we would have a whole day available on Friday. A revolutionary aspect of the whole expedition is that we would be travelling light (i.e. hand luggage only) and the girls would basically have only spare underwear and a toothbrush with them. (In all honesty, this was really a revolutionary concept for Lucy, too, and it was quite a struggle to get that one through the approval process. I think I won out on the argument that it would save us at least 30 minutes at Xianyang airport, and we were already going to be getting to the hotel very late.) Partly, I think that my life—and the lives of the girls—will be a lot happier in the future if they can internalize the concept of travelling light. So, from this tiny seed, I hope that a very whippy sapling will grow.

The weather was forecast to be 29°C and sunny—if rather hazy—so seeking somewhere cool seemed to be a good idea. Hence, we decided to spend the day visiting the terracotta army at the tomb of Qin Shi Huang ("Chin She Hwang"). He is called the "First Emperor of China" because he unified most of China and brought the Warring States Period to an end in 220 BCE. At the same time, he founded the Qin dynasty—although this lasted only until 202 BCE, when the Han dynasty seized the throne (more on this later). Everything about the tomb of Qin Shi Huang is mind-boggling in its magnitude. You will doubtless have seen the "standard" photo of the terracotta warriors, all lined up and ready for battle (or queuing for entry at the Glastonbury Festival, depending on your point of view). But what you have to realize is that Qin actually recreated his entire world in his tomb.

So the "standard" photo shows about 8000 life-sized terracotta soldiers lined up in "Pit 1" (originally complete with real weapons). But there is also the cavalry (complete with chariots and horses) in "Pit 2" and the command centre (complete with generals and so on) in "Pit 3". Presumably, this was essential because the emperor's vanquished enemies, from the Warring States period, were lying in wait for him again in the afterlife to get their revenge. In fact, if he had only known, I think that he was going to meet rather more annoying people than that in the afterlife. Presumably, Marx, Lenin and even Mao are now up there—and they have probably incited Qin's long-suffering troops to overthrow him and institute a republic. The three warrior pits are open to the public. But then there is also the "Acrobat Pit" (since no self-respecting emperor would want to go to the afterlife without the ability to entertain guests), the "Waterfowl Pit" (not sure if this was for ornithology or as a source of Peking Duck), the "Prisoner Pit" (wouldn't want to be short of people to punish with extreme rigour), the "Craftsmen Pit" and so on.

Apparently it took 700,000 workers—a mixture of slaves, convict labour, royal artisans and private craftsmen—36 years to complete the tomb. You also have to realize that every terracotta figure is unique: the bodies were formed in moulds but the heads were individually finished and each face is different. They were also painted! So, when the emperor was buried, the terracotta army was not the plain brown that you see now. They had black armour held together with red ties, coloured trousers and so on. The soldiers were also not left exposed to the elements: they are housed in underground barracks with tiled floors and timber roofs. The chapter by Gideon Shelach in the book *Birth of an Empire* (edited by Yuri Pines et al.) is very good on this. He estimates that the tomb and other mega-projects occupied 15–30 per cent of the adult male population during Qin Shi Huang's reign and may have constituted a key cause of the dynasty's downfall (it was overthrown within three years of the first emperor's death). The whole thing is basically insane—narcissism on a stupendous scale. It makes Hitler look like a reasonable person, rather than a megalomaniac with grandiose ideas and a low value of human life. This comparison is more than a cheap shot. Yuri Pines argues that Qin Shi Huang is distinguished amongst Chinese emperors by his Messianic mindset: he portrayed himself as a "True Monarch", uniquely gifted to lead the people to a stable and prosperous future. As soon as he seized power, he imposed a new socioeconomic system on the empire and implemented a *gleichschaltung* (as they called it in Germany in the 1930s); he also burned books that were out of step with the new ideology (does that sound familiar?). Since he was more gifted than any of his advisors or ministers, he also insisted on making all important decisions personally (again, does that sound familiar?). Some scholars stress that Qin Shi Huang was an effective and intelligent leader, able to create and administer an empire. I can see this point of view—but I don't see that it contradicts the view that he was a Messianic and narcissistic megalomaniac. I think that Hitler was both, and so was Qin Shi Huang.

Our visit made me ponder the symbolism of UNESCO World Heritage Sites (a club to which the tomb belongs). Yes, the tomb is an extraordinary example of craftsmanship and human organization. But it is also the product of enslavement and working people to death (since slaves and convicts were required to do hard labour for 365 days per year in really punishing physical conditions): most of the population was living in poverty while the emperor was (literally) burying an entire army's worth of resources in the ground. I expressed the hope to a Chinese friend that a modern president would not take all this as a template for strong leadership but she assured me that this would all be far too low-budget and something much more grandiose would be necessary to celebrate his accomplishments. Another friend suggested that he would take a terracotta TV and HBO subscription into the afterlife—since entertainment must be at a premium over all eternity—or a terracotta laptop and high-speed internet connection. This is obviously ridiculous: I don't think that anyone can dream of having high-speed internet access in China (although I do often wonder if the connection is made of clay, since it is so slow). In any case, I assume that Emperor Qin foresaw an eternity of slaying his enemies in bloody battles—a bit like watching the Lord of the Rings Trilogy or the Hobbit, but thankfully a bit shorter.

Now, I have to tell you that—amazing as they are—the terracotta warriors are not even 10 per cent of the reason to go to Xi'an. For 1500 years, Xi'an (then known as Chang'an) was the capital of China. The city and the whole province are replete with incredible historical relics and monuments and culture. Beijing is just a Johnny-come-lately in Chinese history, beloved of barbarian hordes from outside the northern borders but rather marginal to the Han Chinese.

So now jump forward to around 750 CE, the height of the Tang dynasty. The Tang Emperors were doubtless the world's most powerful monarchs in their time. Remember that western Europe had fallen into the Dark Ages following the collapse of the western Roman Empire. The eastern Roman Empire was operating out of Constantinople, but scarcely on the scale of the Tang Empire. Chang'an was a magnet for wealth, sophistication, learning, culture and military power. The pull of that magnet could be felt along the Silk Road into the Middle East (which was geographically far closer to Constantinople than Chang'an). The first mosque was built in Chang'an in 742 CE—an incredibly early date, considering that Mohammed started preaching only in 610 CE. A culturally important aspect of the Tang era is the peregrination of Tang Seng (the "Tang Monk"). He left Chang'an in 632 CE and travelled along the Silk Road to India, where he spent 17 years learning the true meaning of Buddhism. He then returned to China—carrying thousands of scriptures with him—and was given a hero's welcome. Tang Seng has been immortalized in the mythical story of *The Journey to the West*, which is a key element of East Asian culture. I return to this fascinating story later because it has left its physical footprint in Xi'an.

Let's get back to the Tangs. Not content with meeting the terracotta warriors, we zipped off in the evening to the Winter Palace ("Huaqing Palace"). Although it is built on a steep hill—which you would think would make it undesirable as a winter residence—it is also situated on a hot spring. There has long been a palace there but much of the current structure dates from the late Qing (i.e. nineteenth century). The old palace was rebuilt and expanded in 723 CE by Emperor Xuanzong as a love nest for his concubine Yang Guifei, before being destroyed in a rebellion (a key incident to which I shall return). The palace is very pretty and distinguished by having a beautiful lake. The whole area is actually very nice—with fountains and many bronze statues of historical figures in the gardens and walkways outside the palace itself. We arrived in the evening and did not take a detailed look at the palace itself because we actually went to see a Tang-influenced dance show.

WOW. It was the most amazing theatrical experience ever. If you have the time and money, then I advise you to fly to China to see it. It is based on a Chinese poem called "The song of everlasting sorrow" ("Chang hen ge") written by Bai Juyi in 809 CE. It recounts the tumultuous and doomed love story of Emperor Xuanzhong and Yang Guifei. In the pantheon of Chinese literature, it is around the level of Shakespeare—it is on the school syllabus, so everyone has heard of it and many have even read it. I fear that the facts of the case do not flatter either of the two protagonists. The emperor ruled for 43 years and was a diligent monarch for the first half of his reign; thereafter, he became dissolute and mostly interested in his concubines (of which he had thousands). In particular, he fell in love with Yang Gufei—who was unfortunately his daughter-in-law.

He arranged for Yang to become a nun—thereby voiding her marriage—and for his son to marry someone else. Yang then left the nunnery and the emperor took her as his concubine. Yang and the emperor had a shared love of drinking, dancing and being dissolute, in which they indulged endlessly while leaving the affairs of state to ministers. Happily, ministers were not in short supply because Yang had many relatives who needed employment. Ultimately, An Lushan (a senior general) revolted and almost succeeded in overthrowing the Tang dynasty. Although the Imperial Princes managed to destroy An Lushan in the following decade, the emperor had to win back the loyalty of his troops by having Yang strangled and killing all her unpopular relatives. He abdicated in favour of one of his sons shortly thereafter and died six years later, a broken man. Although the Tangs re-established their state, it was never as strong as it had been before the revolt. Now, the clever thing about Bai Juyi's poem is that he portrays the whole episode as a doomed romance—two soulmates, with a shared love of music and culture, destroyed by the ambitions of a ruthless and barbaric general. The emperor orders her to commit suicide to save the kingdom and then dies himself from a broken heart.

So much for the history. What about the show? WARNING: Plot spoilers follow for the most extraordinary and beautiful piece of theatre you are ever likely to be able to see. In fact, it was so good that we seriously considered buying tickets for the performance the next night, so that we could see it all over again. I may fly back to Xi'an just to watch it again before we leave. The show was created by Zhang Yimou, the man who created the opening ceremony for the Beijing Olympics. He is a respected film director but has lately been creating spectacular shows around China—such as the *Impression Lijiang* show (which is good), the *Liu Sanjie Impressions* show in Guilin and so on. I think that he surpassed himself this time.

The audience is relatively small—a few thousand—sitting on a bank of seats in the palace courtyard and looking out over the palace lake, with (real) temples and pagodas on the far side. So far, so magical. Unlike an English summer evening, the temperature is perfectly pleasant (no sweater required) and the sky clear. A spotlight goes on and an angel flies across the sky and lands on the far side of the lake; there is some nice dancing and then the angel departs again. Now a huge moon suddenly appears in the sky (yes, really). It is high up on the steep hill behind the palace and the size and colouring is such that it looks like the real moon. Cue gasps from the audience. Now a waterfall appears below the moon (a sinuous ribbon of white light running down the hill, covered with mist—presumably created by dry ice). Cue more gasps. Now the stars suddenly appear—they have covered this entire hill in thousands of lights so that it really does look like a starlit sky. (You could obviously never do this in Europe because you wouldn't get planning permission. I can just hear the local planning and environmental officers—"You want to create an artificial moon, waterfall and starlit sky in an area of outstanding natural beauty and historical significance? Well, I am afraid that we have had complaints from the National Trust and the local residents are concerned about light pollution. Also, it would disturb the birds/rabbits/earthworms, which are of Special Scientific Interest.") Barely has the audience recovered from this shock when a lady (Yang) appears in an illuminated boat in the shape of a lotus flower (cue beautiful music). As it nears the centre, a stage surfaces from beneath the lake. She gets out and dances. Now a curtain of fountains shoots into the air and there is a shadow show—of people dancing—on the curtain of water. The fountains are suddenly cut to reveal a stage, which is a platform in the lake, docked on the far side. The floor of the stage itself is lit, initially in white but changing colour with the mood of the show. (I know that this sounds like a cheesy 1970s disco performance worthy of the Bee Gees with big sunglasses and falsetto voices but, trust me, it is beautiful.) There are 50 ladies on stage doing Tang-era dances (which involves robes with very long pink sleeves, flicking and writhing in perfect synchronization).

Now scene follows scene, with each more extraordinary than the last. We are familiar with traditional Chinese dance because we have been to see Shen Yun several times (which is well worth it, if it ever tours in your neighbourhood!). But this is on another level. There are solo performances, as well as duets between the emperor and Yang; there are dream sequences that use the hill as a screen to project swirling lights; there are 50 armoured warriors performing a martial dance with swords and spears; there are Russian-style dances and Middle Eastern-style dances to reflect the cosmopolitan nature of Chang'an and the cultural influences flowing along the Silk Road. There is a rebellion is which rockets are fired into the lake and it catches fire (honestly—it is so intense that you can feel the heat in the back row of the auditorium). There are love sequences where you can smell the blossom. There is an episode where the stage submerges slightly (still illuminated, of course) and the dancers are actually dancing *in the lake*. When the emperor is sad—after Yang's demise—there is a thunderstorm where it really rains and lightening appears. Yang reappears as phoenix with a beautiful feather tail around 4 m long. And there is a clinch at the end—where the emperor joins Yang in heaven—that involves two enormous arms (made to appear like stones) rising out of the lake and spinning around so that the lovers meet in the middle, 7 m above the water. It is breathtaking. I am sure that it sounds contrived and gimmicky from my description. But it flows so seamlessly and naturally, and blends so well with the surroundings of the palace and the hill and lake, that it is spellbinding.

There are so many things to see and experience in Xi'an that one follows another like raindrops falling in the monsoon. The next morning we got up late (having been out way past the children's normal bedtime) and decided to run off some energy. Being only five, Elizabeth (in particular) has only a limited tolerance for historical sites and had been very good the previous day. So we decided to cycle around the city walls. Xi'an has the most complete city walls in China. They are very thick and there is *de facto* a two-lane road all the way around the top, so you can make a 20 km circuit on hired bicycles. We hired three tandems, with one adult driving each and one child on the back of each. (The hiring process was a little tricky because the children are supposed to be over ten years old. Of course, the bicycle renters are happy to disregard the law as long as they are not obviously doing so. Hence, we parked the children around the corner and hired the bikes before collecting the children and heading off on our expedition.) It was fun! The walls must be 15 m high and there are great views in to the old city and out to the new city. The existing walls date from the Ming dynasty; Chang'an—which is believed to have numbered about a million inhabitants—was surrounded by an even longer wall. The Muslim quarter and the mosque are inside the wall; we planned to see those but ran out of time on our trip. There is a beautiful Tibetan Buddhist temple, with a gold roof, at one corner of the old city wall. There are also a couple of impressive barbicans defending the main gates.

It was mid-afternoon by the time we had finished, so a little between normal meal times. But we managed to find a well-known restaurant serving a traditional local dish. This was basically lamb or beef soup (mostly broth, with one slice of meat placed on top) into which you have to crumble a kind of hard bread (almost like sailor's hard tack). I cannot say that it was the greatest dish ever, but it was perfectly fine and the children had fun crumbling the bread—which was surprisingly tough on the fingers—and it kept them out of trouble while we were waiting for the soup to be ready. Then we headed down to the Big Goose Pagoda—a place whose interest we had rather underestimated.

The pagoda was built by Emperor Gaozong in 652 CE to store the thousands of manuscripts brought back from India by Tang Seng. It is a seven-storey brick and stone structure—and you can walk up the stairs to the top! WOW! I cannot think of any other multi-storey building from such a date that is still standing and in good condition, and certainly not one that is open to the public. I have been to the Pantheon in Rome—which is awe-inspiring but not multi-storey; maybe there are some tall Mayan temples—although I think that they are of a later date. It is really extraordinary to be able to go up the pagoda, and see the places where monks travailed for years on end to translate the sutras brought back by Tang Seng. You can look out of the large windows—one on each side, on each floor—over the city and imagine what the view would have been when Chang'An was a city of a million people. There are precious samples of the sutras on one floor, sealed carefully into glass tubes (the sutras are written on leaves, not paper, because paper was far too expensive a medium at that time). On another floor, there is a small, highly decorated stupa with a relic of Buddha inside.

Outside the temple complex is a huge square boasting a big bronze of Tang Seng, as well as bronze statues of vernacular street scenes from the Tang period (men wrestling, musicians playing, a birthday gathering). A park linked to the square contains a formal area with cherry trees—magnificent with blossom at the time of our visit—and a large informal area of grass and groves with more statues. Not surprisingly, this is the place in Xi'an to hang out at the weekends and it is crowded with people meeting friends and relaxing. It is a popular place to fly kites and the Chinese are passionate about this. Elderly men have huge spools of yarn strapped to their waists (like an upside-down fishing reel, but bigger) and fly big kites really high in the sky. Some of the kites are multi-deckers—kites attached to kites above and below them, flying in a tall stack. The kites even have LED lights and continue flying into the night, flashing and flitting and making lovely patterns. At the north end of the square, there is a massive fountain area, the size of a football field. It is paved with fountain spouts set into the floor. Every night at 8:30 p.m. there is a *son et lumière* and the fountains dance to the music.

The next day we went to the Shaanxi History Museum. WOW! With 1500 years as the capital of China, there is a lot of beautiful and amazing craftsmanship to be dug up around Xi'an and you will find much of it in this museum—more than you can appreciate in one visit. Some of the gold dishes are extraordinary—beautifully shaped (not simply circular but something much more complicated) and covered in chased patterns. And the pottery is fascinating—from relatively simple pieces over 2000 years old to extraordinary Tang era figures of people, horses and camels. After a couple of hours, we were rather overloaded—especially the children—and we went off to do something more fun for them. If we had more time in Xi'an (without children), then I would have been tempted to go back another day. I should also say that the museum was extremely crowded; it made the V&A in London in half term week look empty by comparison. Disregarding the museum plan completely, the logical order in which to view the treasures is to start with the room that is least crowded (since you anyway cannot actually see into the display cases in the other rooms) and work your way up through the levels of intensity until your cannot stand any more (which might be "Black Hole of Calcutta" level for a dedicated antiquities hound, but only "Squashed on the Tube at rush hour" level for normal people).

In true Chinese fashion, there is an odd method for allocating tickets that engenders complicated stratagems to circumvent the system. For each morning and each afternoon, there are 3000 free tickets available, for which you can register online. Naturally, these had all gone by the time we got around to searching for tickets. OK, we can pay—no problem. But when you get to the museum there is a *massive* queue to buy tickets; people were queuing round the block. This is not good if you have three small children. But it is OK because you can contact a "tour operator" who can get you special tickets (for a commission, naturally), which involves entering through the turnstile in the gift shop—where there is no queue at all. I have no idea how these things work (have I broken the law here, or has someone paid a bribe to make this happen?); but Lily sorted it all out for us without batting an eyelid and I just played dumb (which was easy for me, obviously).

After a couple of hours we went off the Lotus Garden. This is a Tang-themed park created recently on the site of a genuine Tang palace and garden. At its heart is a splendid lake, complete with a "marble boat". A marble boat is not actually a boat at all. It is a pavilion built out into the water so that it looks like boat that is miraculously floating, despite being made of stone. In fact, the stone is anyway commonly wood that is painted to look like marble! The most famous example of the genre is in the Summer Palace in Beijing. The original boat there was built by Emperor Qianlong in 1755 to emphasize the solidity and permanence of the Qing dynasty. This architectural statement of intent was itself harking back to the comment of the great scholar Xunzi that "Water can carry the boat as well as overturn it"—meaning that the people can either support an emperor or overthrow him. An irony of the Summer Palace marble boat is that—having been burnt down by the Western powers in their punitive expedition of 1860—it is rumoured to have been rebuilt in 1893 by Empress Dowager Cixi using money diverted from reconstruction of the Qing navy. (The Qing navy continued to be heavily outgunned and was eliminated in the tumult of 1899, in which the marble boat demonstrated no significant maritime or military capability.)

Some argue that the Dowager Cixi story is a falsehood perpetuated by the Republicans to discredit the Qing regime. This certainly fits with the idea that when things go wrong in China the wife of the emperor or great leader must take the blame—an argument put forward in the fascinating BBC Radio 4 podcast about the Soong Sisters, for example. (By contrast, in England it is not the king's wife who takes the blame but his advisors. This tradition goes back at least a thousand years to Æthelread the Unready, who was not really "unready" but rather *unræd*, which is Old English for "ill-advised".) The issue of sexual equality in China is an interesting one. If you ask educated Chinese women, then they will tell you vehemently that there is no sexism in China—that they never even had the idea when growing up that women and men were treated differently. I then ask them how many female members there are of the Politburo (i.e. the 25-member body that *de facto* serves as the cabinet). That answer is zero. As far as I know, there has never been a female member of the Politbureau. Can you imagine a Western government in which there were no female ministers? There would be public outrage. Obviously, there has never been a female president, nor indeed an empress (I mean a woman who ruled in her own right, rather than as the consort of the emperor).

My brush with Tang culture left me wishing that the current Chinese Government would aspire to recreate the vibrancy and openness of the Tang Empire, rather than the rigid and closed formalism of the Qing Empire. An obvious contrast between the view from Beijing in 2016 and the view from Chang'an in 716 concerns the role of the Silk Road, which is currently being reinvented as the "One Belt, One Road" initiative. This involves building train lines to Pakistan and across central Asia, as well as sea lanes to Africa and accompanying train lines into the interior (amongst other projects). I will discuss the economics of this initiative elsewhere, but the point here is that it is partly designed to project Chinese power and influence into central Asia and Africa. There is certainly no notion that this will be a conduit for foreign influences to enter China. In fact, this is clearly the last thing that China wants, since it might bring calls for changes such as increased democracy or greater freedom for religious minorities. In 2013, President Xi created the "Central Leadership Group for Internet Security and Informatization" and made himself its head. (People have argued that this is the way that President Xi moves to monopolize power within China. He does not start a war with his political rivals in the Politburo by removing them from their roles; instead he creates a new role and takes it for himself. He takes one bean off the plate at a time and eventually his rivals will find that there are no beans left.)

This innovation gives President Xi indirect control of the "General Administration of Press, Publication, Radio, Film and Television". Just last month (March, 2016), new regulations outlawed foreign ownership of internet publishing services (which includes things like iTunes and film streaming services) and required all material visible to Chinese web users to be stored on servers based on the Chinese mainland. This will obviously make censorship much easier: first, the state can more easily monitor what is on the servers; and, second, no one will have any justification for crossing the Great Firewall and searching the web outside China. This move is considered essential to "combat terrorism and foreign ideas that could prove harmful". It is true that foreign ideas may be harmful: my guess is that the new train line to Pakistan will greatly help the Taliban or Al-Qaeda in sending equipment and training to Uyghur separatists who are intent on murdering people. But I don't think that greater censorship of the internet is going to hold back that particular tide. By contrast, it will shut out many beneficial, stimulating and enriching foreign ideas and concepts. If the Chinese really want to make the next step to modernization, to complement the economic modernization that has occurred over the last 30 years, they should move the capital from Beijing to Xi'an. This would be a real statement of intent about moving China from the rutted remnants of the Ming and Qing empires (in which China is, in many ways, still ideologically stuck) into a new mindset embracing the world and standing with it on an equal footing (culturally and politically, as well as economically and socially).

I have read that China's population of 1.4 billion includes only 40,000 foreigners who have acquired citizenship—hardly the sign of a society that is open to outside influences. Yet Chinese people think that they are open to the world because a very few Chinese (relatively) study abroad and then bring back Western technical knowledge. They fundamentally do not understand that being open to the world requires much more than this, and their society (and economy) will get precious little push from the trickle of returning PhDs. Even if those returning PhDs have observed how academic endeavour works, they are soon crushed under the weight of Chinese hierarchy. If you go to a university research seminar, then the atmosphere is really dead. Essentially, no one will ask questions during the seminar; and the few questions that arise after the seminar are taken in strict order of academic hierarchy, where that never descends below the level of assistant professor. Questioning is a key tool in the Anglo-American method of education—a way to increase one's understanding of the ideas being presented and also to challenge them. But questioning authority is alien and dangerous in China, so you can understand why few people are willing to do it. While you can have brilliant scientists under this kind of regime—as we saw in the Soviet Union—it does not seem to be enough to maintain intellectual or technical progress at the scientific frontier. Unless China really opens itself to the world and welcomes challenge and innovation (in the very broadest sense) its progress will fade away. And it will always be behind the US—which the Chinese find so annoying—because the US attracts and welcomes the brightest and the best (people and ideas) and absorbs them into the US economy and culture.

The Monday (Tomb Sweeping Day) was our last in Xi'an, and we had to catch a flight at 5:30 p.m. So we decided to see the tomb of Emperor Jingdi. One advantage of this arrangement is that the tomb is only 20 minutes from the airport, so there was no stress about possible traffic hold-ups. (Like everywhere else in China, the traffic in Xi'an is very heavy; you wouldn't want to be driving out of the city centre at rush hour with a flight to catch.) Also, there is less to see at Emperor Jingdi's tomb and it is not a whole day expedition.

Jingdi was an emperor of the Han dynasty and his tomb was built around 153 BCE (i.e. around 70 years after Emperor Qin). To keep up with the Joneses, he was buried with 50,000 terracotta figurines who were all dressed in silk robes (none of this painting nonsense, like Emperor Qin) and replica accoutrements (thousands of bronze belt buckles and coins and weapons and chops). However, these figurines are not life size—only about knee-high—and the excavated pits do not look as immediately impressive as Emperor Qin's. The figures were turned out using moulds—although the sculptors still had to create a large number of anatomically correct moulds to reflect the rich array of fauna inhabiting Jingdi's palace, such as males, females and eunuchs. Everything that you might need in the afterlife was present and correct: terracotta barns and granaries and millstones, so that agricultural production need not be interrupted; thousands of sheep, pigs, goats and cows; terracotta stoves and bronze cooking utensils to transform it all into a feast fit for an emperor. The whole thing is like a Barbie and Ken playhouse on an insane scale. A nice aspect of Jingdi's tomb is that the excavations are covered with a glass ceiling (as well as being inside a building, of course) so visitors can actually walk over the dig and watch the archaeologists at work (which is particularly child-friendly). I don't know of anywhere else that you can do this, and get a real feeling for what archaeology is actually like (hard work and mostly dull, I think, to be honest: digging an entire pit several metres deep with a paintbrush, to make sure that you do not miss the tiniest artefact, must be very tiring and tedious 99.9 per cent of the time). Still, I have the greatest respect for these people and I appreciate the work that they do and the objects that they bring to light.

Of course, there is always a sting in the tail whenever you do anything with children, such as an embarrassing meltdown on the way home. In fact, our children were as good as gold for the entire trip. The elder two even spent their time at the boarding gate and on the flight doing their homework, without a whimper, which was pretty heroic. Since we left Beijing straight after school on Thursday night, they had two days' worth of homework to do—Thursday and Friday—and we wanted to make sure that they were up to speed on Tuesday, so as not to test the patience of the teachers. Taking your children out of school for frivolities such as travel—even rather educational expeditions—is basically unheard of in China, so we already felt that we were pushing the limits of social acceptability a bit.

The sting in the tail on this occasion was entirely external. It turns out that if you take your child out of Beijing, then you have to keep them out of kindergarten for three days after you return! So Elizabeth was not allowed to go back to school until Thursday. It should really have been Friday—since we effectively kept her at home only on Tuesday and Wednesday—but we negotiated with the teacher and she agreed to count Monday as a day in Beijing, rather than a day out of town. This is, of course, a very Chinese solution to a ridiculous problem. Can you imagine having such a rule in England, or Europe more generally? Children would spend more time out of kindergarten than in it, given the frequency with which they leave their home town or city. It also makes you wonder about the motivation for this rule. China must be filled either with ridiculously over-zealous bureaucrats or with virulent (but heavily localized) diseases (which affect children of kindergarten age but not older). You can take your pick.

This rule is entirely consistent with other aspects of child health, though. For example, every morning the teachers inspect the throats of every child as they enter the classroom (using a torch and lollipop sticks) to ensure that they are not sick. We are also obliged to take our child's temperature before leaving home and enter it into a register outside the classroom door. Since our thermometer has run out of battery (we have several child thermometers but none of them ever seem to be working when we need one?!), our child's temperature is 36.5°C every day. I notice that the temperatures of all the other children are all in the low 36-point-somethings; since the temperature of children generally averages 36.8°C, I assume that all the other parents are erring on the side of caution—like me—to make sure that there is no excuse for the school to send the child home. I hope that no medical researchers try to use these data in the future to assess the health of Chinese children because they would get some pretty weird results: we would probably be told that increasing average height is accelerated by keeping your child's core body temperature below the biological norm, or some other complete tosh.

The Chinese kindergarten is similarly careful when it comes to readmitting children after a day of absence through sickness. You are supposed to get a doctor's letter saying that it is safe for the child to return to kindergarten, or the child has to be checked by the school nurse. Elizabeth's school seems to have an entire sick bay staffed by three people. Obviously, this is a strong disincentive to keep your child off school if they are feeling off colour (which is a pretty common occurrence, in our experience of having three children), especially since these episodes typically do not escalate into anything serious anyway—so you might as well risk it and save yourself the hassle and expense of a pointless trip to the doctor. Happily, we were ignorant of all this when Elizabeth was sniffly, so we kept her off school on the Friday and sent her in as normal on the Monday. No one actually asked us for the doctor's letter—presumably because it was too much trouble to have to talk to us and explain the protocol in English—and the school nurse just signed off on it.

Anyway, the requirement to keep Elizabeth off school effectively scrubbed out another two days of work for daddy, since someone had to look after Elizabeth while she was at home. Hence, a long weekend for the family turned into a week off work for the parents. Still, it was definitely all worth it. Whenever I mention Xi'an to my Chinese friends, they say: "Actually, I have never been to Xi'an. All the Westerners go there and say that it is great." It really is great. It really was worth having a week off work to see it. I wish that all Chinese would see it—it is really a cultural gem and an alternative template for Chinese society.

OK, I am going to send this right now. It is still Sunday morning where you are, so you might even be able to find time to read this today if I am quick:-)

Very best wishes,

Liam.

References

BBC Radio 4, "The Soong Sisters—The Consorts", Episode 5 in the series *China: As History is my Witness*, presented by Carrie Gracie, 2012.

Pines, Yuri, Gideon Shelach, Lothar von Falkenhausen and Robin D. S. Yates (eds.), *The Birth of an Empire: the State of Qin Revisited*, Berkeley: University of California Press, 2014.

Letter 8

A Week of Firsts
17 April 2016

Dear Aleks,

Since you have been a good boy and replied assiduously to my emails, you can be the first to get this week's instalment. And I think that you deserve an award, anyway, for being a Hero of Socialist Labour and driving three children 2000 miles to take a holiday (what are you, some kind of masochist?). If you make it all the way back without a homicide or suicide en route, then I promise to send you another instalment next week.…

Having just about recovered from our Xi'an trip, we launch into another hectic week. Our first first was to see our youngest daughter perform as part of the team raising the national flag and singing the national anthem. Of course, it was the Chinese flag and the Chinese national anthem. But we have never seen her raise the UK, US or French flags—any of which would be more expected, given our nationality and place of domicile—or sing any of those national anthems. So this definitely counts as a "first". They do this every Monday at the kindergarten and the children take it in turns to be part of the flag-raising crew. Parents are invited to witness the proud moment, so we went along to video our budding Good Citizen and potential Communist Party official starting out on the long road to obedience and self-sacrifice. (President Xi Jinping recently remarked that

Chinese journalists should "make the Communist Party their surname", although I would have thought that this would make life awkward when filling out official documents. In any case, I think that "Brunt" is more concise and potentially more accurate.) We felt privileged to be part of the occasion and we really appreciate the non-discriminatory and inclusive ethos of the school. And I am sure that any Chinese parent would be equally proud to see their children raising the Stars and Stripes and singing the "Star-spangled banner", or raising the Union Jack and singing "God save the Queen" (except, of course, that we do not do that type of thing in English schools). In fact, the British are remarkably non-jingoistic in this respect. It is very common in Norway and Sweden and Switzerland, for example, to fly the national flag outside one's house. This is just weird if you are English.

But we always try our best to fit in with local custom and we enjoyed the kindergarten flag-raising ceremony very much. And so did our daughter—she was very proud, torn between wanting to smile at us and wearing her really SERIOUS face for the occasion. The crew wears a special, bright red uniform and marches purposefully across the courtyard carrying the flag. Then it is attached by a teacher, hoisted by two members of the crew, and the national anthem is sung.

This is how Chinese children learn to socially cohere and subsume their individuality for the sake of the nation. A while ago I noticed a young boy in a hotel lift wearing an interesting T-shirt. It bore the silhouette of the famous statue of the US Marines raising the flag on Iwo Jima in 1945 (a little ironic, given the rest of the story). Underneath was the legend: "The Xisha Islands—Chinese Forever". And I thought to myself at the time that this child (and his parents) had truly absorbed the empowering message put out by the Communist Party of China, and this must evidently be a great and powerful thing. And now I have seen this process of empowerment in action: from such tiny seeds as three-year-olds attending school assembly, mighty and uncompromising oak trees are grown. Of course, we hope that the children of Vietnam will also be empowered in the future (probably wearing T-shirts stating "Hoàng Sa—Vietnamese Forever!") and I am sure that this is a great way to spread peace and prosperity in the world. You can see why the Hitler Youth Division of the SS was the most fearsome fighting formation of the

Second World War: they were the first (and only) generation of recruits to be schooled entirely within the Nazi propaganda regime. I am sure that the Young Pioneers in China would also gladly sell their lives dearly for the cause if they were told that it was necessary.

Lucy took video of the whole proceedings and we showed it later to Catherine and Annabelle. Not to be outdone, Catherine immediately launched into "We are the heirs of Communism", which is the song they use to indoctrinate elementary school children: www.youtube.com/watch?v=vo3K-BHMBf4. They cleverly have jingoistic songs for every age, you understand, with different ones for middle school and senior school students. But not everyone is invited to sing them—only the best students, and it gets more selective with age. Interestingly, Catherine seems quite susceptible to this type of propaganda. She is very competitive and wants to be the outstanding student in the class, in every discipline. Her best friend at school is the class leader and gets the best grades: Catherine is determined to be at least as good as her, so I guess that this is generally a positive development. A few weeks ago, the junior children (Catherine is in first grade) received a visit from some fourth grade students whose task was effectively to inspire them to join the Party. So Catherine came home excitedly with a leaflet describing the stripes—one, two or three—that you can get as you rise up through the ranks. She was also awarded a red neckerchief. Now, everyone in Annabelle's year (second grade) wears a neckerchief with their uniform, in which they are required to turn out every Monday and on special occasions. But first grade children are *not allowed* to wear the neckerchiefs, and they are given out only as a form of special recognition, to be kept safely until the child enters second grade. We were therefore pretty flabbergasted when Catherine, and only one other girl in the class, were awarded their red neckerchiefs. I even wonder whether I am living through a remake of *The Manchurian Candidate* (they have already done it with a black actor, in the form of Denzel Washington, so maybe it is time for a girl to take on the role). I am not entirely sure what Catherine does at school, but it seems to make her very popular with students, staff and Party officials! Catherine then launched into the Chinese national anthem.

In fact, Catherine came home very happy on Thursday. One of the parents had given a presentation about "travel" to all the first grade classes—and there are 400 children in first grade in total! There were various quiz questions thrown to the children on the way through the talk, to keep their attention, and if you answered a difficult one correctly, then you got a prize. The presenter asked for whom the terracotta warriors in Xi'an were made. Catherine was one of the few children to raise her hand and, when called upon, answered correctly that it was the Emperor Qin Shi Huang. Obviously, she was very proud to be able to demonstrate her superior knowledge of Chinese history to the rest of the school, and won a cuddly brown rabbit into the bargain (which is, of course, the best possible prize for my most bunny-loving daughter).

I must say that Annabelle does not fit this mould at all. She sits diagonally behind the class leader and cannot stand the girl. She thinks that she is too bossy and should mind her own business. She told Lucy that she used to fight with her all the time. Lucy said: "Do you really mean fight, like hitting each other?" Annabelle said: "No, just with words. The trouble is, she always wins because it's all in Chinese. So now I just ignore her instead." Smart girl! Just wait until Little Miss Bossy comes to school in Boston and has to debate in English or French—then we'll see who's the boss…. In Annabelle's class, they keep the same seating arrangement throughout the year, except that each week they move one chair to the left so that no pupil spends more time than any other immediately in front of the teacher. Annabelle tells us that she is looking forward to the week when she is in the far left column—at which point the class leader will be over in the far right column and she will be unable to speak to her for an entire week!

Annabelle is by far the least gregarious of my three daughters and is generally rather aloof: she can happily go through life without needing the company of other humans, and makes no effort to hide it. In fact, yesterday she was evidently very self-satisfied when she confided in us that she has found a secret passageway into her classroom, which means that she can get into the classroom more-or-less unobserved and with no pushing and shoving. It seems that there is a back staircase—which she noticed on her way to and from the music room—that no one else uses. So she has adopted it and swans around serenely while all the other children jostle up and down the main drag. Some people might find this aptitude for solitude an unattractive trait, but I rather like it: it reminds me very much of me! Of course, this is not the best way to get ahead in life, so—rather hypocritically—I always encourage Annabelle to be more sociable and I extoll the virtues of teamwork and so on. But I am apparently rather ineffective in this endeavour. She made me laugh when I discovered that she can do the "Moonwalk": I showed them a snippet of Michael Jackson and Annabelle could copy him straight off, whereas her sisters struggled to get the step. I was a bit surprised by all this because Annabelle is not the most natural dancer among our children, but then she explained why. In case you have never thought about it, I should say that when you do the Moonwalk, you make a kind of exaggerated movement of the arms and knee (they swing backwards and forwards vigorously) to make it look like you are walking forwards. But when your knee bends forward and you heel lifts up, you keep your toe on the floor; then, as your knee straightens back and your heel goes down, your toe slides backwards a little. So you have shuffled backwards while looking like you have stepped forwards. How did Annabelle discover this technique? At recreation, they have to assemble in long lines outside in the courtyard and do various exercises, such as marching on the spot. She couldn't be faffed with all that marching business, so she developed a style whereby it looked like you were marching vigorously but you don't actually have to pick up your feet! From there, it is but a microscopic movement to the Moonwalk—one small step for man, one backward step for dance. The secret anarchist in me applauds the way she subverted the system. In fact, I wonder if this is a metaphor for the whole of China....

Our second first this week is that Annabelle went on a school trip, and it was a particularly appropriate one. They took her off to the Chinese Nationalities Park. This is a sort of theme park designed to celebrate the 56 recognized "nationalities", or ethnic groups, of the People's Republic of China. Annabelle is fascinated by the Chinese minorities—their costumes, their music and dancing, and their architecture. China certainly pays lip service to safeguarding and celebrating its many nationalities and minorities. It is difficult for me to judge how these minorities are really treated, since I have not yet travelled to many of these places and spoken privately to any of the people from minority groups. Obviously, I am aware that many Tibetans and Uyghurs feel that they are being overwhelmed by the inflow of Han Chinese and that this is (perhaps deliberately) destroying or suppressing their culture. On the other hand, minorities are given preference in education. For example, they require lower grades in the high school exam that determines entry into higher education (the dreaded "Gaokao"). In fact, the Government has tightened up the eligibility requirements recently to stop Han Chinese moving to minority areas for a couple of years in order to register their (well educated) children as coming from a minority area and thereby gaining an unfair advantage for university entry. (Does this sound familiar? Of course, it is just like the parents who put down false addresses, or move house, in England or Norway in order to be in the right school catchment area for the best schools.) Minorities were also exempted from the One Child policy and so, in principal, could come to comprise a larger share of total population. (A more cynical view of this, though, is that the Han Chinese needs worker bees. If you have only one child, then you can pump many resources—such as further education—into that child and they will do well in life. This is exactly what has happened over the last 30 years: educational levels of Han Chinese have risen massively. But those families who are having multiple children end up stuck in poverty trap of low paid or migrant work.)

The celebration of the minorities does bring to the fore the fact that China really is, and always has been, an empire—a collection of separate and distinct kingdoms under the rule of one monarch (the Emperor). For hundreds of years, neighbouring monarchs—such as the rulers of Tibet and Korea—recognized the Chinese Emperor as their suzerain or overlord. New kings sent tributes and received official recognition—such as Imperial Seals—in return. Korea was a client kingdom of the Yuan Emperors from 1270 CE to 1354 CE; it accepted Chinese suzerainty when the kingdom was refounded as Joseon in 1392 CE; and it recognized the Qing Emperors as suzerains again in 1636 CE. Tibet came under Yuan authority following the Mongol conquest of China and Tibet around 1250 CE and it persisted through the Ming and Qing periods, when Chinese forces were garrisoned in Lhasa. This partly explains the Chinese view that Tibet is an integral part of China. Of course, it was never populated historically by Han Chinese, nor ruled directly from Beijing, in the way that it has been since 1950. I am not seeking to legitimize what has happened in Tibet. I am merely explaining that the Chinese have quite an encompassing and imperial concept of "China" and they see modern efforts to assert their control in neighbouring regions merely as a continuation of longstanding tradition. Moreover, at various times following the unification of China by Emperor Qin, the country has been split into competing centres of authority. For example, from 1038 CE to 1227 CE there was a western Chinese kingdom, generally known as the Tangut Empire, based in Yinchuan. The Tangut Empire—which covered 800,000 km^2—was reunited with the rest of the Chinese Empire after the Mongols eradicated it in 1227 CE, and then went on to conquer the rest of China. As far as the Chinese are concerned, the Tangut Empire was an errant province for 200 years. Hence the view from Beijing that Taiwan is an errant province that will be reunited with the rest of China in due course (where "due course" could be several hundred years).

Since Annabelle had enjoyed the park so much, we decided to visit it ourselves with all three girls on Saturday. It was a beautiful day—about 20°C and sunny, with blossom everywhere and no pollution. In truth, the pollution in Beijing has been nowhere near as bad as we feared. True, there are some days with horrible pollution and then you need to wear a mask and you wouldn't want to go cycling or jogging (which we don't, anyway). But there are also many days with little or no pollution and the air is no worse than many cities in Europe or the US. It is much better to have this variability than to have the pollution spread evenly across through the week: then you would always have to wear a mask and never get a clear view of the sky and the mountains outside the city. I understand that the pollution situation is better in the spring than in the winter (when more coal is burnt for heating and so on), so I don't want to downplay the severity of the problem. But—in our limited experience—the pollution is not the worst or most constraining aspect of life in Beijing.

The park was indeed very interesting, and very large. We spent about five hours touring only the northern half of the park, which is constructed around a fine lake. The northern half mostly consists of about 20 replica "villages" from various minorities, typically built by craftsmen from the minorities (either *in situ* or in pieces and then shipped to Beijing for assembly). The southern half of the park has more cultural exhibitions and shows, and we hope to go back and see that another time. The villages in the northern park are very varied. They include minorities from the far north (such as Koreans in Jilin province and Oroqen from Heilongjiang) to the far south (the Li people of Hainan Island); and from the west (Tibet and the Salar of Qinghai) to the east (the Gaoshan of Taiwan). The traditional Korean and the Salar dwellings have beds constructed like stoves: they are made of clay and you light fires inside them! Obviously, it gets very cold in those places in the winter (easily down to −20°C) so the houses have to be well heated. The buildings are of a heavy, wood construction and feature beautiful carving—both outside (on balconies and eaves, and so on) and inside (on furniture and doors). By contrast, the southern Li villages are made of bamboo covered with mud.

In fact, we had visited a Li village when we were travelling through Hainan in January and we were greeted there by young girls in traditional dress. The cloth from which their clothes are made is quite extraordinary: it typically has a black background and is shot through with very colourful woven designs, often geometric but also incorporating animals and flowers. The material is very thick and strong and is all hand made by the villagers from local plants, such as tree bark, that they harvest in the forest. To spin and dye and weave those threads is extremely labour intensive and essentially uneconomic: it is a dying art, maintained only by the elderly women of the village. Sitting flat on the floor, they use a very interesting loom that has a foot bar to stretch out the warp while the weft is passed backwards and forwards by hand. The Li have been famous for cloth making for hundreds of years. As long ago as 1270 CE, a woman called Huang Daopo travelled from Shanghai to learn their skills and then went back to Shanghai to set up her own cloth factory. The Li village that we visited is essentially a "living museum" and there was also a really extensive and interesting display of artefacts and historical material—such as traditional costumes from different minority groups in the area (who have different ways of earning a living and therefore clothing that is adapted differently to their needs).

The Li are also interesting because their society is matriarchal: it is the men who have had to work the fields and woo the women with gifts. Why? Perhaps because the women have this special skill—high quality weaving—that makes them the primary breadwinner? The Li women decorate their legs all over with tattoos and chew a lot of betel nut—which makes your teeth go brown—and this reminds me quite a lot of the women in my home town (you can see why I left). In fact, one of the tests that a male suitor has to pass is to collect 49 betel nuts from 49 different trees in an hour; they do this by climbing up the vertiginous trunks (which have no branches because they are a type of palm) armed with a knife. Their customs and history are portrayed in a spectacular piece of song and dance theatre at the Li village. The whole thing is well worth visiting if you are ever in Sanya. (Sanya is a beach destination on the southern side of Hainan Island and a good place to go to escape the Chinese winter: it is reasonably warm and unpolluted. You also do not need a Chinese visa to go to Hainan for tourism—it has a special exemption—so it is relatively easy and cheap to arrange.)

The Li village is part of a complex that includes a Miao village. They are more of a mountain people and traditionally earn their living from hunting rather than agriculture (in contrast to the Li people). The Miao people are one of the largest minorities in China, numbering over seven million and being spread over a vast area—from Hainan Island up to Guizhou, which is about a two-hour plane ride away! I think that there must be a lot of diversity within the Miao culture, given the great distances and rough terrain that separate the various populations. Even a fairly small country, such as Switzerland, demonstrates enormous linguistic and cultural diversity precisely because it has historically been difficult for villagers in one valley to talk to villagers in the next valley: they are separated by high mountains. The Miao village—located further up the hill than the Li village—somehow has a more "Disney" feel to it than the Li village. At the entrance to the village there are skulls and warning signs written in red (which is presumably supposed to be fake blood) and a large wooden pig trap (i.e. a spikey contraption that drops onto the pig when animal accidently pulls the trigger). Although the Miao may have used skulls and warning signs and pig traps, I doubt that they were placed at the entry to the village; hence it all seems a bit fake and overplayed. Whereas the old Li ladies demonstrate cloth and basket weaving while you watch, the attractions of the Miao village focus on tanks of poisonous spiders and snakes—again, hardly something that I suppose the typical Miao village had on hand.

The children had great fun in the park—mostly finding sticks in the undergrowth and fishing tadpoles out of the lake (and putting them back in again, I hasten to add). The cultural aspects were a less prominent part of the experience for Catherine and Elizabeth than for the adults and Annabelle. Still, it is always surprising what the children remember about these things: Elizabeth will often make a comment a month later about some very detailed observation that she made during a visit and it makes you realize just how much she does absorb.

My personal first this week was to speak to a westerner—the first to whom I have spoken since I arrived in China in January. It was purely a work affair: I was at a conference and it seemed polite to speak to as many people as possible, including the two other barbarians present (some of whose hair was even fairer than my own!). I realized that my goal of total Chinese immersion has been working quite well, and I am happy to say that I have no regrets or problems (at least, no problems that would have been better solved by talking to another westerner). The children seem to have missed Western society even less than me. To get them to write to their Boston school friends is a struggle—partly because we are always whisking them away to see something, partly because they have had enough of book work by the time their free time comes around, partly because they are not good at typing (so even a very short email takes a very long time to write), and partly because they are reasonably well entertained by all the new friends that they have made in Beijing. Even Annabelle seems to have made some friends (or, perhaps more accurately, some kindly classmates seem to have befriended her). In fact, we have been racking up some IOUs in the classmate stakes because we have not been entertaining other people's children as often as they entertain ours/ have homework play dates, especially in Annabelle's case. This is basically a scheduling issue: the classmates have after school activities on several evenings per week, so it is difficult to find a mutually convenient slot when we can have them over to our place.

Lily suggested that we arrange a climbing date at the rock gym on Sunday afternoon with a couple of Annabelle's classmates. We ended up with seven children (our three girls, plus two classmates, plus a sibling, plus the daughter of a friend of ours) and six parents (two who came to belay—Lucy and me—plus two who wanted to climb, plus two others who preferred to watch). It was fun. Not surprisingly, our girls raced up the walls multiple times—they have done it before—while the others were content to boulder on the lower parts of the wall. ("Bouldering" is where you try to chain together several challenging moves in a very benign setting—such as a few feet off the ground with a crash mat beneath you—where it is not scary if you fall off.) Of course, our girls also bouldered with their friends and everyone tore around and burnt off lots of energy. We have been to this particular rock gym several times before. It is fairly average (not very high or large) but perfectly adequate for a couple of hours' entertainment; and it is always surprisingly empty on a Sunday afternoon. I would have thought that in Beijing—where it is often polluted outside and the winters are fairly cold—lots of people would want to go to the climbing wall but that seems to be not the case, perhaps because it is expensive by local standards. Also, the adults whom we see at the gym are not very good. In a British rock gym you tend to see either children or dedicated adults, who are therefore typically rather skilful. I guess that this type of bourgeois leisure activity it fairly new in China (like cycling or skiing) so maybe there is just not yet a cohort of comfortably off 40-year-olds who have spent many years climbing for pleasure. In any case this place has a very casual air, which is ideal if you want to show up with a bunch of noisy children because you do not feel that you are interrupting any serious training sessions.

From the outset, we deliberately left our weekends unencumbered (no regular clubs or formal activities, unlike in Boston) so that we are able to travel and see things in China. But we are not travelling every weekend—which would be totally exhausting—and we often have some days or afternoons free to meet with other children and families. Since we have three children, and two (at least!) are fairly gregarious, we have ended up doing quite a lot of socializing with Chinese families. Sometimes this is easy because many of the parents speak English (a high proportion of them being university professors, or similar). Sometimes it is difficult because the parents either do not speak English or are rather out of practice. Smartphone translators are then a useful tool, although not as useful as smartchild translators: I recommend that everyone should take a smartchild with them when they travel. In years to come, I will even have someone to programme my electronic devices for me when I cannot be bothered to read the instructions. My smartchild is even voice-activated (although that particular function is a little erratic in the model that I have). And—just like other smart devices—your smartchild will often give you the information that it thinks you ought to want to know, not the information for which you actually asked.

The fourth first occurred on Tuesday morning: it rained in Beijing. I understand that it must have rained before in Beijing (although I could be persuaded to the contrary) but not in the seven weeks that we have been here (thereby making it a first for us, at least). Not only that, it even hailed for about 15 seconds. We took photos of a puddle in the school playground. Seven weeks without rain is a bit unusual if you are English—and completely unheard of if you live in Bergen in Norway! (Bergen is the European city with the highest number of rain days per year, at 202, and it has been known to rain for 85 days in succession.) Beijingers are obviously not used to precipitation. I saw a man take a tissue and carefully wipe the rain drops off both his car wing mirrors, so that he could see properly when pulling away. I admire his dedication to safety but fear he would get very little done in a day in Bergen. And he would get through a lot of tissues. The concierge of our apartment building obviously felt that it was a red letter day, too, because when we got home a red carpet stretched from the outside porch across the foyer. In fairness, this may simply have been a ploy to make the tiles less slippery and avoid anyone breaking a hip, or reduce the amount of mopping that she has to do in the day. But I did feel that we were getting star treatment for a special occasion. Sadly, I don't think that there was enough rainfall to clean the façade of the building or the windows, which are constantly grimy from the pollution. In fact, my five-year-old noted that the rain was probably very dirty, and the puddles certainly smelt like there were a few dead dogs in the bottom. I remember it raining in Dubai (this was a couple of decades ago, when Dubai was not like it is today) and the effect was somewhat similar. I think that a point is reached when a place gets so little rain that it might be better off with none at all; Beijing may just be at that tipping point.

The fifth first was seeing someone get a parking ticket. Parking in Beijing could best be described as "freestyle". Gateways seem to be a favourite; painted traffic islands are also fair game (on major junctions and elsewhere). In fact, the painted traffic islands at junctions, and pedestrian crossings, are particularly favoured stopping zones for carts—both hand-drawn and horse-drawn—carrying retail goods. I regularly see a moth-eaten, furry pony standing patiently while a sun-baked son of the sod tries to sell a cartload of oranges or durians to passers buy. You might think that this would dangerously impede the traffic (vehicular and pedestrian) but it is usually at night, when the roads are a bit less busy; of course, all these carts are entirely unlit, so I am not sure that this is a net safety improvement. The gaps between the trees on the wide pavements of the boulevards are also a handy parking option for those who don't like to walk too far (i.e. cars just drive straight up the kerb and park across the footpath). This is particularly troublesome when trying to collect my daughter from school because the parked cars block the whole width of the footpath and the only way to circumvent them is to walk in the road and risk getting run down. Some people seem to have assigned on-street parking, which they defend with metal triangular bollards. Imagine having a contraption with two arms bolted to the road in the middle of the parking space; now flip up the arms and join them at the top with a padlock; this prevents people occupying the space unless they have the key. Or, at least, it prevents them occupying the whole space: they just park half in the space (i.e. pull right up tight to the bollard) and leave the rest of the car hanging out in the road. Now you have successfully parked your car, blocked an innocent person's parking space and blocked half the roadway. On the morning when it rained, I actually saw two people out giving parking tickets (to cars that were actually parked in parking spaces, rather ironically). Personally, I think that the traffic officials just wanted an excuse to leave the office and enjoy the rain!

I assume that traffic rules in Beijing are conceived to apply only to cars because motor scooters do just whatever the hell they like. Seeing them zip the wrong way up the divided highway is normal, as is riding on the footpath and using pedestrian crossings when they have a red light. That is, their way ahead is blocked because they have a red light; so they pretend to be a pedestrian and cross with the multitudes on foot; and then they carry on their way on the road once they have passed the intersection. I should note that you can turn right on a red in Beijing—as in most of the US—so there is a perpetual game of "chicken" going on between the pedestrians and the traffic. When the green man is illuminated and the allotted time for pedestrians to cross has arrived, cars turning right legitimately try to force their way around the corner and through the throng. Obviously, there is safety in numbers: one assumes that running down one pedestrian could be viewed as an accident by the driver but running down a dozen or a score could be viewed as mass murder. So the pedestrians surge forward together to establish their property right to the crossing and face down any drivers who try to exercise their right to attempt to turn right on a red. It is at this point that cheating scooters—who do not actually want to turn right but carry straight on—can sneak forward with the plebeian masses to cross the junction and then accelerate onwards on the other side. I have never seen any kind of traffic enforcement operation that might deter this type of behaviour. I am told that this is typical of many East Asian countries—and indeed Kuala Lumpur may be the regional champion—but this is the first time that I experienced it myself, so it was quite stressful (especially with three small children in tow, none of whom are used to this kind of thing).

I am pleased to report that one of the most popular scooter liveries that we see in Beijing is the Union Jack, which is extremely common. By contrast, I have almost never seen a scooter in the livery of any other nation. (I have seen precisely one Stars and Stripes and two German Eagle scooters.) In fact, the Union Jack logo is surprisingly common—you regularly see it on sweatshirts and rucksacks and so on—so I think that Britannia is still pretty cool over here. I am not sure why: is it because the London Olympics followed the Beijing Olympics, or because Cameron and Osborne have been busy flattering the Chinese in recent years? Although the UK does not get a royalty for using the Union Jack, we must get a lot of goodwill and that can only be a benefit for UK exporters. By contrast, I am amazed that I never see Vespa or Lambretta scooters. That style of scooter is one of the main modes of transport and Chinese consumers are willing to pay over the odds for anything that is chic. Given their history and Italian cachet, you would have thought that Vespa and Lambretta could command the kind of mark-ups that other Italian brands achieve (Dolce & Gabbana, Versace and so on)—even if the machinery inside were made cheaply in China. In fact, the insides being made cheaply in China would probably be an advantage because they would then be easy and cheap to maintain. I really question whether Vespa and Lambretta are under good management. And another market that is yet to be exploited is motorcycle helmets! You hardly ever see one. If someone could persuade the Chinese that helmets are wise and/or chic (back to Vespa and Lambretta again, or Dolce & Gabbana?), then they could make a mint, even if they earned only ten cents on every helmet sold.

Now, the Chinese are very much into "gaming the system" (i.e. bending the rules to breaking point). Three-wheelers are treated the same as motorcycles so many people—private individuals and businesses—use them. They come in all kinds of fascinating shapes and sizes. The most basic kind have a flatbed on the back and you see them chugging around carrying huge loads—overhanging the three-wheeler itself on every side, so that it takes up the same amount of space on the highway as a small lorry—and grunting noisily (this particular variety of three-wheeler generally seems to be powered with a smoky old two-stroke engine, circa 1940). Some have a truck-style bed on the back, and I have even seen a tipper version! There are also more modern, electric cargo carriers with neat aluminium cargo boxes, beloved of courier companies (of which there seem to be many in China). Then there are old-fashioned people carriers, which look rather like a nineteenth century carriage: they have coachwork on the back to protect the passengers but the driver sits up front under a little roof. There are also more modern versions that are totally enclosed and very square, like a tiny bus (and which always seem to be painted red); in fact, I am only surprised that the Chinese have not had the idea of creating double-decker three-wheelers in order to increase capacity. You even get futuristic three-wheelers that have a Perspex dome on top, which can telescope back in hot weather or forwards in winter to keep out the bitter winds. They look rather like moon buggies, and I suppose that the Beijing atmosphere is often rather similar (unbreathable exterior environment, covered in a thick layer of fine dust). Of course, you would rather have the luxury of a car, so you obviously want to construct a three-wheeler with full coachwork. Hence, we see many "deluxe" three-wheelers circulating that look like small cars (akin to the old Reliant Robin). I have even seen a four-wheeler! It was the size of a small car—such as a Suzuki—but it still had handlebars, rather than a steering wheel, so I suppose that made it a motorcycle?! I leapt out of its path as I was innocently walking the children to school and noticed it speeding silently up the sidewalk behind me, like a shark circling for a sneak attack.

In fact, my sixth first this week was seeing night work at my local newspaper kiosk-cum-motorcycle repair shop-cum-spot welding clinic (motto: "If your bike ain't right, then we'll fix it tonight"). The Chinese are nothing if not entrepreneurial. Most of the newspapers, magazines, ice creams, playing cards and so on are anyway stacked outside the kiosk, right? So there is plenty of room inside for a set of tools and an electric arc welder. And the kiosk is right next to some cycle parking. So people can—and do—pop in any time to have their bikes straightened out or joined back together. This seems to involve a lot of hitting things with a really big wrench.

OK, my wife is pointing out to me that it is late and we have to go to work tomorrow. So I am going to call a halt here and wish you a very happy holiday. We are in the process of planning a long weekend ourselves for the end of the month—I'll keep you posted.

Don't spend too long in the sun, or someone will mistake you for one of those lobsters that your daughters are ogling.

Very best wishes,

Liam.

Letter 9

Safety and Security
25 April 2016

Dear Tim,

A downside of our trip to Xi'an was Lucy losing her bankcard (actually, leaving it in the ATM—silly sausage!). She realized almost immediately that she had left the card and was able to phone the bank and block the card, so no financial damage was done. However, she did then have the fun of getting a new card when we returned to Beijing. Dealing with banks in China is an interesting experience. They are obsessed with security, but their concerns seem to centre on fraud by insiders as much as crime by outsiders. For example, when you go to open an account you have to complete the standard sort of paperwork. You then have to show your passport, so that the bank clerk can check your face against the photo. She then uses a machine to scan her fingerprint to confirm the fact that she has checked your face against the photo. She then gets a senior colleague to check your face against your passport and scan *her* fingerprint to confirm that she has checked your face against the photo. This is presumably to prevent people opening banking accounts illegitimately to undertake illegal activities, such as money laundering. I suppose the logic is that it is more difficult to bribe two bank clerks than one bank clerk (i.e. even if the first clerk is opening false accounts, this will be detected by the second clerk). To me, this seems self-evidently ludicrous. I am sure that these bank clerks work together every day and many of them must be good friends. If one of them is open to being bribed to falsify documents, then it seems likely that they would be able to recruit someone else in the branch to assist them. And I am quite sure that criminals are able to find branches employing staff who are open to persuasion. In any case, Lucy had to go through this process a second time in order to order a replacement bankcard.

There are then additional layers of bizarre and pointless security. For example, the bank wanted to send someone to physically meet Lucy to verify her identity. This was tricky because it is not clear that Lucy speaks (or reads) enough Mandarin to complete this transaction—depending on what questions need to be answered or papers signed. Also, the branch did not know when and where the verification would take place; this is arranged directly by the verification officer. So Lily gave the bank her own phone number, so that the verification officer could call Lily to set up the appointment (since the caller would probably speak only Mandarin and therefore be incomprehensible to Lucy). It was also planned that the verification officer would come to our apartment to do the verification— even though the address that we have registered with the bank is the office address, since it is easier to receive mail there. So the verification officer is going to call *not* the registered account holder and go to *not* the registered address to be sure that he is meeting the true owner of the account to authorize the delivery of a new bankcard. Well, I am feeling safer about my money already. In fact, the verification officer called Lily and decided that it would be easier to meet at the branch, which makes some sense, and the appointment was set for Friday lunchtime at the university, where our branch is located.

Unfortunately, it turned out that the university was on lockdown on Friday because the Chinese Prime Minister was visiting, so the verification officer was unable to get onto campus. I noticed that something odd was going on as I walked into the office: the footbridge that crosses the main road, on the edge of campus, was occupied by the Goon Squad—fit and aggressive-looking young men brandishing walkie-talkies, all dressed in white shirts (no tie) and loose-fitting black suits with lapel badges sporting the Chinese flag. You occasionally see them marching around together—which is a little odd, since they are all wearing lounge suits but clearly not doing much lounging—at official events. For example, we saw them when we went to Tiananmen Square because the Peoples' Congress happened to be on and it was important to intimidate any would-be protesters who might have wanted to gather outside. Anyway Lily (who had fortunately taken the precaution of planning to show up at the meeting, in case there were any hitches) diverted, with Lucy, to the South Gate of the university to meet the bank representative. He had a grainy photocopy of Lucy's passport to compare to her face—although that was anyway a bit pointless, since every Chinese knows that all westerners look the same—and signed the form for Lucy to take to the bank. It is interesting that they did not do this verification when they issued the original card. So if you want to steal someone's Chinese bankcard, then I recommend that you steal the original card and not a replacement because you will find it significantly less troublesome.

China is generally very hot on non-sensical security measures. Travelling by train is akin to travelling by plane. In fact, this almost seems to be a gold standard to which the Chinese train operator must aspire, whereas—as a European—I have always found the fact that the train is *not* like the plane to be one of its key attractions. As train stations become ever more like airports, so I seek to avoid them more assiduously (not least because it makes driving a relatively quicker option). When you arrive at a train station in China, you find raised police cabins outside where officers can stand and survey the crowds. Then you have to go through security before you can physically get into the station; this was a response to the attack by Uyghurs a few years ago, when they rampaged through Kunming station and stabbed around 20 people. First, you show your ticket to pass through the outer gate (the ticket office is outside, obviously). Then you put your baggage through an x-ray machine and pass through a metal detector to get to the platform area. Then there is a set of barriers to stop you getting onto the platforms until the train is ready to receive passengers. This is not like passing the barriers at Waterloo, but rather like going through the boarding gate at the airport: ticket and passport must both be checked by the ground crew and you can access only the platform for your train. The fundamental problem with this set-up is that we are in China: there are thousands of travellers at every station. There are sometimes *hundreds of thousands* of travellers.

For example, at the beginning of February, just before Chinese New Year, we were travelling from Hainan Island to Hong Kong. I had considered going by train in order to see the countryside but Lucy persuaded me that it would be too boring for the children—it takes about a day—and that we should just take a two-hour flight instead. This turned out to be prescient because there was—very unusually—snowfall in Guangzhou, the Chinese mainland city that is closest to Hong Kong and which used to be known in the west as Canton. The trains in Guangzhou were therefore cancelled and a crowd of *100,000 people* was left stranded in and around the station. Navigating that with three children would have been terrifying.

So the first thing that happens when you block entry to the railway station is that you get big crowds outside. A terrorist can kill people just as easily outside the station as inside the station—maybe even more easily—before he even has to go through security. This is why the US Embassy in London moved to a system of timed appointments for people applying for visas: someone pointed out to them that having people queuing round the block created a wonderful soft target for a terrorist with a nail bomb. It does not matter whether the bomb goes off inside the Embassy or outside the Embassy: the civilian casualties, and the damage to US reputation, will be the same. Hence, you need to disperse the crowd by giving timed appointments. Of course, one problem arising from having people crowding outside is that it blocks the traffic. It also makes it easier for a terrorist to kill people with a vehicle (either with or without a bomb in it). Then the next "logical" step is to shut the road outside the railway station, as they have in Kunming. So now you have to walk miles to the station with your luggage if you get dropped off, and when you arrive it is quicker to walk to your hotel—even with suitcases—than try to find a taxi (which is exactly what we did). Travelling is so glamorous, isn't it? Of course, we are not immune to this kind of stupidity in the UK, either. The drop-off area in the revamped Gatwick Airport is practically in Crawley; if it gets any further away, then they will need to lay on buses to get people into the terminal. (The fact that you have a flight of steps to get from the drop-off area to the terminal—with all your luggage—is also not particularly well thought out, in case anyone from Gatwick Airport management gets around to reading this.)

Obviously, the Chinese authorities are aware of this crowding problem. So the baggage x-ray and metal detector process is really just a charade. You throw your bag onto the belt and drag it off at the other end, but no one is actually looking at the x-ray machine. In fact, Lily accidentally took her pocketknife with her to Tiananmen Square and put it through the x-ray machine with no problems at all. And if you really had to open your bag, then there would be no space to do it because the security area is cramped and jam-packed with people. And if the line were held up for just a minute or two, then the queue would stretch into the next street, or maybe the next town. The Beijing subway is the same: every bag passes through an x-ray machine and every passenger passes through a metal detector. And there are multiple security agents standing around, not paying attention to either. The final stage of the train process—waiting at the barrier to be allowed onto the platform—is the most dangerous. Just like going to the airport, you want to turn up in good time at the station for your train because you never know quite how long it might take you to queue through security and shove your way through the crowds to your platform. So there is always an entire train's worth of passengers waiting at the barrier by the time they open it—and many of them have been waiting some considerable time—so there is a powerful human surge towards the train. People are trying to sprint past you, dragging bags, to make sure that they can monopolize the overhead baggage rack. You usually have to negotiate long flights of stairs onto the platform and there is no lift. Instead, each flight of stairs has a ramp at the edge for dragging suitcases up or down. When we took the train in Lijiang, we moved *en famille* to the bottom of the stairs and posted one adult at the top and one at the bottom. The children then stayed at the bottom while the third adult (me!) mounted the stairs six times and carried up six suitcases to relay everything from the bottom guardian (Lucy) to the top guardian (Lily). I physically carried the suitcases—around 23 kg each—because there were so many people mounting the stairs that the ramps were permanently occupied, often by little old men moving very slowly with heavy loads. After finally carrying up the last suitcase—heart bursting, gasping for air and lathered in sweat—we then had to run for the train because whistles were blowing and station masters calling. Having sprinted with all the luggage to the door of our coach, we were then halted officiously, and frowned at, and told that we could not board until we had shown our tickets for the fifth time. That is what I call customer service (Soviet-style!).

The first train that we took in China was the sleeper from Lijiang to Kunming. We had flown into Lijiang from the far north (Harbin). Lijiang is a beautiful old town, high in the mountains, now known as a tourist destination—which reduces its charm in the view of some people, but means that it is nicely renovated. (I mean, there are still open gutters beside the streets but they are no longer full of rubbish and dead animals, as they would have been historically; and they run in concrete channels with little bridges over them, rather than making you wade across through choleric mud pools. I personally regard this as a decent compromise between architectural authenticity and modern amenity. But then I am also the kind of person who has my children vaccinated, rather than harking back to a "golden age" when people just caught a healthy dose of scrofula and got on with life.) Flying into Lijiang had actually been rather stressful, not least because we had lost Lily when changing planes at Beijing airport (don't ask) and she had to rebook on a later flight. So two Western parents with three young children pitched up at Lijiang airport at midnight with huge amounts of luggage (some of it Lily's), little Mandarin and only a hazy idea of how to get to their hotel (which was in the historic pedestrianized zone—oops.)

We first had to screw up our courage enough to leave the terminal. China is a country of mass underemployment—on which matter, more shortly—so everywhere you go there are crowds of people just hanging around. You know, maybe something will show up tonight and they can earn a dollar; or maybe it won't and they can sit around into the small hours, smoking and spitting with their friends. When a family of five fair-haired foreigners show up—looking like the advance guard of a much larger force, given the amount of luggage they seem to be dragging—this is a cause of enormous interest and entertainment. There are all kinds of whoops and laughter and cat-calls and staring; you are soon surrounded by 20 people thrusting themselves in your face, offering incomprehensible advice and deals while you try to keep track of three children and 20 items of hold baggage and hand luggage. All credit to Lucy, she took charge—I think that being brought up in Hong Kong and taking all those holidays to chaotic places in the South East Asia created significant human capital in this regard—and she dealt firmly with the throng in pidgin Mandarin. None of the official taxi drivers would take us, since we were five people (when four is the limit) and had way too much luggage. And, of course, the airport security personnel are supervising the taxi rank to make sure that Rules Are Enforced. Except that there is a huge crowd of unlicensed taxi drivers walking up and down the queue, touting for business, which must surely be against the rules? The fact that they were so brazen was actually one of the reasons that we engaged them: if they were going to rob us and leave use dead in a ditch on a dark and deserted road then they would soon be caught, since everyone outside the airport (including the security personnel and twenty taxi drivers) had seen them collect us. I credit Chinese criminals with a little more common sense than that. So Lucy engaged two young men with SUV-type cars to transport us in convoy into town. This was rather stressful ("I have only one child in this car—does Lucy really have two in the other?" and "Is the town really so far from the airport? I wish I could read the road signs!"). But the young men were perfect gentlemen and took us as close to the hotel as possible by road and called the hotel to send someone to collect us—which was essential because the old town is a complete rabbit warren.

The hotel was a really beautiful traditional Chinese house—two storeys, with wooden balconied landings surrounding a courtyard, and looking out over the neighbouring rooftops. The courtyard had a small pond with goldfish swimming around in it, and was delicately decorated with a rockery and small plants (which we managed to leave intact, despite the fascination of three small children). Our room was very large, containing two king size beds with sumptuous duvets (ideal for accommodating the parents and three small children) and interesting indigenous artwork. The hotel had recently been acquired by a group of young people (seemingly early 20s) who were extremely pleasant and helpful. (I don't have the impression that the welcome was primarily pecuniary—I think that they were just genuinely very warm people.) The next morning, one of them kindly guided us through the backstreets to find breakfast in a traditional eatery, where we feasted on fried dough sticks and all kinds of other goodies that we had never sampled before. The little row of eateries was in a jumble of old brick buildings; they all had open fronts that faced across street to a little temple, with seating in the back on simple wooden stools and low tables. The cooks were mostly jolly middle-aged ladies. As we walked through the alleyways from the hotel, we could peek into the courtyards of the other houses and it was like stepping both backwards in time and into the footsteps of a local Chinese squire: the private courtyards were filled with many fine carvings, in both stone and wood, as well as interesting ironwork and dainty ponds. Each courtyard seemed to be its own little oasis of tranquility and reflection; you could imagine cultured minds sitting there creating poetry or paintings that embodied the peace of their surroundings. As we meandered back to the hotel, the shopkeepers were just removing their shutters (which are traditionally like rows of carved doors that are taken out and stacked to one side) and setting out their wares. Being a tourist destination, there is a massive overrepresentation of jade dealers and silversmiths—some of whom were sitting making bracelets (with a hammer and anvil, and sometimes a blowtorch) while they waited for customers to take an interest.

The Lijiang area is known for wonderful hiking up the Tiger Leaping Gorge (which sounded just a bit too adventurous with small children) and the spectacular Jade Dragon Snow Mountain (a 5600 m peak with the most southerly glacier in the northern hemisphere—a big, sprawling beast that clings tenaciously to the rocky outcrops that thrust up through it and around it). The massif has ten tops—that is, the main summit (which has been climbed only once!) and nine satellite summits. It is so huge that you can sit and marvel at its beauty from the landscaped gardens of the Black Dragon Pool on the outskirts of Lijiang, 25 km away, while drinking tea beneath a shady ornamental tree (which I highly recommend). There is also a small cultural museum at the Black Dragon Pool which is very nice for a brief visit and has some exquisitely carved tree roots (more on which elsewhere). Finally, there is the *Impression Lijiang* show by Zhang Yimou, which is well worth attending—not least for its extraordinary setting in a purpose-made (fake) rock amphitheatre at the foot of the Jade Dragon Snow Mountain itself. You can sit and admire the Jade Dragon's spiny back—a massive rock arête—as it twists up towards the summit, and clouds swirl across the glaciers and snowfields. I can think of a few shows around the world where nature providentially provides such a majestic backdrop—the music festival in the Cirque de Gavarnie in the French Pyrenees, for example—but they are rather rare. (Do take warm clothes, though! Even if the forecast is for warm weather, you can get quite chilly when a persistent wind blows down from the mountain.) The purpose of all the *Impressions* shows is to celebrate local culture and we are led through the songs and dances that accompany various life moments of the Naxi, Bai and Yi people who inhabit the Lijiang area. The attraction of some of these rather passes me by: watching a hundred young men getting drunk and rolling around on wooden tables reminds me too much of Oxford undergraduates horsing around in Eighth Week. But having 50 or more men on mountain ponies galloping hell for leather around the amphitheatre (literally around it—up on a narrow *passerelle* that runs behind the audience and up round the top of the stage scenery, 15 m above the floor of the stage) is quite spectacular. Then there are songs about falling in love and doomed young lovers who cannot stand to be parted, which are more touching. My daughters were sufficiently inspired to demand that we purchase native costumes for dressing up (an inspiration that seems to occur to them very frequently) and Lucy and Lily were convinced that the girls looked so cute that it was all worthwhile.

The logical way to transfer from Lijiang to Kunming was by sleeper train. It was an efficient use of time to spend the whole day in Lijiang and then have the train convey us gently (and slowly) through the mountains to Kunming, arriving around 6:30 a.m. when the children normally wake up anyway. I have always thought that sleeper trains should be a trump card for that very reason. Why can't you get a sleeper from London at 7 p.m. on a Friday night and then wake up in the Alps (at Geneva or Bourg-Saint-Maurice) at 7 a.m., ready to hit the ski slopes? Sleeper trains should be particularly good in Europe because airports lay on few late evening flights, in order to avoid upsetting the local residents. Sleeper trains also use the network when it is least used (i.e. at night) and can have trains that travel rather slowly (since you don't want any journey to take less than eight hours in order to get a good night's sleep!). In any case, sleeper trains are very common in China—which makes sense because there are very long distances between cities and the track is often slow—and they work fairly well. You can either go "hard sleeper" (no mattress, six bunks opening onto the companionway) or "soft sleeper" (mattresses, four bunks in a cabin with a door). We bought five soft sleeper tickets—thereby having one whole cabin to ourselves, plus one extra berth in the neighbouring cabin—and put the two smallest children in one bunk, so as to have a completely private compartment.

The cabin was perfectly nice—there was even a cut flower in a tiny vase on the table beneath the window. Obviously, the children thought that it was all extremely exciting. It was wise of us to book a fairly late train (around 10 p.m.) so that they were so tired by the time they got into bed that they went straight off to sleep; otherwise we would have had high jinks from three bouncy children in confined space, which would have been a recipe for disaster. Since Kunming was not the last stop for the train, we had to be ready to get off fairly smartly when we arrived and I set my alarm good and early. No need. The same Soviet-style customer service bade us farewell, just as it had welcomed us. I had been told that the conductor would knock at the door sometime before we got to Kunming. I did not realize that he would actually throw open the door at 5:30 a.m. (a good hour before our stop), turn on all the lights and switch on patriotic piped music at high volume. Memories of my (brief) time in the Royal Naval Reserves came flooding back to me and I was mentally preparing to jump into a cold swimming pool before breakfast when I remembered that I was actually on vacation. Of a sort.

There are officious security personnel basically everywhere in China—any car park or major road junction, school or university, plaza or shopping mall. They mostly dress in black uniforms (combat boots and trousers, military-style shirts, baseball hats) and sport red armbands with yellow writing—in the style of the Red Guards from the Cultural Revolution or Mussolini's Black Shirts (is there much of a distinction between the two?). I am never quite sure whether they are official law enforcers or private security, which I think is probably part of the plan on the part of the people who dress them. Frankly, it is a form of hidden unemployment: all these people (mostly young males) get paid but don't actually produce anything. This is why GDP per head in China is so low: it is not necessarily the case that people who work are unproductive; it is just that only half the working population truly works. The output of those workers is then *de facto* shared with those who do not do any work (i.e. the millions of people employed by the Government to stand around and do very little all day, in tasks that we would not even bother to allocate in the west). Security guards are a prime case of this but there are others, too, such as the army of workers sweeping up the dust in the streets with brooms made out of bunches of twigs. When I exited the back of our complex recently there was a rather elderly man from the sanitation crew—decked out in Day-Glo orange—sitting on the kerb, using his hands to scoop up tree blossom that had blown into the gutter and put it into a big metal dustpan. It was such an extraordinary sight (so very inefficient, so totally unnecessary) that I wanted to take a photo but felt that it would be too intrusive. I am told that some of these jobs are allocated to people in receipt of social benefit payments, so I guess it is what we would call "workfare" in the west.

Many apartment buildings in Beijing are arranged in little squares; then they have a gate to control entry into the communal parking area in the centre. And the gate has to have a security guard sitting in a box. But what does the security guard actually do all day? A cluster of apartment building containing thousands of apartments generates a lot of traffic (both vehicular and pedestrian). Residents have an electronic key to get through the gate, so we just ignore the guard. (In fact, my children do not even need the key—they are skinny enough to slide between the bars in the gate!) Visitors on foot or scooter are ignored by the guard: they just wait until a resident enters or exits (never more than a minute or two) and pass through the gate unchallenged. Obviously, there are a lot of deliveries and so on every day, so it would be completely impractical to question all these people, or even to check their ID and keep a log of their movements. Occasionally, cars show up. Residents have an electronic beeper to let themselves through the barrier. Visitors—such as taxis or deliveries—stop at the gate and have long discussion with the guard, but I have never seen anyone turned away. Maybe the guard is defending us from armed robbers or passing bandits? If any armed robbers did show up then I would recommend him to wave them straight through because there is no point in being gunned down to save the pitiful store of goods that we have in our apartment. (We have quite a few nice pictures that our daughters have produced in their calligraphy classes, but I cannot imagine a third party really coveting them that highly.)

We anyway have more senior security officials who can defend us from armed robbers because there is a police station at the far end of our apartment complex (about two squares over, so to speak). This is where we had to go to register—five times—when we came to live here. And everyone knows that we have these lovely police folk watching over our neighbourhood because their happy faces—all tight smiles and clear skin, framed with wonderfully starched collars—beam down at us from posters on every bulletin board. This phenomenon is not limited to our residential area: all around Beijing, and especially on the subway, you see posters of clean-cut law enforcement officers—men and women lined up in solidarity, ready to protect the good people of China. If I were a member of Falun Gong or a Christian Church, or if I were a pro-democracy or anti-sexism protestor, or a human rights lawyer or a publisher, then I would definitely watch my step around these people. It was interesting when we went to Tiananmen Square to visit the Forbidden City. You have to queue up and go through security (including baggage x-ray and metal detector, or course) to gain access to the square. But we had foolishly left our passports at home (which is technically against the law because you are supposed to carry a passport or ID card at all times). Having spent an hour on the subway with the children, we did not want to abandon the expedition so we just carried on queuing. When they asked for ID, I showed them my US driver's licence and Lucy showed them nothing (since she was carrying no form of picture ID at all): they did not care one bit and just waved us through. By contrast, they were assiduously checking the documentation of Chinese citizens: they carry little hand scanners to read the ID cards and immediately throw up any suspicious information about you, so that you can be taken aside for further questioning. It really brought home the fact that the Chinese security apparatus is focused on controlling the domestic population, not combatting potential foreign threats. I was reminded of the time I visited the Archbishop's castle at Albi in France: it was not built to protect the country against invasion by outsiders, but as a tool to oppress the local peasants and a place to store the crops that were taken from them. And it was all paid for, of course, by taxes on those local peasants. (It is a beautiful castle, though, and well worth a visit if you are ever in the south of France.)

The closest that we have come to a brush with the law is when we took a local train in Kunming. Our first challenge was getting train tickets.

Lily had reserved them for us online but when she tried to collect them at the station, the clerks refused (or were unable) to issue them because they could not handle foreign passports: they just could not work out how to put the registration numbers into the computer system. Lily had to escalate the situation to a senior manager, who eventually somehow issued the tickets. We then dashed for the train—running about 30 minutes later than planned, by now—and followed Lily through security by pushing into the long queue (or "cutting the line", as they say in the US). We felt really bad about this because we were obviously Caucasian, so we felt like we were playing to the stereotype of arrogant Westerners who felt that they were better than the local Chinese. Of course, that was not true—we were just in serious danger of missing our train and the next one was not until the afternoon, which would be far too late for our day trip—but we were unable to explain this due to a lack of time and a lack of vocabulary. The train itself—being a slow, stopping service—was just as you would imagine it to be. It was packed to the gunnels with noisy Chinese: groups of young people travelling together, families with mountains of luggage and travellers with huge bundles of wares in old sacks. It was getting towards Chinese New Year and some of the train occupants were going to stay on the train for its whole journey, taking around 24 hours to reach their families in Guangzhou. (People take these trains long distances partly because they are cheaper than the high-speed trains and partly because around New Year there are no tickets left for the high-speed services.) But people were very friendly—enchanted by our blonde children—and we were perfectly happy.

Unfortunately, the ticket inspector was not happy. He was not used to having foreigners on his train and could clearly sense that no good would come of it (perhaps a self-fulfilling prophecy?). He sucked his teeth as he checked our (perfectly valid) tickets and asked Lily about us, which apparently put her back up. He passed on down the carriage but a few minutes later two policemen came back and asked to see our tickets and passports. Lily was outraged and related their request to me in a very stroppy tone. Naturally, I smiled politely and handed over the passports—since I had no real choice and anyway had nothing to hide. Let's face it, I am a university professor in his forties (which some people apparently regard as middle-aged, can you believe?) travelling with a wife and three small children to see a National Park famous for its funny-shaped rocks. It is hardly the stuff of derring-do or international espionage, is it? If I was operating undercover, then it was so deep that even I hadn't been kept informed. The policemen dutifully photographed the passports with their phones—except that they photographed the pages with our US visas, not the actual passport information pages—and then asked Lily which were the names and which were the passport numbers because they had no idea. I am sure that they then wrote up a long report, complete with photographic evidence, and forwarded it to their superiors—who then forwarded it to their superiors and so on until it ended up in a large filing cabinet in the far corner of a large office. And there it will remain until the bureau moves offices and it all gets chucked in the bin. But all the relevant boxes have been ticked and the policemen cannot be disciplined for any infringement, and nor can their superiors, and we have all wasted a lot of time.

The most amusing aspect of all this was Lily's reaction. She is still happily young and naïve and believes that the police are there to catch criminals and protect innocent people. She blithely assumes that people who get hassle, or beaten up, must deserve it somehow. So it was a real eye-opener for her to be travelling round China with some innocuous westerners because she got to see something of what China is like for foreigners. Booking train tickets is virtually impossible unless you speak enough Mandarin to argue with the ticket officer manager (which excludes most westerners, for a start); the police demand to see your travel documents for no reasonable reason; taxi drivers drastically over-charge you (or worse—more on that later); hotels don't take foreign credit cards; and so on, and so forth. She was rather embarrassed. (I should say that some events in England embarrass me in front of foreigners—such as a London yob yelling at my French friend's wife and three-year-old daughter to "Go back to France!" when he overheard them talking in French on the street. She happily cut him down to size by noting that: "Actually, my daughter is Canadian"—which was true, she had been born in Canada—and the yob mumbled: "Oh, sorry" and walked off.) Train travel in China is becoming more difficult, rather than less. For example, there are agencies that can get train tickets for you to save you the trouble of going to the station; you then pick them up locally for the princely additional sum of 5 RMB (50 p). But a new rule instituted in 2015 means that anyone using a passport to buy a ticket (i.e. anyone foreign) has to go to the ticket office in the train station to get the ticket. This means that I have to make an hour round trip to the train station on the subway to collect any tickets that I order. (I realize that I could decline to collect the ticket in advance, and just rely on my ability to collect it when I begin my journey, but this is rather risky. If I cannot get the ticket, or if it takes me an hour to get it, then I will miss my train and my travel plans will be destroyed.) Obviously, this makes air travel relatively more attractive for foreigners, since you automatically save an hour vis-à-vis the train.

The other elements of safety and security that I should mention before signing off this letter are the ambulance service and the fire service. In Beijing, they are even rarer than rain! I saw my very first ambulance a couple of days ago: if it had only sped past me a week earlier, then I could have added it to my "week of firsts". And scarcely had I seen my first ambulance when I saw a fire engine (the next afternoon and in a different location, in case you were wondering—which makes them count as independent events, in a statistical sense). The absence of fire engines must mean that Chinese buildings are super safe, I am sure; and it is true that I have not yet seen anything else on fire (not cars, nor people, nor one of the many roadside food wagons). This is despite that fact that when you go to various locations in Beijing—such as the Temple of Heaven—you are warned not to use mobile phones in thunderstorms, suggesting that lightning strikes are a realistic possibility. But—although the dearth of fire engines may be a testament to fire safety—I definitely haven't worked out how the Chinese manage to operate without ambulances. Does no one get perilously sick or have an accident? Or do they just make their own way to the hospital? Or do they plan it well in advance to minimize the inconvenience? We live in a very busy area and it is hard to believe that no one has fallen urgently ill there in the last two months. I shall make further enquiries amongst our Chinese friends.

Well, I hope that you had a lovely long weekend. We did, too, and have just got back from the airport; I will relate that particular Amazing Adventure in my next letter. In the meantime, I am going to send this one off—which I had originally hoped to do last Wednesday!—before the May bank Holiday is completely over for you.

Very best wishes, and hugs to all,

Liam.

Letter 10

A Cup of Tea and a Nice Sit Down

14 May 2016

Dear Antonio,

WOW! That was another special trip. Sometimes, it is a real privilege to be me. Not very often, I hasten to add: I seem to spend the lion's share of life skivvying for other people (children, wife, head of department, several governments…). But just sometimes I feel really privileged, and this was definitely one of those occasions.

It was another long weekend here owing to International Labour Day (or May Day, as we call it in England—where we'd rather celebrate the coming of spring than the coming of class warfare). Naturally, this is a holiday in the People's Republic but, since the first of May fell on a Sunday, the holiday was observed on the Monday. In fact, the Chinese attitude to any kind of public holiday—even ones designed to stick it to the capitalist overlords—is a bit weird. For example, many people were actually working on Monday, including people doing rather non-essential tasks such as laying grass on the verges beside the roads. They also designate a certain number of days as holidays, but the workers then have to make up the lost time on the following Sunday! Dragon Boat Festival is a case in point. So it is not really much of a holiday, is it? In any case, the Monday was a school holiday, so we decided that the children should bunk off school on Friday so that we could take a four-day break.

10   A Cup of Tea and a Nice Sit Down

The family of a former student of mine, Yang Yang, owns a tea plantation on Mount Wuyi. This is on the border of Jiangxi and Fujian provinces and is the most famous tea producing area in China, a fact of which I was not fully aware until this weekend. Yang Yang had invited us to visit him as soon as he had heard that we were coming to China, and we had hoped to see him immediately after Chinese New Year. This proved impossible because we had to fly back to London that week to change our visa status. This weekend presented the next available opportunity—and a rather superior one, as it turned out. My interest was more than purely personal. I have been doing research on tea production, so I wanted to find some data on tea output and prices and Yang Yang had offered to help me. He has a connection with the Dean of the Agriculture Department in the neighbouring county—also known for its tea production—and he was therefore able to set up an interview for me. Yang Yang had already been to the Agriculture Department and determined that they did not have any data, so I was not overly optimistic about the outcome and therefore not exactly ecstatic about the excursion. Neither was Lucy: my going to meet the Dean of the Agriculture Department meant that I had to travel down on Wednesday (to do the interview on Thursday), leaving her to fly down on Friday morning with Lily and the three children. Not only that, but Annabelle had her "summer ball" on Thursday—which was a bit stressful for Lucy, what with arranging a ball gown and all—and the only flight down to Wuyi City was at 6:40 a.m.! This meant them getting up at 4 a.m. on Friday to get a taxi to the airport at 4:30 a.m., which was brutal.

I had to meet Yang Yang at Shangrao, a city on the northern side of the mountain range, which was most conveniently reached by train. I could have travelled overnight on Wednesday and met Yang Yang on Thursday morning but that did not sound at all like fun. Also, I was very curious to see the landscape between Beijing and Shangrao—since I work on agriculture, after all—and this necessitated taking a train in daylight. So I took the bullet train at 12:30 p.m. on Wednesday, arriving in Shangrao at 8 p.m. I will confess I was nervous about taking the bullet train. I have always felt that a man-made object travelling at 200 mph should have wings and depart from an airport, not be balanced on a couple of iron rails. (I agree that this may seem a bit irrational, from both mechanical

10   A Cup of Tea and a Nice Sit Down

and statistical perspectives, but high-speed trains have been known to crash—certainly in China. I similarly do not like staying in skyscrapers because they strike me as inherently unsafe: if there is a fire, then smoke and flames will be travelling upwards at exactly the same time that I want to be travelling downwards, which is a scary combination. The recent fire at the skyscraper in Dubai—suitably named The Torch—merely confirmed my reservations.) However, I braved everything in the pursuit of intellectual enlightenment.

The train was great. I have to confess that I went Business Class—which, interestingly, is superior to First Class. Ah, the joys of Communism. How apt, on International Labour Day. We basically had a third of the carriage (suitably partitioned from the hoi polloi, of course) with five seats in it—really big, wide ones that move in all kinds of fascinating ways like the first class seats on an airliner. If a Transformer were to disguise itself as a seat, then I am quite sure that this is the kind it would choose. We also got a snack and, later, a full meal served to us by a dedicated hostess. There were slippers to accompany the pillows and blankets (it's true, I swear it) and in-seat power for laptops—everything a harassed businessman needs to work, rest and play. While enjoying the scenery and cat-napping, I was actually able to knock off several hours of good quality work. I wish I could take the bullet train every day.

Yang Yang met me in Shangrao. He had been to high school there and was keen to show me some of the local colour. The main problem was that it has changed so much in the six or so years that he has been away that he didn't know where anything was! Whole new suburbs have been built, with major new roads and bridges to boot. He kindly came to collect me from the station in his car but that was a major trauma because the station is huge (about the same scale as a medium-sized European airport) and hadn't even existed when he lived in Shangrao. The presence of a major armaments factory in Shangrao could explain why it is served by both the bullet train and superfast internet—a lot faster than we enjoy in Beijing! The thing to do in Shangrao is to hang out late into the night and drink beer and eat barbecue in the local restaurants (where "restaurant" might be over-selling it a little). So after we had driven into town and dumped our bags at the hotel around 9:30 p.m., Yang Yang was keen to show me the town. Unfortunately, when Yang Yang hustled me over to his favourite barbecue joint we found that it had shut down. So he called up some friends to get a recommendation and we ended up joining them in their new favourite haunt. Since Yang Yang knows that I am not keen on spicy food, he kindly ordered it non-spicy—so the meat skewers were only eye-wateringly hot when they arrived, as opposed to combustibly hot. Like most Chinese meat, it was essentially fat with the occasional speck of flesh on it. (I assume that Chinese livestock also carry muscle, so that they can get up and move around and so on, but you will find little evidence of it in the meat that you are served in restaurants here. I wonder what actually happens to the flesh on slaughtered animals; it seems to disappear without trace.) But we still had fun and the company was top notch!

Following our late night, we had to be up early to drive an hour to the next town, where the county Agricultural Department was based. So we grabbed some noodle soup and dough sticks at a local breakfast place that Yang Yang used to visit regularly. If you are a Westerner, then it is a little odd that the Chinese seem to eat roughly the same stuff for breakfast, lunch and dinner. Mantou (steamed) buns and noodle soup are suitable for any time of day (the culinary equivalent of "the little black dress"); only the dough sticks are normally reserved for breakfast, since the Chinese like to get off to a healthy start. We ate our food to the gentle accompaniment of "The animals went in two-by-two" blasting out over loudspeakers, from which I inferred that there was a kindergarten nearby. I am familiar with this ambience from dropping off my own daughter at kindergarten: it is wall-to-wall cheerful music blaring out at you from 7:30 a.m., as if a manic Butlin's manager has been put in charge of the school system. It doesn't leave space inside your head to think, let alone have a conversation, which I assume is the goal. My personal favourites include "Hello *Hello Kitty*, baby/You're such a pretty baby" and "Why can we smell with our nose/see with our eyes/etc." (which seems to me to be an excessively metaphysical question for five-year-old). You see, they are keen to introduce the children to the heights of Western culture as well as traditional Chinese culture. The loudspeaker phenomenon is pretty general around China. We have them all around the beautiful lake out the back of the department that I am visiting: you can sit and admire the blossom and historic buildings across the water while being pulverized by loud, patriotic music. Anyway, with breakfast done, we dragged ourselves away from our musical interlude and headed off to work.

The Dean of the Agriculture Department was very welcoming, along with the Head of the Tea Section. I took the precaution of presenting some swanky chocolates from London as a sign of my esteem. Of course, one has to be very careful these days owing to the Chinese crackdown on corruption: it would be rude to arrive with nothing in hand, but dangerous (for the Dean) to arrive with something expensive. I think that the chocolates managed to hit the sweet spot, so to speak. (Decent chocolate is ferociously expensive in China—about three or four times the price in England.) Since I knew that it was pointless asking quantitative questions—about tea prices and output and so on—I had come prepared with some questions about the change in government policy on tea production that occurred in 2012. The Dean politely listened to my question and then responded by telling me about the history of tea production in his area. This was actually very interesting, although it makes for uncomfortable conversation if you are British.

The Chinese reluctance to allow access to British merchants in the 1840s—in particular, to sell unlimited quantities of Indian opium to Chinese drug addicts—led to the First Opium War of 1839–42. This is hardly an episode to burnish the halo of the British Empire, not least because the main motivation to sell the opium was to allow the British East India Company to recoup the cost of maintaining its occupying army in India (a plan seemingly hatched by the an evil genius!). The Chinese regard this episode as the onset of foreign oppression and degradation, which reached a crescendo with the Japanese occupation of the 1930s. Happily, the Brits do not continue to be as reviled as the Japanese, although the current drive for economic growth and modernization is generally portrayed as a kind of Chinese Manifest Destiny to return the country to the economic and political superiority that it achieved before foreign intervention, and to ensure that such degradation does not occur again. (Obviously, China was not actually in a state of economic and political supremacy in 1839—otherwise, it could not have been so easily overwhelmed by a few thousand British troops operating 9000 miles from home. Rather, China was already in a state of economic and political decline. But it is always more attractive to pinpoint foreigners as the cause of your distress than to take a long, hard look at your own shortcomings.) I was aware that the peace treaty of Nanking had opened up China to British merchants, at least somewhat—they were still nominally limited to the area within one day's travel of one of the five "Treaty Ports". I was also aware that Robert Fortune had used this opening to steal tea technology (plants, processes and people) and send it to India (more on which later). But the Dean was eager to tell me that the Opium War had sent the tea industry in his area into a steep decline, with a reduction in acreage of around 75 per cent in subsequent years. Although I agreed politely and expressed concern, in truth I find the supposed line of causation somewhat implausible. The Opium War was fought a long way from Jiangxi province; and Robert Fortune did not take tea to India until 1851 (and, even then, the industry almost failed in the beginning). But by 1850, the Taiping Rebellion had broken across southeast China and the Taiping's "Heavenly Kingdom" included Jiangxi. The destruction of the Heavenly Kingdom by the Qing armies through to 1864 is estimated to have killed 80 million people—making it potentially the bloodiest conflict in history—and this seems a more plausible explanation for the decline in tea output.

In any case, I learnt a lot of interesting things about tea production generally and about Chinese Government policy in this area in particular. It was getting on for noon and I felt that we should make our excuses and not trespass further on the Dean's time. At that point he revealed that he had laid on lunch for us as his honoured guests—which was embarrassingly kind. And it was a very nice lunch, too. The agriculture building was rather bizarre because it was mostly a posh hotel. When it was constructed, a few years ago, the building was apparently somewhat oversize; therefore, the Agriculture Department moved into the upper floors and a hotel company leased the lower floors. You somehow cannot imagine this happening in the UK or the US: there would be questions raised by the National Audit Office about the use of government funds to build excessively large premises. In any case, it meant that we were able to pop downstairs to a deluxe dining room and have a wonderful Chinese meal (five of us, including the head of the Tea Section and the Dean's assistant). Conversation was a little stilted because I speak no Chinese and the

10 A Cup of Tea and a Nice Sit Down

Dean spoke no English, but Yang Yang was an able translator. They were curious about some of the issues that seem to be afflicting Europe—particularly migration—and I hope that I was a useful and impartial window on the West for them. As the lunch wound down, the Dean had another surprise: he had set up a series of visits to tea plantations for the afternoon, if we were free? Free? Absolutely! Again, this was way beyond my expectations for help and hospitality. In fact, I did not realize quite how lucky I was: I learnt later that it is illegal for foreigners to tour tea plantations unless accompanied by a government official (something about evil Englishmen stealing tea technology and exploiting it elsewhere, I think—some people have long memories). But, more than that, I will state for the record that I have generally found Chinese people to be extremely hospitable whenever you have more than a passing contact with them. This may be due to the requirements of "face" (more on which elsewhere) but also because they really want to present a good impression of their country, I think. It puts Westerners to shame, really: they must find us very cold and indifferent, by comparison.

The Dean and the head of the Tea Section headed off in their government car (a chauffeur-driven four-by-four) while we followed in Yang Yang's jalopy. I assumed that the tea plantations would be fairly local—there are tea plantations down in the flat areas near the city, as well as up in the mountains—but the Dean was determined to give me a good show by taking me to plantations that produce some of the finest teas. So we wound up and up into the Wuyi massif, along ever narrower roads, until we were tearing along a single strip of concrete: the Dean is a busy man, you see, with a professional driver who tackles these roads every week and thus sees no need to slow down. It was notable that these concrete roads were fairly new, as were some of the installations that we visited, and this was all evidence of the government-ordained push into tea production since 2012. When the Chinese government wants something done then it shall be done, whatever the barriers or the cost. I discovered that the head of the Tea Section visits the plantations about once a week during the tea-picking season (which, admittedly, is only a couple of months per year up in the mountains) to check how things are going. This is a level of government interest and support that you cannot imagine in UK or US agriculture.

We first stopped at a plantation specializing in white tea. This is made from the finest tips of a particular variety of tea bush which, when processed at the correct temperature, go white. It is very popular in Taiwan. The plantation building itself was fairly basic and workmanlike, but the manager had a magnificent table and chairs in the foyer—which I was to discover is common in the region—where we sampled the tea. It was basically a huge slice of tree trunk—maybe 5 feet across by 10 feet long and 8 inches thick, which the bark still on the edges—all beautifully finished. It stood on massive chocks of the same wood and was surrounded by stools made in the same fashion. When you come from a small island that was largely denuded of hardwood 200 years ago to build warships to fight the French (6000 oak trees per ship-of-the-line!), then to see that amount of timber used so extravagantly in one piece of furniture is an amazing sight. The white tea season was already over because that plantation was lower down and because the white tea has to be picked when the tips are very young. So we then headed further up into the hills to visit some producers making green and black teas. Although I had not realized beforehand, the days of our visit were the height of the picking season and production was in full flow. As we wound along a narrow road above a reservoir, a white car shot past us, beeping its horn. We pulled over and a small man jumped out, all smiles, and dashed over to shake the hand of the Dean. When he heard that the Dean was taking some guests to visit tea plantations, we immediately had to head off to this man's plantation. This was particularly lucky for me, since both his green and black teas had won prizes in recent competitions. This plantation was really at the end of the road, so we wound further and further up into the mountains, with the government car zipping off ahead. We rolled into a small village to find the Dean's car waiting for us; we had not arrived at our destination, but the Dean was growing impatient. So we abandoned the jalopy and crowded into the Dean's car—he in the back and me embarrassingly plonked in the place of honour in the front passenger seat. And off we went at high speed again.

We drew into a cobbled courtyard, enclosed by a house on one side and single storey tea factory buildings on two others. We were welcomed into the foyer, past the magnificently carved, life-sized wooden Buddhas, and offered tea. I did my gracious best to hide my continuing embarrassment as I was given the chair of honour while the Dean sat slightly off to one side. Chinese tea tables are a work of art in themselves. Making Chinese tea is a fairly messy procedure. You put a palmful of leaves into a small bowl—no bigger than a mug—then add boiling water. You put the lid on the bowl and, in the case of black tea, let it brew for about ten seconds. (Yes, that's right folks, about ten seconds! Longer than that and it is massively over-brewed.) You then pour this out into the tiny teacups, about the size of shot glasses, and immediately tip it all away; this is just to wash the tea and the cups. It is traditional to offer the lid or the bowl to your guests at this point in order to smell the aroma and gauge the fineness of the tea. Then add more water, for about ten seconds, and serve the first round of tea to be drunk. A polite guest first smells the tea (as with wine), then tastes and holds it in the mouth before swallowing. Each tiny teacup contains about one mouthful! But, with good quality tea, this process can be repeated about eight times ("eight waters") before the taste is too weak, so there it still ends up being a reasonable quantity of tea for four or five people. The second or third water is generally considered to be the best, with a strong but clean taste.

As I mentioned, this process starts with a mugful of water being poured away, and typically involves a fair amount of spillage because the bowls pour very imperfectly. So tea tables have been developed for the purpose. You can have a table with holes in it (often a bamboo lattice) with a catching tray underneath; or a table with a rim and a drain in the corner with a bucket on the floor; or a table with a heated stone in the middle, which makes the water or tea evaporate off. The last is the most deluxe setup, and typically comes connected to water and electricity for filling and boiling the kettle; and the whole is encased in some magnificent piece of hardwood cabinetry, usually with a trapdoor to cover the heated stone when it is not in operation. If J.D. Rockefeller had drunk Chinese tea, then his office desk would have looked like this.

After sampling the prize-winning product, we were whisked off for a tour of the factory and I was shown the production process in detail. Tea factories are very pleasant places. There are some ultra-modern ones, with people wandering around in white coats, but most of them are fairly traditional. The building is simple concrete, kept clean with a broom; the machinery is sturdy but unsophisticated; and tea workers are the same. It is a joy to see the fresh green leaves unloaded from huge bags by the pickers, invariably female, who have just come down off the mountain. The leaves build up into huge piles as the bags are emptied. The production process is continuous, so you can see all the stages of production at once as you tour the factory. By the time you get to the room where huge sacks of black tea are being stockpiled, ready for shipping, the aroma is overpowering. I should say that the aroma is nothing like putting your nose into a bag of PG Tips, or similar. I find Indian teas—which is generally what people drink in the West—to be strong and bitter, even harsh. Most Chinese teas are much less bitter and the tastes are more subtle (more on which later).

In the absence of my children, it was my turn to play at being a movie star: everywhere I went that day, I had to have many photos taken with the Dean, plantation managers and their staff. I have never considered myself to be photogenic but I managed to put on my best smile as a small sign of my gratitude. Having had my photo taken for about the twentieth time that day, we bundled back into the car and headed back down the valley and up the neighbouring one to see the next plantation on our tour. This plantation was more newly and lavishly constructed than the first two. Coincidentally, the Chinese government was a major shareholder in this particular enterprise. This is one way in which the government makes people fall into line: becoming a significant player enables it to use moral suasion to herd everyone in the approved direction. For example, if it wants new technology introduced, or a new umbrella branding for the regional tea, then owning a major tea plantation gives it a platform from which to launch those projects. The plantation gateway was flanked by two massive retaining walls that held back the mountain, while the driveway defied gravity to snake up a steep hill to the main building (unlike the big blue lorry that had succumbed to gravity and was lying on its side in the driveway—something that I have never seen before). The interior had tiled floors, glass walls and workers in white coats—more like a laboratory than a traditional tea factory—but it was redeemed by the fact that all the windows were open, so there was still plenty of opportunity for foreign matter to enter. Since tea leaves are anyway not washed before processing, I am sure that there is plenty of foreign matter in them habitually (hence you pour away the first water when you make the tea). The Chinese approach to food hygiene is comparable to the approach to public security: build an extensive and onerous system that ticks all the boxes but is ignored or ineffective at the point of delivery.

Having sampled the tea at the "Government" plantation—at yet another magnificent hardwood table—and had the obligatory photo shoot, we headed off to our final appointment at a modern, private plantation. We passed through another old village. Desiccated middle-aged men with white hair were leaving the muddy fields and ambling alongside the road: barefoot, and dressed in coarse, blue cotton outfits with hoes over their shoulders, they would have looked more at home in the year 1816 or 1716 than in 2016. As Yang Yang said, this is the China that no one is interested in showing you: it doesn't fit with the image of modernity that the government is pushing or that young people are seeking.

The car climbed the steep road to the hill station and we finally drew up outside the plantation as it was getting dark. The ladies were just dumping the days pickings—probably 9 m^2 of tea tips, 15 cm deep—at the door of the factory. We watched the men scoop them up and deposit them into the preparatory drying beds, as other men removed the previous set of pickings from the twisting machines (in which the leaves are wrung to rupture the cells inside and promote fermentation) and bundled them into baskets for fermentation. We passed the special secondary driers—where the fermented leaves spin on bamboo baskets in big ovens to thoroughly dry them for packaging—and exited through the tea store, which was piled high with enormous bags of premium black tea (hundreds of thousands of dollars' worth, at least). Then we were conducted upstairs to take tea in the grand, balconied reception room looking out across the valley and talk business. It was getting on for 7 p.m. by the time we had finished and we were promptly invited to dinner, which had been set out for us in another building.

I am just not used to being fêted in this way and, after a whole day of it, I was feeling like Dravot in Kipling's *The Man Who Would Be King* (which is also a great film, if you ever get a chance to see it). I was terrified that this remote mountain tribe would realise that I wasn't really a visiting god after all—even though they had been treating me like one—and plunge me into the precipice in their fury and disappointment. Another fine meal followed, including local specialities that you can't find elsewhere (mostly, I think, because they do not grow elsewhere—some particular kind of marinated root, for example). Like the grand lunch, it was washed down with some sickly sweet Chinese herbal drink that comes in cans and is very popular. It was hard to do the meal justice because I am not used to eating that much food in a day. I notice that Chinese friends whom I have known in the West as students or professors come back to China and rapidly "bulk up". Doing business in China requires attendance at a lot of lavish meals and expressing your appreciation by eating a lot; coupled with reduced exercise, owing to time pressure and pollution, this is a recipe for obesity. I am obviously given some latitude, as a Westerner, but I do my very best to sample everything and make appreciative noises. I am fortunate that I am pretty handy with a pair of chopsticks—I just happen to find it fairly easy—so I don't embarrass myself too much. Most meals require multiple toasts taken at seemingly random intervals and not being able to make a toast (or even understand the toasts) is slightly awkward, particularly when you are the one being fêted. I find that just smiling broadly goes a long way.

After dinner, and the obligatory photo op, we were given tea samples (not the first that day!) and wished on our way. Yang Yang headed his car up towards the town of Wuyishan on the crest of the massif. Our peregrinations had already taken us most of the way there and we were speeded on our journey by a big new highway, the fruit of Chinese infrastructure investment that seemed rather underutilized. We soon arrived at our hotel, the Wuyi Mountain Villa. As you may guess from the name, this was a deluxe resort hotel and rather a cut above the hotel that Yang Yang and I had used in Shangrao. But that was work and we are men, whereas we were to be joined on Friday morning by my lady folk for a holiday, so only the best would be good enough. The hotel was situated in the National Park so, naturally, it was a beautiful setting as well as being a beautiful hotel. The foyer featured exquisite carving and fascinating tree root formations, as well as a dedicated tearoom where you could sample the finest local tea. And the local tea is some of the finest in China.

Wuyishan is the home of a tea called Da Hong Pao ("Big Red Robe"). As noted in the recent BBC News article, "The drink that costs more than gold", it is the most expensive tea in the world and can sell for thirty times its weight in gold. This is because an official sent some Wuyishan tea to the ailing mother of an emperor and she was miraculously cured by it. The emperor then sent red robes to cover the tea bushes in winter to ensure their good health (given that it can snow up on Mount Wuyi in January). The tea is said to "Look fit for a beggar, be priced for an emperor and have the heart of a Buddha". Those original tea trees still exist, some dating back a thousand years to the Song dynasty. Descendants of those trees are also cultivated to produce modern Da Hong Pao (this is known as "Mother Tree Da Hong Pao" and is about the most expensive kind still produced—surpassed only by dried samples from the original trees, which have not been harvested since 2006). When I say "descendants", they really are direct descendants and not just the same variety growing in the same place. This is because tea trees are propagated by taking cuttings, not seeds, so that the genetic stock is preserved. Later, we were to see some the original trees ourselves.

* * *

We collected the girls from Wuyishan airport next morning and headed off to the National Park. The rivers running through the crazy karst landscape have created swooping walls of rock that rise up, sheer from the floor. Several summits offer superlative views across the massif, each with a twisting track that winds its way to the top with tiny temples clinging to rocky ledges *en route*. With endless eyries available, we plumped for the Heavenly Tour Peak because the ascent sounded more child-friendly. It started as a pleasant, shady walk on a broad path alongside the river (paved, of course—this is China, so everything has to be upgraded to be able to withstand the foot traffic of hundreds of thousands of visitors). The mountain is cloven in two. To the left is a stupendous rock wall—supposedly the largest unbroken slab in Asia, although this is a little hard to believe since surely there must be something larger in the Himalayas? It is certainly very big—around 200 m high and maybe 300 m across—and very smooth and runs most of the way up to the main summit. On the right is another bulging wall, similarly high but with natural breaks in it; and around two thirds of the way up, nesting precipitously on a ledge, is a temple that you can visit on your way to the second, smaller summit.

The path picks up from the cleft between the summits, following a line of steps incised into the stone. It brings you up onto the shoulder of the sheer face and then turns along the skyline; it is perfectly safe, but may not suit those with vertigo. Then it doubles back into another cleft before cresting the flat summit, complete with temple, gift shop and food stalls. We trotted up, overtaking ladies in summer dresses and high heels (neither of which have I ever seen on sale in Eastern Mountain Sports), and circumventing the selfie-snappers and smokers who had staked out the stopping points. In fairness, given the grumbles I see online about Chinese mass tourism (e.g. on Trip Advisor), I should profess that it was a perfectly pleasant walk and not overcrowded. I have seen substantially worse in the English Peak District on a holiday weekend. And a big advantage of intensive traffic is that there are enough travellers to support an ice cream stand on the summit—which was a most welcome discovery, of which we took full advantage. Having enjoyed the views and the temple to the full, we headed down the back way and wound our way through the deciduous forest to the valley floor. On the way, an artist had set up shop selling pictures in a special style: they were Chinese characters drawn to resemble the Wuyishan mountains. The lady would write/paint/draw whatever you like, so the girls settled on "Wuyishan" and she created an artwork around that (amazingly quickly, too). This whole thing may sound odd if you are Western, but it is fairly common in China; for example, you can get your name written in fancy, decorated characters that end up as a work of art. Of course, Chinese characters lend themselves to this because they are anyway pictograms: the character for mountain ("shan") is 山, which is supposed to resemble a mountain and certainly does around Wuyishan!

We had show tickets for 7:30 p.m. so after our long walk we headed into town for dinner. Travelling in China without a Chinese chum is obviously challenging—not least when it comes to ordering chow. First, there is a bewildering array of eateries from which to choose, so it is handy to have someone who can check the online reviews on their phone to focus on a suitable establishment. Second is the problem of ordering.

There are just so many dishes on every Chinese menu that, unless you had spent a lifetime eating in China, you could hardly know what most of them were—not least because they vary a lot regionally so, even if you learnt the menu of a restaurant serving Beijing food, you would still be lost when you travelled outside the capital. They say that in New York you can eat out every night of your life without eating in the same restaurant twice—partly because there are many restaurants and partly because they turn over, so that by the time you have been through the whole list some new ones have opened. I think that in China you could eat in the *same restaurant* every night of your life and never eat the same thing twice—because by the time you had got the end of the menu the beginning would have changed. Chinese people must find it very odd when they go to a Western restaurant and there are only 20 things on the menu (or only five things in some particularly posh places). Now, if you are feeling particularly cruel to your Chinese eating companions, then you can turn this cornucopia to your advantage by asking them what is in each dish. Leaving aside the language barrier (how many of us can name obscure vegetables or animal parts in a foreign language?), they will have great trouble answering because they frequently eat things which even they don't really know what they are. I was once eating Dim Sum with a friend in Hong Kong when this rubbery, curly white stuff (think blanched curly kale, but made of animal) appeared on the table. When I asked him what it was, he answered—after a long pause—"fish buoyancy material". I was impressed: I didn't even realize that fish *had* buoyancy material. Mind you, he is a biologist, so he might have had the inside track in this instance.

The town centre was full of shops selling amazing tree roots and wood carvings. There was a tree trunk lying in one shop, maybe 7 m long (I am not even sure how they managed to get it into the shop) and 2 m high; it was split in half and carved down the middle were two rows of about 20 horses, each horse about 20 cm long, stampeding from one end of the sculpture to the other. I cannot imagine how much this sculpture would cost to buy or transport. There were tangled tree roots with a Buddha growing out the top (i.e. carved into the lowest metre of the main trunk, which was still attached to its roots). The best designs take the natural shape of the root and create the sculpture around it. For example, the tree trunk typically widens (fans out) near ground before narrowing again into the roots. So one sculpture of a phoenix used the roots as legs, the fanning out part as the tail feathers and the narrowing trunk as the neck and head. It was fantastically clever of the sculptor to be able to see that design in a tangled tree stump before he set to work—almost like a skilled diamond cutter sees a brilliant, finished stone in an uncut diamond. Wood sculpture seems to be one of the things to buy in Wuyishan, judging by the number of sellers. I had not realized that Wuyishan is such a tourist trap but half the city is apparently tourist accommodation, so they obviously get many thousands of visitors every year. I am told that they really started targeting the tourist market around 2000 and it has built very fast since then.

Our walk past the shops brought us to the *Da Hong Pao Impressions* show.

As you may have realized, top-rated Chinese tourist destinations nowadays require an *Impressions* show and thus Wuyishan bought one (sorry, "had one created to celebrate its unique history and culture"). As elsewhere, it is performed in a spectacular purpose-built venue that harnesses the natural surroundings. [WARNING: plot spoilers follow. If you think that you might want to pop down to Wuyishan at some point to catch the show then look away now.] You meander down a broad, curved path, past some nice bronzes depicting life in China in olden times, and take your ease in a steep bank of seats. In front of you is a high—maybe 15 m—stepped wall in the style of rice terraces, perhaps 100 m wide; at the top of the wall is a small building, which is used as part of the backdrop to the show, with a tall tree to its right—one of the original Da Hong Pao tea trees! To your left is the curved lane and gate by which you entered; and to your right is a grand valley, maybe a kilometre wide, looking across to Mount Wuyi. Between the seats and the precipice of the valley is a flat, grassy strip about 15 m wide, which is edged with a wall (a haw-haw, effectively) which gives you a sense that you are perched on the brink and the valley is spread out below you; but you cannot see into the precipice because it is obscured by mist.

A spotlight falls suddenly on a man standing alone. He launches into a lengthy and theatrical monologue about a cup of tea: the timelessness of drinking a cup; the fact that it can carry you far away from your current circumstance; its ability to give you physical and mental strength; its symbolism. The whole show—like this monologue—is rather "zen": it is a set of moments or feelings woven together in a stylish way to celebrate Chinese history and shared culture and make people feel good about one of their simplest shared experiences (i.e. drinking tea—even if most them do not get to drink Da Hong Poa on a very regular basis, given its price!). Suddenly, the seats start spinning—yes, the whole grandstand turns out to be built on an enormous turntable and it spins slowly 90 degrees anti-clockwise to present you with a new stage. This is a stylized historic Chinese town, with a long façade of multiple two-storey buildings above a street. There are 50 ladies in traditional Chinese costumes—giving the impression that they are courtesans—dancing on the upper, balconied level and down at ground level. It is a wonderful, vibrant, colourful sight. Don't ask me exactly what the plot was at this point but it all looked very nice.

Then the seats spin a further 90 degrees and you face a large, flat grassy area. The spotlight falls on two men in historical costume who are drinking tea and arguing; there is a quasi-kung fu fight. More lights go on and 50 men with long bamboo poles (5 m long?) are revealed and they launch into energetic and complicated dance patterns in a vaguely militaristic fashion. I have no idea what is going on—in truth, I am not sure there is a "plot" as such, more of a "mood"—but it is spectacular and clever. Then the seats shift another 90 degrees and you are facing out over the precipice. Suddenly the smoke clears and we are presented with the most extraordinary video show. Somehow, there are enormous screens set up on the far side of the valley, to our left and right. You cannot see these screens under normal conditions—it is not as if there are huge white screens that are clearly visible, as in a lecture theatre—but when lights are projected onto them, they can act as screens. Now there is a love story going on. A herd of magnificent white horses appears to gallop up the valley through the forest while a woman is lamenting the absence of her lover. There is a to-and-froing until finally a white horse seems to leap across the precipice from one side to their other and the woman gets carried off. WOW! I don't understand what technology makes this possible but it is an amazing sight on a grand scale.

After ten minutes they suddenly kill the lights and plunge the show into darkness and the seats spin again, back to your original direction, and we go through another cycle of scenes. When we eventually turn back to face the valley the smoke clears and powerful lights come up and you can see for the first time that you are actually looking down into a beautiful, twisting river valley—a real one, not an imitation. There is a whole flotilla of real old-fashioned boats making their way down the river, carrying tea (and, by implication, happiness and well-being) to those who need to drink it. A final twist is that ladies in traditional outfits mount the steps of the grandstand and offer us a cup of Da Hong Poa to savour at the end of the show. Overall, the show was not as cohesive at the one at the Huaqing Palace in Xi'an and not as breathlessly intense. I preferred the Xi'an show because I like a linear plot: I am rather Anglo-Saxon in that respect. I can imagine that other people would prefer a kind of "mood" show that was more loosely woven and perhaps more cerebral. But the show was certainly interesting and surprising and colourful and a technological triumph. And it takes wonderful advantage of its natural setting.

The next day dawned fine and warm—contrary to the forecast, which had warned us to expect cloudy skies and thunderstorms. Tea plants like damp places and are not really fond of strong, direct sunlight; so it is no surprise that Wuyishan is famously rainy and misty. In fact, it had been a very wet spring (the tea harvest was less than usual) and it had rained every day for more than a month. We were therefore lucky to enjoy four straight days of warm, sunny weather: 25°C and big sun every day from Thursday to Sunday. (But don't worry—the weather was to take its revenge on Monday....) We headed off to the famous Curtain Waterfall. One side of the valley has a smooth rock face with a massive rock roof (i.e. it is overhanging, as if the face has been scooped out with an enormous dessert spoon). The Curtain Waterfall cascades over the lip of this rocky overhang—perhaps 40 m above your head—into a pool below, and you can walk behind it into the deep, expansive recess. (Although "Curtain" is perhaps overselling it slightly: "Rope" might be more accurate. We were visiting in very a wet spring, so it is hard to believe that the waterfall ever really extends to being a curtain). But it is perfectly pleasant and the site is of some historical significance because several famous scholars taught there about 800 years ago. It certainly offers a spectacular amphitheatre [very similar to the cover photo on this book, which was taken nearby]. I wish we had teaching rooms like that at my university.

Our main event that day was a raft trip. Catherine had complained to us previously that: "You like *seeing* holidays, mummy, whereas we like *doing* holidays." Since we like happy campers, we do our best to lay on "doing" as well as "seeing" on our trips. The rafts consist of two narrow bamboo rafts, with a turned-up bow, lashed side by side with six bamboo seats tied on top (i.e. three on each half). Since safety and security are a high priority in China, we were each given an orange buoyancy aid, sized to fit a man weighing upwards of 100 kg (and therefore of no use whatsoever to 99 per cent of passengers, since it would just float off over their heads if they actually fell into the water). The raft trip winds its way through the National Park down the Nine Bends Gorge, passing the place where we had walked up the Heavenly Tour Peak. Some sections have slightly rougher water and it washes over the floor of the raft, so you can buy plastic bags to cover your shoes (which is what most people do) or just take them off (which is what we did). The rafts are guided around the shallow river by two boatmen, one at each end, armed with long bamboo poles. Apparently, it is obligatory to tip them before you begin your journey if you want good service, so we took the precaution of giving them 120 RMB (which we were told is the going rate).

The scenery is magnificent and the descent is relaxing and interesting. There are sweeping faces of smooth rock rising sheer from the river, carved by the constant motion of the water. You pass some caves halfway up a sheer rock face, maybe 50 m high, in which they have found stone coffins dating back 3000 years; the mind boggles as to how they got them there, or why (archaeological mysteries yet to be solved). The river was alive with fish, not least because the tourists buy small packets of biscuits to feed to them. The procession of rafts is more-or-less continuous and so is the feeding. It is like a upside down sushi bar—instead of the fish coming past on plates to be picked up and eaten the humans, the human pass on plates and throw down biscuits to feed the fish. It is lucky that fish don't eat in the winter, when they are not growing, or they would get rather hungry between tourist seasons. Some of the rock faces have been carved by man as well as nature—they have philosophical inscriptions that were incised by monks hundreds of years ago. The boatmen bounce the rafts off some of these faces with their bamboo poles as the current swings the flimsy vessels from one side of the river to the other around each of the nine bends. It is a bit like Oxford punting, on steroids. Many of the rearing monoliths *en route* have local nicknames—the three sisters, the bottom (because it has a crack down the middle), the frog's mouth and so on. A wider section of the river passes sedately under a bridge, across which we had walked the day before to get to the Heavenly Tour Peak. There is a great waving and hollering at this point between those on the bridge and those in the rafts. My daughters decided to regale the flotilla with a rendition of the Communist Party song for young pioneers, which caused considerable amusement and bemusement, as you might imagine.

Eventually you end up at a purpose-made quay in a little riverside park, next to *The British Café*—although I am not exactly sure what is British about it, in all honesty—which forms a pleasant and convenient end to the expedition. The only inconvenience was a surprising lack of eating options; since we had skipped lunch we needed to find something to fill up the children. Lily discovered that there was a little local restaurant half a mile away on the local bus, so we hopped on and were soon eating. Since it was really between meal times, we had the restaurant to ourselves: our balcony table looked out across tea fields to Wuyishan, and chickens were scratching around in the yard. Very fine chickens they were, too, and tasted delicious once we had one in the pot: fresh, free-range and local—what more could you ask for? Suitably fortified, it was time to embark on the next stage of our adventure—on to Yang Yang's village, about two hours away, to visit his family and their tea plantation.

* * *

Yang Yang's village is at the end of a long valley, where the road runs out. His house is in the narrow main street, which is lined on both sides by small shops selling all of life's essentials and a fair few inessentials. It was humming at 6 p.m. on a Saturday, with shopkeepers sitting outside chatting and children running around. We became the centre of attention the moment that we got out of the car—especially my very blonde children! We had seen previously that in China it is not considered rude to stare, especially not for children, and we were soon surrounded by people staring and pointing and chattering. I act regally in these circumstances ("smile and wave, smile and wave") but my daughters find it a bit overwhelming—understandably because they are smaller and almost physically overwhelmed at times (people walk up and touch their hair and sometimes grab them to have photos taken).

Yang Yang spirited us off into his house, which also doubles as a business premises and tea factory. His parents were very welcoming and his mother immediately put some food on to cook—not that we were really hungry, given our late lunch, but the Chinese are never to be faulted for the enthusiasm of their welcome. Interestingly, the stove was identical to designs that I had seen in the museum of the tomb of Emperor Jingde in Xi'an! It was a large brick or clay structure, with a wood fire inside and some depressions for cooking pots in the top. The meal was a kind of stew served in a wooden pail with a lid. The stove was not the only traditional item in the house: Yang Yang's tiny, wizened, white-haired grandmother was enchanted with our girls but unable to communicate directly because she spoke *only* the local dialect (whereas our children speak Mandarin, but obviously no dialect). After the civil war, Mandarin was imposed throughout the Chinese education system (i.e. people may speak dialect at home but must speak Mandarin at school) so that everyone has at least some mastery of Mandarin. The Government recently complained that only 400 million Chinese speak "proper" Mandarin—that is, can distinguish reliably between the various "s" and "sh" sounds in speech, for example—but Mandarin is nonetheless effectively understood and used fluently for communication by virtually all 1.4 billion Chinese. There cannot be many people left who really speak only their dialect, but Yang Yang's grandmother is one of them.

After dinner we sat in the back of the shop taking tea, while the pickers were still bringing in their bags of tea tips and getting paid. The local children really wanted to come and gaze at our children but were not quite brave enough to come in. Annabelle and Catherine were too shy (or tired of being admired) to appear but I persuaded Elizabeth to go out and make friends, in the interests of international diplomacy. (I am always conscious that our girls are probably the only Western children that the local kids are ever going to meet and I would like them to think that the English are an open and pleasant and friendly people.) Elizabeth ingratiated herself with her party piece of picking up much bigger children and carrying them around, which the Chinese children seem to find a bit mind-boggling. (Elizabeth is rather strong for her size, and gets a lot of practice in school at carrying around other children.) After a while, Yang Yang's family were free and took us for a stroll around the village—down through the narrow lanes, past the old buildings falling into ruins, to a wide street of new and deluxe townhouses (many still under construction). Most young people leave the village—as with most villages in rural China—but the villagers who leave have formed a close-knit business community in the nearby city, where they are frequently very successful. To demonstrate their success back home, they have grand houses built for themselves in this street—even though they never actually intend to live there—which may well cost as much as $300,000. Apparently, this is a common phenomenon in China: the villages are denuded of young people but populated by expensive empty dwellings. Just along the street the proud new Communist Party offices preside over a posh town square and this is now the heart of the village.

There is a dancing mania in China, to be witnessed most nights from 8 to 10 p.m. in every town: gangs gather, ghetto blasters blaring out loud music, and block local squares and sidewalks and even bus stops. But this is not the young impinging on the elderly—it is the elderly imposing on the young! Hordes of middle-aged ladies line up to strut their stuff. Passing middle-aged aren't safe: in the blink of an eye, they can get dragged into the clutches of these shuffling dervishes. "Dad dancing" is for pussycats: these ladies need a lion tamer. In fairness, many of these ladies are very tastefully attired and some are rather good dancers—it is more *Sergeant Pepper's Lonely Hearts Club* than Darby and Joan Club. It seems to keep them slim and mobile and in good spirits: if mature English or American ladies were doing this, instead of watching Coronation Street or Downton Abbey, then the world would probably be a better place. This is actually part of a more general phenomenon: the elderly have primacy in Chinese society. This is not so much due to the showing of respect to one's parents—although that is a traditional tenet of

Confucian thought—but to sheer weight of numbers. The One Child Policy that has limited population growth since 1978 has generated a rapidly aging population; the Chinese population is expected to age substantially faster than any other in the next 25 years. A striking feature of Chinese towns is that you never see a park for children (swings, slides and sandpits) but always find a park for pensioners (weights machines and elliptical walkers). We increasingly have these in the UK—which is a good thing—but the balance of power is out of kilter in China. It is no wonder that Chinese children have seen a steep increase in obesity rates: they spend a lot of time in school and there is nowhere for them to exercise out of school. I would like to get a photo of granny gang dancing but, whenever we appear, my children create such a stir that they all stop dancing and crowd round. And so it was in Yang Yang's village, so we glad-handed the crowd for a while and then moved on, drawing a few of the more curious children with us—following with their flashing roller blades as we inspected the big war memorial (which they have in every village in China) and wended our way back up the hill to the house.

This village was the birthplace of Yang Yang's father and his four brothers. Yang Yang's uncle still lives on the fringe of the village, in a large villa, and he had kindly offered to accommodate us for the night. Everyone was very tired so we drove to his house—which really was at the very end of the road—and we tumbled into bed and were soon all asleep. Yang Yang and his parents were going to take us tea picking next morning on their plantation and we had to be up early enough to be breakfasted and boarding a boat at 8 a.m. Yang Yang's mum, who is a very energetic lady, showed up next morning with dumplings and mantou buns. We ate fast and then trotted off up the track next to the house. The track led to a large reservoir, which was long, narrow and very pretty—although much of it was invisible to us because it curves like a crescent moon around the mountain. Yang Yang's uncle is the official overseer of the reservoir and runs the ferryboat, amongst other things. The boat was a dirty, noisy, smoky, beaten up old beast: for me, it was a trip down memory lane as it reminded me of the heavy machinery that I used to ride around my father's building sites when I was a child in the 1970s (which would now be illegal twice over—the having children on the machines part, and the machines belching smoke part). A half-dozen tea picking ladies were already sitting on the bench on one side of the boat; there were a couple of other passengers on the bench on the other side; and there was a motorcyclist sitting on his bike in the mid-section. He looked very 1950s, the kind of thing that my father would describe to me from his youth: his bike was deep blue and shiny, clearly his pride and joy, and he was looking dapper in his Sunday best—a fawn jacket and slacks and slip-on shoes (all rather incongruous for riding a motorbike over rough mountain tracks), with neatly trimmed hair and moustache. He smiled diffidently when I asked to take a photo and it was quite a charming scene.

I previously asked Yang Yang whether they ever had problems with illegal tea pickers. After all, the plantations are hard to police (often being up in the mountains and fairly remote), the tea is quite valuable and there is a lot of local underemployment. He said that illegal picking is a problem, but not on their plantations—because the only way to get there is by ferry, and his uncle runs it! After a short journey we were deposited beside the lake (by the simple expedient of running aground and throwing a gangplank out the front) and then the ferry carried on up to the far end of the reservoir to deposit the other passengers at the road head of the next valley. We scrambled up the bank and followed a track up the hill. We passed several graves on our way—simple mounds of earth in a quiet clearing, some with headstones and all of them littered with a few flowers and burnt out joss sticks. Only in the last couple of years had Yang Yang's family got permission to cultivate tea in this area, which is in the confines of the National Park. Tea had actually been grown here for many years—before the area was designated as a National Park—and there were many old tea trees. But if tea plantations are not managed, then they get rapidly overgrown by brush, so they have had to do a lot of work to clear the brush and bring the tea trees back into production. Old tea trees produce very fine tea because they are already well established (and so turn relatively more of the nutrients that they absorb into leaves, rather than into new roots and trunk) and because they have always been entirely organic.

We followed instructions to pick either the buds (just the buds—the single, green needle growing on the end of each twig that had yet to unfurl into a leaf), or the tips (a little cluster of three light green leaves—the one on the very end and its two neighbours). The tea made from buds (called "Jin Jun Mei") is one of the most expensive kinds because it is highly sought-after and expensive to produce (you need an awful lot of buds to produce a small amount of tea!). Even for regular tea, it takes about five pounds of tips to make one pound of tea, an amount that requires a fair amount of gathering. The girls were very focused and had great fun picking. It made me think that the small girls making lace in the Industrial Revolution were probably equally cheerfully dedicated until their eyesight failed them and they ended up in poverty. Once the tips are no longer light green, it is not worth picking them because the tea does not taste as good; to ensure that the tips are always young and light green, the pickers come every day to the bushes to take only the freshest ones. In fact, the picking season is also very short—especially as you go higher into the mountains, where the finest teas are cultivated—and may run to only 30 days per year! Lower quality teas, from down in the valley, can be harvested for much longer periods (maybe six months per year). Having done some picking low down on the slope, we headed further up the track to the area of a deserted village. The landscape was still scarred by its experiences: the slopes were terraced into defunct rice paddies, which Yang Yang's family was now repopulating with baby tea trees to boost future production. In the meantime, they were harvesting the mature trees that covered the slopes above the village. By about 11 o'clock the ferry was due back from the far end of the lake and this was our opportunity to head back for lunch. So we rounded up the children and headed down a slightly different path, past a dilapidated Daoist temple. (Most Chinese villages have a temple at which offerings can be left in order to bring good fortune to the village; this is a traditional part of Daoist belief.) On the way, Yang Yang pointed out the fast-growing grass-like plant—a bit like a spider plant on steroids—that takes over the tea plantations but which is also an economic crop in its own right, being traditionally used to make paper (for which the county is historically well known). As I travel round China, it amazes me how many different local plants have been used to make paper and cloth; it is fascinating to see the ingenuity of man in exploiting local natural resources.

When we got back to the landing area and headed back down the track to the edge of the village, there were people fishing in the reservoir (for which they have to pay by the hour). The reservoir was not so clean—there was an awful lot of trash washed up around the sides—and I was not thrilled about the prospect of consuming either the water or fish that came out of it. Which is a shame, since that is exactly what we were getting for lunch. Yang Yang's aunt and uncle kindly cooked us another fine lunch with duck, fish and other dishes. The problem with most Chinese fish dishes is that the fish is cooked whole and has a lot of bones, often very tiny ones if it is a freshwater fish; it is tedious to remove them, especially using chopsticks and having to do it also for your children. These fish were no exception, so the duck was definitely our preferred platter. Afterwards the children went off to play in the yard while the adults digested for a while and then packed the luggage. Once Yang Yang's uncle has woken from his afternoon nap—a traditional Chinese pastime—we loaded up for the short hop back into town in two cars (Yang Yang's jalopy and the uncle's truck) and I was in for another highlight of the trip.

First, we stopped halfway to see the family home of Yang Yang's father, where he and his brothers were raised. It was a traditional Chinese house, of the kind that is falling rapidly into ruins in villages across China because no one wants them (or even to be reminded of them) any more. Yang Yang's family are a little different and actually want to preserve their old home; so, instead of spending money on a fancy new townhouse to keep up with the Joneses, they have started renovating the old house. They have re-roofed it (i.e. replaced some rotten beams and re-laid all the old tiles) and made good some holes in the walls (exterior walls being made of rendered stone and interior walls being wattle and daub). A family member had been living in the house until five years ago, even though the only running water is a stream that comes down the hill and across the back yard. The house is one of a cluster of half a dozen. Again, this is traditional in China because the communities historically grew organically: when your son moved out, he built a house right next to yours. So all the owners of the housing cluster have the same family name and are fairly closely related. We looked in several houses: each had an earthen floor; each contained a huge, freestanding wooden cupboard—made of massive timbers—that was used as a grain store; and each contained a brick or clay stove of the variety that we saw in Yang Yang's house. While wandering between the dwellings, we also met an old man spreading night soil. He was carrying a yoke with a bucket on either end—one filled with slops and the other filled with water as a counter-weight—that he was taking out to fertilize his plot. He reminded me of the blue-suited agricultural workers, like something from another century, that I had seen with Yang Yang when we were whizzing around tea plantations. He was happy to be photographed and even offered to let me try his yoke—an opportunity about which I was genuinely curious but politely declined, on the basis that a small mistake would be hilarious for two minutes but horrendous for two days (since I had brought only one pair of trousers).

Now, you know that I have more than a passing interest in this kind of thing, having worked extensively on agricultural history. But I never actually imagined going back in time to experience these things first hand. So I was over the moon with my next discovery—a man ploughing with oxen! Well, actually a water buffalo. Water buffalo plough teams are like London buses: you wait all that time for one to come along, and then two show up at once. Within the space of half a mile, Lucy spotted two different men goading a water buffalo into dragging an araire through the heavy, damp soil. If you had told me that I would see men ploughing with buffalo in India or Cambodia then I would not have been surprised. But I was pretty shocked to see it in China. They produce so much cheap machinery, for example, that it is very surprising to me that farmers do not have some tiny tractor that can complete the work more economically than the buffalo. Of course, I asked Yang Yang to stop the car and took many photos—which his uncle thought was very funny because he could not see anything extraordinary or interesting about it all, of course.

We took our leave of Yang Yang's family—expressing our heartfelt appreciation of their hospitality—and headed off to spend the night in Shangrao. This was a two-hour drive away and about halfway to the next day's destination: Jingdezhen. This is the historic capital of porcelain manufacture in China and has been renowned for its pottery for at least the last thousand years. Its rise is partly due to a fortuitous confluence of factors: it is near Kaoling, which offers a superior type of clay for porcelain manufacture; it is near the Yangtze River, which offers ease of transport for fragile goods; it is upstream of Nanjing, the historic capital that generated a high demand for the finest tableware. Jingdezhen remains an important centre of porcelain manufacture and a great place to buy fine china. With three young children in tow, our objective was more modest: to visit the site of the historic kilns on the edge of town, which is set up as a working museum and craft centre. Jingdezhen also has the advantage that you can fly direct to Beijing, which would enable us to get back on Monday night (in preparation for school on Tuesday morning). The drive from Shangrao to Jingdezhen is also very pretty, through rolling forest-covered hills and soaring mist-covered mountains, made all the more spectacular because the weather was about to deliver those long-promised thunderstorms. I should say, in passing, that China is a remarkably mountainous place; it almost seems that there is really rough terrain everywhere you go. Of course, that cannot be exactly true—and I myself zipped through some good agricultural areas on the bullet train—but European geography certainly seems more benign and better suited to human settlement.

As we neared Jingdezhen, it absolutely hammered with rain. I have never seen so much rain on the roads of an urban area with my own eyes (I have seen it on TV but never in reality). Since we did not want to drag our luggage round with us all day, we called via the airport to drop it in left luggage—which was a fine plan, except for the fact that the airport did not have a left luggage facility. The best that they could offer was to rent us a car for the day for 400 RMB as a place to leave the bags. Then the drivers that we had hired in Shangrao—two friends who had driven the six of us in two saloon cars—offered to stay with us for the rest of the day for 400 RMB! That was obviously a lot more convenient, so we nipped straight off to the historic kiln site, which was quite close to the airport, and there the fun began. The site was flooded. I mean seriously flooded: the courtyard on the other side of the turnstiles was a foot deep in water. They had lifted the manhole covers and water was pouring into the drains like Charybdis with a thirst. We entered the park and picked our way across the courtyard—keeping a tight hold on the children's hands, lest they get sucked into the open drains and drowned. (I am being deadly serious: any small child going down there wouldn't have stood a chance; it was unbelievably dangerous to leave off the manhole covers.) Once through the courtyard, we followed the wide path alongside the lake. I realized later that the park was not flooded by chance. The porcelain works were built here precisely because there was waterpower, which was harnessed using hammer mills to crush the Kaoling clay. The hammer mills were quite ingenious: the water wheels turned spiked drums; the spikes catch on the ends of several see-saws (each about 3 m long) and push them down, thereby raising the hammers on the other ends; as the drums turn further, the spikes disengage from the see-saw ends and the hammers come crashing down on the clay boulders beneath. The lake then captures the water running out of the millraces.

A striking feature of the museum is that the whole design was very artistic, if that doesn't sound strangely self-evident for a museum. The lake had an islet with a teashop on it; the wooden footbridge to the islet had sections of wood panels that were inset with broken tiles—a really striking confection owing to the contrasting textures and colours of the tile and the wood. Slightly further on, there was a small garden with some lawn and a shrubbery. Enormous blue and white porcelain pots—bowls, vases, and even a giant teapot, decorated with dragons and phoenixes and willow pattern—were lying, half-buried in the lawn, as if you had stumbled across a crazy archaeological dig in full swing. I wondered if the pots had been created to be buried, or simply cracked beyond repair; in fact, they were historical fakes (i.e. they were genuinely old but merely copies of original Jingdezhen pottery), so this was an inventive way of destroying fake goods while still being able to appreciate them! The garden path led out to a spacious plaza and on one side was a row of blue and white porcelain columns, maybe 5 m high, decorated with historical scenes—a town with merchants gathered round a mill, monks trekking to a temple high on the mountain. It was very unexpected and novel.

We moved rapidly on to the workshops where craftsmen create works of art in front of your own eyes. The basic setup was probably unchanged for hundreds of years. The traditional grey brick buildings were rectangular, single-storey affairs, arranged around a central open-air courtyard, onto which all the craftsmen's work areas opened to benefit from natural light. Tile gutters and downpipes drained water from the roof into huge ceramic pots standing in the courtyard (maybe four feet high by four feet in diameter). The water in these ceramic butts was used to wet the clay (in preparation for working it) or washing tools and hands.

The first person you meet in the workshop is the potter throwing bowls and vases on his wheel. Interestingly, the wheel is large (a metre across) and he sits on a bench that is above and across it; he sets it spinning by twirling it repeatedly with a stick and then he works the clay until the wheel slows down, whereupon he twirls some more and continues working. I had often wondered how they physically threw those huge vases; I can imagine that getting up above it, and having a bench aslant the wheel to get closer, would reduce the strain on the back from reaching over and lifting the clay. The children were able to sit with the craftsman (for a price) and throw their own vase. The job of the next man that you meet in the workshop is to scrape out the excess clay under the foot of the bowl. Yes, it's really true! When you flip a bowl over, you will see that the foot is not flat but indented. After the bowl is first formed, and allowed to dry, the foot is solid. So someone has the job of taking every bowl, twirling it upside down on a wheel and using a special tool to excavate the foot; it takes just a few seconds, so skilled are they.

After the bowl is fired once comes the turn of the decorative artists. Interestingly, the bowls are still biscuit-coloured at this point, and the paint looks black: but when the bowls are glazed and fired again, the background becomes white and the design becomes blue. The children were able to sit (you guessed it—for a price) and paint their own bowl. The bowls are still fragile at this point, as two out of three children discovered by picking them up by the rim and breaking them; you have to hold them gently by the foot until they are fired for a second time. Once you have painted your bowl, they put it in the queue for firing and then post it to you, which I think is a great service (although we are still waiting for ours to arrive at this point!). The next workshop contains the professional painters; they sit and work all day, next to displays of their work, and you can sit and watch for as long as you like. The porcelain is not just painted: it has texture, as well as colour. There is a tradition of incising patterns into the pottery—often interlocking spirals made of thousands of tiny dots—when it is still soft; you can see the ladies working endlessly on this. The painters often put several coats on parts of the pottery—such as the leaves of flowers—to give them thickness. It is a joy to watch and learn just how much work and expertise is required to create one piece of porcelain.

The museum also contains several traditional southern Chinese porcelain merchants' houses, which have been moved to the park. These houses are typically a succession of small courtyards that are roofed around the edges but open to the sky in the middle, with a pool for collecting rainwater in each quadrangle. The biggest quadrangle has a grand pond with goldfish in it: goldfish, of course, are important in feng shui because they absorb any bad luck that enters the house. The rooms of the house—bedrooms and meeting rooms and so on—then open off these quadrangles with a series of wooden screen doors. In this way, all the rooms have natural light even though the building has no exterior windows (presumably because glass was expensive and created a security risk). All these screens and wood panels are intricately carved with a variety of scenes (hunting, ploughing, travelling…) and gilded. You would find this kind of artistry in England only in a church or a very fine country house.

Beside these houses was a display of reconstructed historical kilns for firing pottery. The "dragon kiln" was the oldest type, so called because it has a very long, lean, low form with a stepped brick roof that notionally looks like the scaly back of a dragon. The kilns were built going uphill, so that the heat would rise up through the building and generate really high temperatures at the top end. All the kilns were heated using wood and so, to protect the pots against smoke and ash that might discolour them, each pot was actually cooked in the kiln inside another pot (a "sagger"). An improvement on the dragon kiln was the beehive kiln (also called the "mantou kiln" because it looks like a steamed bun); the curved roof of this design was more efficient at recycling the heat and gave a more even temperature distribution. A further improvement was the "gourd kiln", which was a bit like a double beehive with one half slightly larger and higher than the other: the increased height of the back section generated higher temperatures and better firing. It was interesting to see the evolution of technology.

A second, smaller lake featured a spectacular bandstand on stilts in the middle, and a handsome colonnade facing it on the shore. A few years ago, the craftsmen of Jingdezhen set their sights on creating instruments from porcelain—flutes, pipes, glockenspiels, gongs and several others that I cannot name. The museum musicians play a concert using these instruments at the bandstand every day, so we went along to listen. It was very tuneful. The female orchestra was attired in Chinese dress and played traditional music, while a male dancer swooped and leapt and pirouetted. We felt privileged to have been able to see it—like the rest of the museum. We discovered so much and learnt to appreciate porcelain on a new level.

While most of our visit had been dry, the storm clouds were gathering towards the end. We should have been wise and exited early because about another inch of rain fell in about 30 minutes. We were in the workshop at the time and congratulated ourselves on staying dry and being entertained by the artisans at work. The problem was that the path had turned to a stream and the open drains running beside the path had broken their banks. We were literally trapped in the building. As the rain eased we managed to pick our way along beside the path, where the ground was slightly higher, and make it to the next building, which was a Buddhist temple. But you had to pass through a gate in a wall to go further and the whole area was flooded (I mean, it had turned into a lake). We took shelter in the temple for a while, which was very nice. It was slightly surreal the way the monks were sitting peacefully in front of the shrines as the thunder rumbled threateningly overhead. The black sky—which you could look up and see through the atrium—contrasted with the enormous gold statues of the Buddhas. And in the middle of the quadrangle was another grand pond surrounded by a stone balustrade with the fish quietly going about their business.

We felt that we had to make a move after a while because the park was due to close and we needed to get some dinner and get to the airport. So we adopted the simple expedient of running through the flooded area to the drier courtyard beyond the gate. The other side of the courtyard was worse: the path the whole way back to the park entrance was a river. We tightrope walked our way along the raised kerb stones to the exit, leaping across a drainage ditch at one point to outflank another flooded courtyard. Lucy and Catherine had gone on slightly ahead and negotiated the same section when it was still raining and the waters raging: Catherine commented that it was the most exciting and frightening thing that she had ever done! Our drivers were waiting for us back in the car park and whisked us off to a nearby restaurant, which was a mercy because the children, in particular, were cold and wet and tired: they needed feeding up to raise morale. After a good scoff—to which we invited our long-suffering chauffeurs—we were dropped at the airport. We were in plenty of time for the flight, so we were able to change into dry clothes. The rest of the journey went smoothly and we tumbled into bed back in Beijing around midnight on Monday.

Of course, all good trips must have a sting in the tail—and this was an exceptional trip, so it had to have an exceptional sting! Tuesday started OK: the older girls went off to school with no problem, while Elizabeth stayed at home for quarantine purposes (and I now understand why...). By bedtime I was feeling unwell; Lucy came in late and was also feeling unwell. I was violently sick after a half-hour in bed; Lucy followed suit about 15 minutes later. And so it went on through the night, step by step and measure for measure as we traded places in the bathroom—soon joined by Catherine, and later by Elizabeth. We were wading in the stuff. I imagine that this is what it was like for the Pilgrim Fathers when they were battened below decks in an Atlantic gale. It was getting desperate long before the sun came up so we resorted to anti-vomiting medicine. Luckily, we had had a previous experience of family food poisoning when on holiday in Canada and are therefore old hands at this type of emergency. (Let me tell you, when both adults are down and you have young children exploding at both ends, things can spiral out of control pretty fast.) The key is suppositories. The problem with oral nausea medicine is that you throw it up—so it is ineffective and you cannot be sure how much you have taken. But with a trusty old suppository, you are getting a steady dose. There is, of course, one drawback with suppositories that we need not examine in great detail. But I can tell you that it is easier the second time around (something about not clenching too hard, I think). After the storm came the calm—as the dawn broke and the birds began singing (not), we fell into an exhausted slumber. We were subsequently confined to the house for an entire week, too exhausted to move and too frightened to venture far from the bathroom, on a strict bread-and-water diet. Even the Pilgrim Fathers would have pitied us and Lucy was finally forced to make port (i.e. trudge to the local supermarket) when we ran out of food. It was a Sisyphean cycle of dullness, cleaning and vomiting: boredom and tedium *ad nauseam*, you might say.

I was sure that the episode must be due to food poisoning. The onset was so sudden and violent and synchronized that it was obvious. Except that I could not think of anything that all four of us had eaten (since Lucy had not had dinner with me and the three girls), and except that Annabelle had eaten with us but not been sick. But the mystery was later solved. Annabelle came down with the same symptoms about 24 hours later, so it was presumably a stomach bug that somehow missed her the first time around and we happily passed it on to her in subsequent interaction (because we are a caring, sharing family). So maybe quarantine is a suitable policy for kindergarten children in China, after all? Certainly, if Elizabeth had passed on the bug to all her classmates, then productivity would have been drastically reduced amongst the Beijing intelligentsia that week—I know that my own output was approximately zero. I could scarcely get off the sofa for two days.

The children were off school the whole week. We started feeling better on Thursday but everyone was feeling worse again on Saturday. Whatever this thing was that was living inside us, it wasn't going without a fight. I was just hoping that it wasn't going to burst out of my stomach, like that thing in *Alien*. I pressed the Nuclear Button. We had brought antibiotics with us from the US for emergencies: the emergency had arrived. Lucy and I took Cipro (which is a very powerful antibiotic—the kind of thing that you need if someone is throwing anthrax your way) and the children took azithromycin. Lucy and my troubles seemed to clear up pretty quickly and we stopped taking the pills after a day (as instructed—cease when symptoms disappear). But the girls had to finish a three-day course.

The girls finally went back to school on Monday—hurray! But bodily biology was going into overdrive.... On Monday, Elizabeth started to get some bumps on her legs—maybe a mosquito bite, or maybe a rash? I put some hydrocortisone cream on the bumps and sent her to school. It was worse when she got home. On Tuesday, it was noticeably worse (up on her thighs, as well as her calves) and I put on more cream and gave her some antihistamine, since it looked like an allergic reaction to me, and sent her to school. It was worse when she got home. She was very tired and asked to go to bed at 5:30 p.m. (what, is the sky falling in today?) so I gave her more cream and antihistamine. She woke up with a nosebleed at 9 p.m.—which happily distracted her from the fact that she was covered in a severe rash, all over her arms and legs and bottom, and looked like a burns victim. I should say that I am not much into panic: after all, this is my third child and we have met most crises that you are likely to come across with small children. But this was serious: it if got any worse (i.e. spread to the torso or head), then I was clearly going to need to drag her to hospital in the middle of the night, since swelling in core areas could interfere with her respiration. Lucy was out; I don't speak a word of

Mandarin; and I have no idea if Chinese hospitals even offer Western medicine. Elizabeth could end up with a prescription for pickled snake or powdered rhino horn, or some other hocus pocus, for all I know. (Lucy tells me that, in fact, when you show up they ask if you want to be treated with Chinese or Western medicine.)

At times like this, it is a relief that your wife's cousin is married to a paediatrician at a major New York hospital. I surreptitiously took photos of the rash on my phone while Elizabeth was holding tissue to her nose. Once I had dosed her again with antihistamine and put her back to bed, I sent the photos to Heideh in New York—whom I am sure was happy to hear from me, having just got off a night shift and having a small baby of her own to look after. Still, if you can't dump on your friends, then who can you dump on? Anyway, I am sure that she has secretly always wanted to play *House*. Heideh was a rock. We talked through various possibilities (tick bite from the tea plantation? allergic reaction? erythema multiform?) and she checked a few things with a friend who specializes in rashes. The most likely explanation seemed to be an allergic reaction to the antibiotic: apparently, azithromycin is known for this. By the time we had gone through the possibilities, it was close to midnight. Checking back on Elizabeth, I found that the rash had gone into remission: it now looked more like it had at 6 p.m., rather than continuing to progress at the frightening rate observed between 6 and 9 p.m. So we sat tight and saw it through to the morning, when things were mostly better; the swelling had disappeared and some red edges (almost like a tide mark left on a sandy beach) were the only evidence of last night's trauma. We were congratulating ourselves on our cool heads; we dosed her up with antihistamine and sent her to school. Unfortunately, the rash worsened during the day—not much (absolutely nothing compared to the previous night!) but the teacher was concerned that it might be contagious (she was not to know that it was an allergic reaction, after all). So she sent Elizabeth home on Wednesday afternoon.

The problem with this is that Elizabeth could not go back to school until she got a note from the doctor saying that she was fit and healthy. Bummer. So we were going to have to go to the hospital anyway. Having had several friends investigate the possibilities on our behalf—since all the websites are in Chinese—we settled on taking a trip to the Emergency Room on Thursday. We could alternatively have made an appointment at a hospital—including one of the international, English-language hospitals—but this would cost 750 RMB (assuming that no actual treatment would be necessary!) and could not be had before Friday. A friend had offered to call in a favour to get us a faster appointment at a top hospital but, since Elizabeth wasn't even sick, I didn't see the need. So we went with Lily to the walk-in clinic at Peking University Third Hospital at lunchtime on Thursday. And this was not at all a bad experience. We had to register and pay 5 RMB and we had to wait for an hour in a quiet waiting room in the paediatric centre; it was no worse (and maybe better) than going to the Emergency Room in the UK or the US. On the way to the hospital, Lily had asked to see the rash and the only remnant I could find was on Elizabeth's back. When we went in to see the doctor, he asked to see the rash and I raised Elizabeth's T-shirt—to find, of course, that it had totally disappeared in the intervening hour! The doctor thought that it was pretty funny, and I was just happy to be out of there with my form signed so that Elizabeth could go back to school on Friday and I could finally get back to work (two weeks later than planned).

Well, that is end of this week's extreme adventure—from the physical and emotional heights of Wuyi to the physical and emotional depths of the toilet bowl. A microcosm of life in China and my life more generally. Indeed, my letter has come full circle: I started by lamenting my life of skivvying, soared to the summit of Chinese tea culture and crashed back to Earth with a week of the basest skivvying. Why take the direct route from A to B when you can follow such an exciting detour?

OK, I have to go—I need to make some progress on a Monday morning, or I won't get anything done this week!

Very best wishes,

Liam.

Reference

Sutcliffe, Theodora, "The Drink that Costs more than Gold", BBC News, 26 April 2016.

Letter 11

"You're in the Army, Now"
23 May 2016

Dear Tim,

We were invited to go on a trip last weekend to visit the People's Liberation Army (PLA) and stay on an army base. This seemed like an offer that was just too good to refuse, so when the call came out we volunteered immediately (although I was slightly concerned that we would have to sign some kind of confession in order to be released on Sunday). It was arranged by the mother of a child in Elizabeth's class—you know that they like to start them young on the long road of patriotic indoctrination, so you would naturally want to take a bunch of five-year-olds off for their first military experience! Our signing on created a bit of a tizzy. Initially, we were told that we would not be able to attend; then we were told that they would check with the army; and then we were told that we could attend, except for an hour on Sunday morning. I presume that this is the hour when they planned to reveal secret information to a class of five-year-olds, and they did not want us foreigners to hear. Of course, we would never be able to get the information out of them afterwards. "What secret information did they give you?" "I'm not telling!" "What if I give you a lollipop?" "Ooooh! They are going to build an artificial island on the Second Thomas Shoal in the South China Sea to reinforce the

Chinese claim of sovereignty." Of course, I would never really say this to a five-year-old—because my Mandarin would not be good enough! Which is also why I could never collect any secret information by attending the hour-long meeting either. In any case, we got the green light for the operation and swung into action.

I was greatly looking forward to it. As you know, having been in the Sea Cadets—a British youth paramilitary organization that seeks to indoctrinate adolescents into joining the Royal Navy—I have spent a fair bit of time on British military bases, particularly Royal Navy and Royal Marine bases. I was interested to see how things compared, especially since the Chinese military is now such a feared fighting machine. Well, at least it employs a lot of people and is effective at putting down civilian protest; whether it can actually fight for toffee is an entirely unknown matter.

It was very hot last weekend (30°C or more, and substantially hotter on the coach and in our billets). I should say that I am also gradually winning my battle—with the children and Lucy—to get them to wear long sleeves at all times. They have a natural tendency to opt for short sleeves when it is hot. But the reality is that long sleeves are not really much hotter than short sleeves (at least, not if the top is loose-fitting) and a lot more practical: you cannot get sunburnt (to which they are prone, being blondies) and you are less likely to get bitten by mosquitoes or—worse—ticks. (Ticks love the softest parts of your skin—such as behind the knee, or in the fold of your elbow, or under your arm—so it is a good defence mechanism to keep covered.) They are also increasingly in the habit (the older two, at least) or wearing big, floppy sun hats to protect faces and necks. With luck, they may avoid skin cancer when they are older....

We had to assemble at Elizabeth's school at 7:50 a.m. to catch the coach—which was actually a bit brutal on a Saturday morning, when Lucy and I had been up very late the night before sorting out stuff to take. Then we headed off, we knew not where (in true military fashion), for our induction. It turned out that our first stop was the National Aviation Museum, about an hour outside Beijing. This was partly housed inside a mountain: I assume that it was previously a military airbase with underground, bombproof hangars. There was a little bit about civilian aviation—including a dozen dummies with men dressed as pilots and women dressed as stewardesses, to demonstrate the Socialist drive for sexual equality—but it was overwhelmingly about military aviation. The underground hangar vaunted various vintage aircraft—multiple MiG models, a Yak trainer, a Hind helicopter gunship and so on. As you will have gathered, there were many more samples of Soviet aircraft than US aircraft; the few US aircraft seem to have been captured from the Nationalists during the Chinese civil war (a P40, a P54 and several Douglas Dakotas). There also seemed to be a Hawker Sea Fury, which I suppose was shot down during the Korean War when the British offered air support using aircraft carriers and planes left over from World War 2 (and pitted them against new Russian MiG jets, which hardly created a fair contest).

In general, the explanation throughout the museum was poor—in English and in Chinese—and it was notable that there was essentially no signage for the US aircraft. In fact, my guess is that the Douglas Dakotas—the workhorse transport planes of World War 2—ended up in China because they had been carrying supplies over "the Hump". This was the route over the Himalayas, from Assam to Kunming, by which the Allies sent 650,000 tons of supplies to the Chinese to combat the Japanese over 42 months. It was very dangerous because the charts were poor, the weather information was almost non-existent, the elevation was very high (close to the operating ceiling of the aircraft) and the payloads were very heavy. Almost any error engendered a fatal air accident, so 600 planes and 2000 crew were lost. Apparently, the Chinese government is not sufficiently open or magnanimous to recognize the sacrifice of the many non-Chinese who helped them stave off defeat in their darkest hour, when China was almost entirely overrun by the Japanese. (In the interests of fairness, I should call attention at this point to the 100,000 members of the Chinese Labour Corps who helped the British in World War 1, employed to dig trenches, bury the dead and move munitions on the Western Front. Just under 2000 of them died, mostly in the 1919 flu pandemic. All participants were awarded a medal in recognition of their service.)

The museum was also decorated with many supersized Socialist Realist statues. There were heroic men manning anti-aircraft batteries (presumably against the Americans in Vietnam—and other wars in which China "never fought"—since they were firing missiles), pointing at the sky and looking brave. There were bold pilots in flying goggles gathered round a

World War 2-era plane (presumably provided by the Americans), gazing off to the horizon. There were intrepid astronauts (presumably the entire inventory of Chinese astronauts, since they are not even into double figures) standing in front of a planet and contemplating the future of space exploration.

We had a guide who seemed to be in the Chinese Air Force (air force blue military dress with epaulettes and so on). I am not sure what her narration covered, since I do not speak Mandarin, but the tour was at lightning speed (as are most Chinese guided tours, in fact—they are desperate to get you into the gift shop to spend more money). Our family could happily have spent most of the day at the museum, although it may be true that some of the other families would have a lower tolerance for these things. True to form, I think that I did a pretty good job of highlighting key characteristics of the aircraft and keeping the children interested and learning something useful (not that I am at all an expert on planes, I should say). After an hour or so, we were hustled back onto the bus and headed off to the army base, which was another 45-minute drive, and arrived in time for lunch.

In true army fashion, our first task was to make our own lunch as a team building exercise. The two coaches parked up and we all disembarked, to be greeted by a soldier in fatigues, and then formed up into groups of about half a dozen adults and half a dozen children. In a small orchard next to the car park was a line of a dozen or so stoves, the kind that we had seen in the tombs with the terracotta warriors and at Yang Yang's house. Now we were to have the experience of cooking on one ourselves! We walked through a gateway and collected a plastic tote filled with food and cooking utensils; we were then allocated a brick stove. The main compartment is a concrete box about two feet square; one end is open, so that wood can be inserted and air can flow in; at the other end is a chimney about six feet high; and in the top of the concrete box is a circular hole the size of a wok. We broke up the wood bundle that had been left next to the stove and set a fire inside. Once it was burning well, we sat a wok in the hole on the top. Add a bit of oil, and you are ready to stir-fry. It was easy and tasty: green peppers and beef; scrambled egg and tomato (a Chinese favourite); spinach; scallions; pork; some manto buns for good measure. There were stainless steel troughs with running water near the stoves, so we had cooked, eaten and washed up in about an hour. Having packed the crockery back into our totes and dumped the trash, we were marched off to our nearby billets for an afternoon nap.

China is similar to Spain: it is traditional to take a long post-prandial nap to avoid working through the heat of the day. This explains the lengthy lunch break in China that stretches from 11:30 a.m. to 1:30 or 2 p.m.: you have an hour to eat and an hour or more to sleep it off. It also explains why Elizabeth has to suffer a two-hour nap at kindergarten, which she absolutely abhors. Indeed, the only problem that we have had with any of our children at Chinese school is that Elizabeth needs to "nap" every day—which she hardly ever does, so instead lies there being very bored for two hours. This is torture for her and recently she has been in tears every morning going into school, purely at the prospect of having to nap. What a bizarre situation! She is banned from reading books or doing anything useful or interesting; she must lie quietly while the other children sleep (or don't sleep, in some cases). In fact, yesterday Lucy took the three girls to the toyshop at the end of the street for Elizabeth to choose a new cuddly toy to relieve the naptime tedium. She declared that it would make no difference, but she certainly seemed a lot happier next morning when she laid her new Anna (from *Frozen*) carefully on her cot in the classroom. As well as loving Anna, she also confided that it was a good choice because none of the boys around her would want to pinch it at naptime—smart girl! We cannot conceive of a superior solution to this issue so, as far as I am concerned, if we are required to acquire a new cuddly toy every week, then this is a price worth paying to make Elizabeth's days less miserable and stressful. It is not only Elizabeth who finds naptime stressful. It makes it awkward for us to get things done in the day, too. For example, if we want to see a departmental administrator, then *de facto* we have to do this before 11 a.m. each day because by the time they get back from "lunch", we need to be leaving the office to collect the girls from school at 2:45 p.m. If we then drop the girls at their next activity—such as the Monday calligraphy class, which is actually quite close to the university—then by the time we swing back via the department the administrators are on the point of departing and not desperately interested in dealing with any difficulties that we are having. So naptime effectively butchers the day after 11 a.m., certainly if you are dealing with officialdom (who knock off at 5 p.m. or earlier) as opposed to private enterprise (who tend to work late into the evening).

Our billets were a series of luxury tents—really more like a village of prefab huts with canvas walls. They were tall enough to have a standard uPVC front door and a steeply pitched canvas roof; then another uPVC door going into a small bathroom at the back (complete with shower, Arab toilet and washbasin). The tents were raised off the ground and had laminate flooring, electric lights, air conditioners and even TV! There was a long shelf along one wall that was effectively five bed bases side-by-side; and there was a table and chairs. The village was set up in an orchard, with slab footpaths between the tents, large pergolas at the intersections and picnic tables and benches between the rows of tents. So it was more South of France than South Sudan. I couldn't work out why the army would want to create this permanent canvas settlement: if you needed something permanent, then why not use regular buildings (which would not degrade as fast as all that canvas in the capital's climate of harsh winters and sun-baked summers)? And if you wanted soldiers to rough it, then why not give them simple tents with nearby wash blocks? Was this a holding camp for new recruits or purely for guests like us? The camp was obviously used by soldiers, at least some parts of it at some times, because there was a very big assault course near the lunch area—albeit a rather strange one. It looked like a supersized children's playground: it was very new and made of metal girders and chains painted bright blue and yellow; the floor was the kind of rubber tiles that you see in kiddy play areas. However, the assault course was very high (at least 8 m in places) and I don't think that falling onto rubber tiles would have saved you from a broken ankle.

The tents were very hot because they had been shut up until our arrival, so it was way over 30°C and stuffy inside. I considered resting outside but the benches were a little too narrow to lie comfortably. So I settled down for an afternoon nap in the tent, which was most welcome, since Lucy and I have been up very late getting the stuff together for the trip and the girls were content to read their books. As we nodded off, the sound of gunfire erupted nearby—I am assuming that there was a firing range, although we never saw it—and the staccato repetition of automatic weapons sent us off to our slumbers. In fact, gunfire could be heard for much of our stay, which somewhat surprised me. My recollection is that the British Army restricts its use of the rifle range because the annual allocation of ammunition is so miserly. Either the Chinese are generally more generous when doling out bullets or we happened on an establishment where the soldiers happily get to fire off an unusual number of rounds. They should have no excuses for poor marksmanship after all that investment. I noticed on the coach that we passed the Ordnance Research Establishment as we neared the army base; fortunately, they seem a little more abstemious with their shells, otherwise we wouldn't have got a wink of sleep.

We actually saw hardly any soldiers in our time on the base, except a few female soldiers who were exiting the mess hall as we entered it at dinnertime. On Sunday there were a few soldiers repairing the accommodation: two were fixing the plumbing in one of the tents, one was fixing a valve on an irrigation system. Discipline seemed pretty relaxed: they were wearing camouflage trousers (of several different patterns) with any old T-shirt and trainers (Nike, Converse All-stars…). This is quite different to a UK military base. On the one hand, British soldiers would be turned out in a much more homogenous fashion. On the other hand, British soldiers don't do maintenance: you certainly wouldn't find British soldiers fixing the plumbing (I am pretty sure that they wouldn't know how). They don't even repair or service their own vehicles—even the Royal Engineers!—it is all done by outside labour. They don't even guard their own bases—that is also done by outside contractors. I think that you would have to go back a long way (the 1950s?) to find the British Army being self-sufficient in this sense—probably to an era and an area when there simply wouldn't have been outside contractors available to do those kinds of tasks (such as setting up a camp in Malaya or Kenya or some such).

On the one hand, it seems a bit sad that British soldiers are not self-sufficient in this sense. On the other hand, they spend a lot of time soldiering—either on deployment in places like Afghanistan, or training. They are professional soldiers. Hence we have a small military (only about 150,000 enlisted personnel in total) but it packs a punch. By contrast, the Chinese military is huge (about 2.3 million enlisted personnel) but it is unclear how capable they are. We know from Tiananmen Square that they can crush unarmed protesters, but we don't have much evidence from the last 60 years that they can operate effectively against an enemy army.

The Chinese remind me of the Swiss, in this respect. The Swiss are very proud of their army and spend a lot of resources on it—certainly if you include all the off-balance-sheet costs, such as giving prime age workers four or more weeks of paid leave to do military service. But the Swiss haven't fought a war since 1815! I find the idea that they are suddenly going to be up to speed and ready to roll when the call to arms arrives to be completely ridiculous. Training for the last 200 years is hardly a substitute for fighting for the last 200 years. They will be overrun before they even work out what their weaknesses are, let alone fix them. In general, if you get to the stage of cooks having to handle weapons (apart from cutlery), then your army is doomed. Hence I wonder how effective the Chinese plumbers would be if they were ever required on the front lines. Let's hope—for the sake of world peace—that we never find out.... In fact, the quotidian skills of the Chinese army are probably at a premium because the PLA is tasked with a lot of jobs that are typically left to the Fire Department in western countries, such as pulling small boys out of wells and digging people out of earthquakes. This helps to maintain their popularity with the general population, who see them as local heroes.

Of course, the Communist army is a commercial enterprise as much as a fighting force. It owns many facilities and companies—car producers, clothing manufacturers, pharmaceutical companies, fibre optic installers, farms.... At one point it was estimated that PLA plants produced about as much as a Chinese province. These enterprises have traditionally been owned and operated by regional military units, so it is unclear that the central government or military command even knows exactly what the army owns. Many of these enterprises were created almost by accident. For example, there was a lot of spare capacity at the aerospace factory—because no one except Pakistan, Bangladesh and Myanmar buys Chinese fighters—and they started producing motorcycles in order to keep the workforce employed and the factory in operation. Very quickly, the motorcycles became a lot more important and profitable than the aircraft. The situation got so ridiculous that there was a drive to privatize enterprise after 1998 and force the forces to focus more on training and combat readiness. But the increase in PLA budgets has barely kept pace with prices (bearing in mind that the actual inflation rate in China is generally believed to be substantially higher than the official rate) and the military is still expected to maintain some level of self-sufficiency to insulate itself from such resource squeezes. So it is seen as sensible for the army to still own assets such as farms. We had a good example of this on Sunday morning. I was under the impression that they had scheduled some kind of team building exercise for us. In fact, straight after breakfast we sauntered several hundred yards to an orchard and paid 30RMB/lb (which was really a bit overpriced) to pick cherries for an hour or two. It was perfectly pleasant (peaceful, shady, surrounded by superb roses) and the children were endlessly enthusiastic. In fact, a little too enthusiastic, as we ended up with 15 lbs of cherries and have spent the entire week washing cherries and turning them in to pies, tarts and crumbles (as well as eating them raw, obviously). Our pooping pieces are perfectly primed for powerful performance.

After our afternoon nap on Saturday, we were roused around 3 p.m. to rush off on another adventure: a visit to the National Tank Museum, just a short drive away. It is fortunate that my three daughters all like tanks (not something that you would want to bet on, with most small girls). In fact, when we went to the British Tank Museum at Bovington, a couple of summers ago, the girls jumped joyously out the car and ran excitedly over to an old Churchill tank that is parked in one corner. They immediately clambered on top of it, stood on the turret and started singing songs in Chinese (which was odd at the time and even odder in retrospect—three little blonde girls standing on top of a tank singing in Mandarin). Of course, no one batted an eyelid. I wonder what would have happened if they had stood on the turret of a Chinese tank and started singing the English national anthem…? As at the Aviation Museum, there was a preponderance of Soviet weaponry: several IS2 tanks (as used in the Korean War), a T34 and a T54 that you could climb inside. I think that the only US tank was an M3, which I assume was captured from the Nationalists (who were armed by the Americans via the Laredo Road through northern Burma). Again, after a whistle-stop tour at the Chinese Tank Museum, we were bundled onto the bus to head back to base.

Since the sun was sinking, it was sufficiently cool to socialize outside so we assembled in the exercise area alongside the assault course. In addition to the soldier who had greeted us at lunchtime, there was *animateur* wearing civvies and a funny haircut (well—a kind of young, fashionable haircut that you sometimes see on Chinese men, including those who are really too old for it, like this guy). The wonderful French word *animateur* is typically translated as "activity leader", but this hardly does the term credit—the British equivalent lacks the crazy dynamism implicit in the French original. We all formed a circle and held out one hand to each side: the right hand was flat and facing the floor; the left hand had the index finger pointing upwards, so that it was touching the (right hand) palm of the person next to us. On the *animateur's* signal, we had to close the right hand as fast as possible so as to grab the index finger of the person on our right—and simultaneously whip our own index finger away so that our left hand was not grabbed. We played the game a few times; it is quite good to play with groups of adults and children because there is no obvious adult advantage, in terms of speed or experience. Then we played for a forfeit: those who got grabbed had to go to the centre of the circle and offer a short entertainment for the rest of us. Unfortunately, Elizabeth got caught and was in quite a quandary about what to do. In the end, Lucy went with her and assisted with the splits and a backbend/kickover (i.e. bend over backwards until she could touch the floor in a bridge and then kick her feet over to get back upright), which seemed to be good enough. We had tried to persuade Catherine to go with Elizabeth and sing her patriotic Chinese song from the Young Pioneers—which would have thrilled the parents and the soldiers for sure—but she was unusually shy and refused. Several team games followed, such as ping-pong races (where you have to carry balls from one bucket to another using chopsticks) and drumming with a ball.

This drum and ball game is particularly Chinese. Traditional Chinese drums have a bulging red wooden shell with about eight metal rings attached to it. Now tie two lengths of string (maybe 2 m long) to each ring and have someone hold them, one in each hand. So you have a drum like a hub, sixteen strings like spokes and eight people like a wheel rim. When you all pull on the strings, the drum rises about four feet off the floor. Now someone puts a ball on the drum and everyone has to flex their strings at the same time to make the drum jump and the ball bounce ("Boom!"). Obviously, if the flexing is not coordinated, then the drum is not flat and the ball flies off to one side. Then the whole group has to run in that direction—together and without tripping over—to position themselves back under the ball as it comes down. And you continue thus, bouncing the ball on the drum as many times as you can before you lose it. So the two key elements are to flex simultaneously (i.e. keep the ball in one spot as far as possible) and to move synchronously (i.e. get the drum back under the ball as fast as possible). You can see why the army would like to play this game as a team building exercise. There was a gang of dads who were deeply into it—doubtless they're deadly serious about pub games, too—so the mums and children could hardly get a look in. The soldier produced another drum so that the mums could miss the ball for a while and then the children (who were, as you might imagine, absolutely hopeless at it). I just looked on with anthropological interest, and I was not alone as some of the other dads did not feel the need to publicly promote their prowess, either.

After a few games we were dismissed for dinner and meandered off to the mess hall. It was much like a British Army base—metal trays, institutional food—but with chopsticks and spoons instead of knives and forks. We were offered the scrambled egg and tomato dish that we had for lunch and which the children get regularly at school (and fortunately like), and several other dishes. Having happily filled the children with scrambled egg and rice, we tidied up and headed back to our tent. We were all very tired—having risen early and spent a very hot day racing around—and soon went off to a long and pleasant sleep.

Our Sunday morning was equally relaxed: a leisurely breakfast, cherry picking and then letting Elizabeth run around with her friends in the canvas village while the two elder girls read Roald Dahl in their beds and Lucy and I tidied up the tent. Then it was back on the bus to Beijing, stopping for lunch *en route* at a fairly swanky restaurant. We took over a huge dining room and each big, round table of diners (maybe 12 tables) shared a lamb hot pot. This was introduced to Beijing during the Yuan dynasty (i.e. the Mongols brought it) and has been a local tradition ever since. The centre of each table consists of a large circular recess. You then have a special charcoal stove (shaped like a small chimney about two feet high) with an integral stockpot around the outside (perhaps two feet in diameter) that sits in the circular area. This is made of copper. The stockpot is filled with broth and brought to the boil; raw food is brought to the table (finely sliced lamb, tofu, mushrooms, lettuce, dumplings…) and diners drop these items into the broth as they like. After a minute or two, each of them is cooked and you can take it out with chopsticks and eat it. It is good, and not necessarily something you might expect in Chinese cuisine. Of course, talking about "Chinese cuisine" is a bit like talking about "European cuisine". There are certain characteristics of European cuisine (such as the fact that typically each person is served a personal plate of food and this may differ from one diner to the next—as a opposed to the Chinese system where you all partake of several common plates of food at the same time). And there are some unifying elements to European cuisine (e.g. in many places you are likely to be served a lump of meat or fish and some boiled vegetables on a plate). But European cuisine is obviously very heterogeneous (from pickled fish in Norway to veal in cream sauce in Austria), and Chinese cuisine is at least as heterogeneous. We tend to experience a rather selected subset of Chinese cuisine in the west—often derived from Cantonese food because they have historically been the largest migrant group—and Chinese cuisine is actually far more diverse than this.

In fact, we had had hot pot several times in China already, which was useful because it meant that we knew the drill. We first had it in Harbin in January, far in the frozen north. The hot pot there is cooked in a big hemispherical copper pot with a wooden lid, and the stove is in a brick table. Traditionally, the heat source would be charcoal but it was a gas ring in the restaurant. The hot pot there was more like a stew, with all the ingredients—including a whole fish—being cooked at the same time and left to simmer for a while (with the lid recirculating the heat and retaining the humidity). The Chinese cook potato surprisingly often, and they often feature in these hotpot or stew dishes. Our second hotpot was in Kunming in the far south and it was much more like the Beijing affair. There was no chimney—there was a simple brazier of hot coals instead—but the procedure was identical. It was also based around lamb, which is not a coincidence because a substantial proportion of the restaurateurs around China are Muslims from Xinjiang (who obviously won't touch pork and traditionally do a lot of sheep herding). The Chinese love spicy food and central Asian cooking is very popular. So instead of the restaurant trade being dominated by Pakistanis or Indians—as it is in England—it is dominated by people from Xinjiang, the Chinese sector of central

Asia. (I should perhaps point out that China is a very large country indeed: the city of Kashgar, in Xinjiang, is closer to Baghdad than to Beijing!) The restaurant in Kunming was very atmospheric. It was in an old three-storey building, with each storey overhanging the one below and the topmost one closed up with traditional carved wooden shutters, rather than windows (of which there were none). We took a table on the top floor, where the open shutters let in the sun and the breeze did its best to disperse the diners' cigarette smoke and the scent of the braziers. Since the entire length of the wall was open—and the rails and walls and floors were all made of old, weathered timber—the ambience was more like sitting on the balcony of Shakespeare's Globe Theatre than a regular restaurant. The staff were also attired in traditional dress—white taqiyah hats for the men, hijabs for the women—and you could have been dining in a restaurant in 1816 as easily as 2016.

Sadly, hygiene was also on a par with 1816, rather than 2016. This was one of our earliest experiences of restaurants in provincial Chinese cities—Kunming is the capital of Yunnan province—and it was an absolute eye-opener. The table had perhaps been given a cursory wipe after the previous meal (or maybe not); paper napkins were an optional extra (available for purchase); and a crockery set for each diner came shrink-wrapped in plastic direct from the dishwashing factory to prove its cleanliness (in theory—when you open these shrink-wrapped crockery sets, they are often not especially clean, we have found). In most Chinese restaurants, you are served free hot water to drink—hot because it has just been boiled to sterilize it. You can always order additional cold bottled water, often order fruit juice, and sometimes order tea. We have found the tea supply to be surprisingly erratic: for example, the Harbin restaurant that served hot pot did not serve tea on the basis that tea was not traditional in that area; we have been to many restaurants that do not serve tea for one reason or another. Tea is certainly more widely available in the UK or the US than in China, which is a little ironic. In any case, the first use of your hot water or tea is to fill your bowl and cup to ensure that they are sterile (pouring away the water or tea after a minute or two). Chopsticks are usually wooden and come in a small plastic packet, still joined at the hip to prove that they are new; you snap them apart before use and discard them afterwards.

Unfortunately, we were still recovering from a previous stomach bug when we visited the Kunming hot pot restaurant. Stomach bugs work their way slowly through the family because we suffer them sequentially. One of the children thoughtlessly puts their disgustingly dirty digits in their mouth and digests the bug—I tend to think of children as "disease vectors" because they are the primary source of entry for any malady—and then falls sick. They then give it to the other children, with a day or two's delay, and eventually the adults who are caring for them. Since life must go on—and those who had the bug first, and were unable to eat for several days, end up ravenously hungry by the time they recover—we then end up going to eating establishments to feast even while the last person to get the bug (usually me!) is still sick. What fun. For one thing, sharing dishes is a nightmare for infection control: sending stomach bugs to your dining companions is a good way to shed friends and I have declined to dine with colleagues on occasion on the basis that I then cannot be held responsible for spreading sickness. (Hot pot is actually benign in this respect because boiling broth sterilizes your chopsticks. But in Kunming I used one set of chopsticks to serve myself and another to eat as a precaution. This is now common in Hong Kong and becoming standard in decent restaurants in China). The second issue is that as soon as I stuffed myself with scran—being starving as well as sick—I was in speedy need of the sanitary facilities (notwithstanding my status as an imodium junky). Now, lavatory provision is entirely optional in Chinese eateries; if you are lucky enough to enter an establishment with an Arab toilet, then it typically has no toilet paper; there is commonly no place to clean your hands and, even if there is, no soap. I went to the men's room and found urinals and a locked Arab toilet: I was supposed to ask for a key (and possibly be charged) if I needed more than a urinal. I exited the bathroom with extreme urgency and found Lucy entering the ladies room. Since we were lunching late, we were the only patrons left on the top floor of the restaurant and the ladies room was empty: I rushed in and Lucy stood guard while I exploded into one of the available Arab toilets. I even experienced the luxury of washing my hands afterwards because—as is often then case—the ladies room was endowed with soap whereas the men's dispenser was exhausted. When I get back to the West, I will never again disdain a restroom, however filthy and unkempt it may be.

So my hot pot history is varied but I would definitely recommend it as a dining experience. It is simple, tasty, unusual and sociable. We left our swanky Beijing restaurant feeling full and happy and headed for home on the bus. When we stopped outside Elizabeth's school, there was the small issue of surviving the trek home with a 15 lb box of cherries—in addition to all our other kit—on a sunny summer afternoon in 30°C. Since we had so many to consume, it seemed best to start processing them straightaway: as soon as the children were settled in front of their school books, I scrubbed some for immediate consumption and then set about pitting a pailful for conversion into crumbles, cakes, pies and tarts. Clearly, if I were in the US or the UK, then I could call into the supermarket and buy these delicacies for less than it cost me to buy the cherries in China—leaving aside the question of how long it takes to cook all this stuff. However, since we had ended up with a crazy quantity of soft and perishable fruit, I bit the bullet and decided to make the most of it by having my wife wear her "homemaker" hat for an afternoon/evening/night and convert it all into tasty treats. And I am happy to report that we have been enjoying our just desserts for the last fortnight!

We also gifted a crumble to the teacher who accompanied us on the trip, as a small thank you. She apparently approved, as she asked for the recipe—which is actually a little difficult to communicate in the case of crumble because the key is the mixing, rather than the mixture. We also photographed our extravagant English delicacies and I urged Lucy to WeChat them to the other mothers. (WeChat is like a Chinese version of Twitter but geared towards restricted groups—such as all the parents of a particular class of school children. Some of the mothers have a "Nigella Lawson complex" and send out WeChats every morning at 6 a.m. with snapshots showing what amazing and healthy breakfasts they are serving their children before setting out for school. They also link their "Fitbit" to WeChat so that everyone can see in real time how much exercise they are getting during the day, gyrating at the gym and running round the park—assuming, of course, that have not just attached their Fitbit to someone else for an hour or two…. I confess that we commonly have other commitments requiring our concentration, so we neither monitor WeChat nor keep people posted on our activities in real time.) In any case, Lucy shied away from starting a culinary arms race—which we would surely lose, since some of the families have cooks on their household staff—so we just stuffed ourselves silly instead and enjoyed the satisfaction of our own private heaven.

OK, this is really all I have time to write right now, and this email is well overdue, so I am going to send it before something else happens.

Love to everyone, and see you soon,

Liam.

Letter 12

Inner Mongolia
7 June 2016

Dear Oliver,

Thanks for your email! Still, I think that moving to Nepal and living as a goat is an extreme reaction to the Brexit vote. It is true that if Britain opts for completely free trade, as Michael Gove is proposing, then life—as we know it—may cease for British farming. But why not settle for something a little simpler? I suggest moving to the Chinese province of Inner Mongolia and living as a dairy farmer. Having seen Inner Mongolia, I can say that your experience would be ideal because your farm is situated on excessively dry land—and everywhere in Inner Mongolia is excessively dry, as far as I can see. I am actually writing this missive while relaxing beside the pool at a luxury oasis hotel in Inner Mongolia's fourth largest desert. Anywhere that has a "fourth largest desert" has at least three deserts too many, in my opinion, and virtually all of Inner Mongolia seems to be on the road to desertification (as I'll explain shortly). I am confident that you could still make money from milk, though, because your trustworthiness—as a foreigner—would be high. If they can afford it, everyone in China buys foreign milk (German, Australian, New Zealand) because they are confident that it is safe to drink. If you could produce milk in China and create a trustworthy brand, then you could make a mint. Anyway, let me tell you how we got here.

Since we were gifted two unexpected extra weeks of school vacation, we had to quickly and radically revise our plans. Our plan to Journey to the West in the footsteps of Tang Seng had to be brought forward owing to a visa complication. But we could not start immediately because Annabelle and Catherine had to be back in Beijing on 8 July for the end-of-year school ceremony. So we had six days to do something, maybe only four days if you take out the travel time at each end. Most tourist targets (such as Guilin or Shanghai) typically have slightly more than four days' worth of key things to see or do—which is annoying because you always feel a bit too rushed. We did not want to go somewhere that was excessively hot—which is hard to avoid in China in the summer, since everywhere is excessively hot! All this suggested that we should go north to Inner Mongolia. You can travel overland from Beijing; it is not hotter than Beijing (although it is not clearly cooler, either); and there is not an excessive number of things to see or do. Also, the key Mongolian festival of Nadam was due to take place from 7 to 11 July, so it seemed like it would be a fun time to visit. (Nadam is celebrated by Mongolians in both Outer Mongolia and Inner Mongolia. It is a bit like the Mongolian Olympics, where men compete at horse riding, archery and wrestling. Obviously, there is also music and dancing and feasting and so on.)

We originally planned to take the overnight train to Hohhot—which is the capital of Inner Mongolia and located roughly in the middle—and start by seeing the cultural exhibits. There are various historic mosques and Buddhist temples and pagodas in the city, as well as a very good museum with many new dinosaur skeletons (Mongolia being the ground zero for dinosaur discoveries these days, you understand) and Mongolian historical artefacts. You can then travel several hours by car to Gegentala (the grassland where the main Nadam festival takes place) or Xilamuren (a closer grassland that is better set up for tourists). Lily was keen to go to Mongolia because she has been captivated since her youth by a famous Chinese poem about the endless grasslands that sway in the wind (a translation—although not necessarily a good one!—might be: "The sky is blue cast/The grassland is vast/The cattle surge past"). But the Hohhot area is arid and the grass is quite sparse—and she thought that it would be rather touristy—so she proposed driving to a place that was closer to Beijing and less parched. If you look at a map, then you will see that Inner Mongolia is incredibly large and extends 1500 miles from west to east. The western end is desert (including the famous Gobi desert, one of the driest in the world); the eastern end is wetter and cooler (being also more northerly) and is known for its greener grass. Driving north from Beijing takes you to a point about halfway between Hohhot and the eastern end of Inner Mongolia. It also takes you to the Hexigten Global Geopark—a massive area containing Inner Mongolia's second largest lake (Dalinur), remnants of volcanic activity, beautiful mountains and a desert. We planned a tour to take in some of the most impressive sights, although this circuit still sampled only the southern part of the park.

It was a six-hour drive from Beijing to Badaying, our first port of call in the Hexigten Geopark. Since we were travelling with children and wanted to avoid a meltdown on the first day, we broke the journey by stopping for a half-day in Chengde—the site of yet another Imperial summer palace (the two in Beijing being somehow insufficient). Chengde is higher in the mountains and presumably cooler than Beijing, although there didn't seem to be any appreciable difference on the day that we visited. The palace has various structures spread around a very large park. A special feature of the Chengde palace is that it includes six temples abutting the park wall. These were designed in different regional styles and used to house guests from those areas (so Tibetan delegations were housed in a Tibetan palace and so on). One interpretation of this set-up is that the emperor wanted his guests to feel at home; another interpretation is that that emperor wanted to overawe his guests by sending the message that "everything you have at home, we have already in Beijing—and more". The park also contains the Imperial library, a pagoda, a temple and a Mongolian camp ground, amongst other things. Having only a half-day at our disposal, we eschewed the outer temples and went straight into the park—walking around the lake sounded idyllic on a hot day. Thousands of other people apparently had the same idea.

The park entrance takes you into the main palace complex, which we rapidly surveyed. The layout is like every other Imperial palace—a sequence of audience rooms, separated by courtyards, in which the

12 Inner Mongolia

emperor sits on a small dais and everyone else seems to sit on the floor. It is true that the buildings were a bit more "rustic" than other palaces, being highly carved but unpainted (which I have not seen elsewhere). But the main palace was not particularly novel or noteworthy. We rapidly moved on to the lake that lies behind the main buildings. It is perfectly nice but, again, not really remarkable. The overall ambience is similar to both the Old and New Summer Palaces in Beijing. We took a leisurely stroll around the lake and then headed off into the parkland on the far side to see some of the more unusual buildings, such as the Wenjin Chamber (often referred to—rather inaccurately—as the Imperial library) and the Mongolian camp.

I must say that the Wenjin Chamber was rather a disappointment, on several levels. It has a fascinating ingress: the path draws you into a grotto in a man-made rock face, which bifurcates and circles round to the left and right. Only after advancing 10 m in either direction do you exit the crag, to be abruptly confronted by the library on the other side of a small pond that must be crossed on steppingstones. It is a dramatic and unique entrance and, once inside, you can imagine yourself in a restful sylvan glade suited to reflection and erudition. The repository's exterior looks like many other Imperial buildings but hides a secret mezzanine floor where the books were kept—so the building appears to have two storeys but actually has three. This seems to be a noteworthy architectural innovation in China, judging from the information panels. The building is not at all large (maybe 30 m by 10 m) and was in the midst of a gut rehab when we visited—so we had an excellent view of the structural design (the front wall being entirely missing) but its grandeur was correspondingly shrunken. The information panels claim that in the era of Emperor Qianlong (the late eighteenth century) this library contained a copy of everything that had been written in Chinese and survived up to that time. If that is true, then either not much had been written in Chinese or it was written in very, very small script. (I certainly wouldn't want to have to read anything written that small—I think I would be blind within a year.) My understanding is that the Wenjin Chamber was actually the repository for a copy of the *Siku Quanshu*, which was more like an enormous encyclopaedia or compendium of approved texts (and its creation involved the destruction of thousands of unapproved texts).

Our tour ended with a walk across the Mongolian camp ground—complete with lush grass and yurts (or "gers", as they call them in China—yurts actually being the Turkic word, although we commonly use it in English to refer to Mongolian dwellings). In fact, the Qing dynasty was founded by the Liao people from the modern province of Liaoning, which is next to Inner Mongolia. (The Mongolians—under Genghis and Kublai Khan—had founded the Yuan dynasty in the thirteenth century. But that was long past by the advent of the Qing dynasty in the mid-seventeenth century.) However, the Liao were a nomadic people with cultural similarities to the Mongols, and the Qing emperors liked to celebrate their heritage by inviting guests to feast on the grasslands of the Mongolian camp at the Chengde palace. There are other campgrounds much further north where the Qing emperors also liked to holiday and hunt in the summer months. We would see some of these later on our trip.

From Chengde, we carried on through the northern part of Hebei (the province surrounding the Beijing metropolitan area), which is green and dotted with latter day yurt encampments—large clusters of polytunnels with funny pointy rooves. Presumably, these produce fruit and vegetables for the Beijing market that is a few hours away by road. The Hexigten Geopark actually spills over into northern Hebei, as does Mongolian culture. As evening drew in, we entered the park—paying 100 RMB per person for the privilege, even though the next day we would have to pay a second time to cross into the Inner Mongolian part of the park! Just inside the park, we stopped at a hilltop observation tower that was seven storeys high and created in reinforced concrete in the form of a pagoda. It was quite kitsch, being decorated throughout with highly coloured Buddhist paintings—like a fantasy version of the Big Wild Goose pagoda in Xi'an. There was even a lift but, since this wasn't working, we stomped up the wooden staircase and happily watched the sun set over a vast expanse of rolling hills and grassland and forest. It was an uplifting end to the day—a beautiful panorama and our first taste of Mongolia.

Booking a trip to Inner Mongolia is not easy, even if you are based in Beijing. It is difficult to dig up any detailed information about things to do or see, either in Chinese or in English. As we were to discover, the road system is also in a state of flux (being greatly upgraded but with many sections still shut) and it is hard to know the best route between two places, or how long it will take to drive. On one of our many detours, Lucy opined that: "It must be hard work to keep the GPS maps updated in China, given how quickly the road network is changing." To which I replied: "Looking at the driver's GPS, I don't think it's too much work." I could see that the screen was perfectly white, except for our car being shown as a blue arrow in the middle! It reminded me of the Elizabethan Blackadder sketch when he has to circumnavigate the globe: they equip him with the latest charts—which all turn out to be completely blank. When Blackadder comments on this, Lord Melchitt replies: "Yes, indeed—we would like you to fill them in as you go along." And so it is in Inner Mongolia. You need to plot your course based on personal experience and I think that our driver, while we were visiting the sights, usefully employed himself talking to other drivers to pick up local knowledge.

We spent the evening at a nearby hotel. We had booked certain aspects of our tour, such as the hotels, through an agent. We always try to avoid using middlemen because they are expensive (they basically charge a 50 per cent markup on everything) and unreliable. We know this because the tour agent failed to book one of our hotels and we had to pay for it on the spot—whereupon we discovered that the regular hotel rate was only two-thirds of what the agent was charging us. (Of course, we would never have found the hotel without the intervention of the agent because it was remote and poorly advertised. The tour agent was quickly on the phone to insist that the hotel refund our payment and accept one from her instead—so that she could then overcharge us for the rooms, as per our agreement before leaving Beijing!) In any case, finding a driver who was willing to collect us in Beijing and drive us around Mongolia for five days was very difficult without an intermediary—someone who had a stable of such people and some idea of routes and costs. When asked by the tour agent, we had opted for comfort over economy in hotels (which is generally a wise choice in China, especially if you have children). Lily had asked to stay in three star accommodation or better—only to be told that there were no three star hotels in Hexigten! The first hotel was OK—decent and clean rooms, a spacious and well-appointed lobby, nice views. Since basically no foreigners travel in these parts, it was geared towards Chinese tour groups and we therefore benefitted from our previous military training. For example, we were awoken at 6 a.m. by noisy groups of people banging around and talking loudly in the corridor (this is normal in Chinese hotels—people entering and exiting late at night or early in the morning seem oblivious to the fact that other people are likely sleeping and hence it would be polite to keep noise to a minimum). And breakfast was army style: you enter the canteen to be given a plastic tray with little compartments, a hardboiled egg, a mantou bun, and the option of some cold spicy vegetable and rice porridge. There was no liquid provided, but we had presciently brought our own water. The benefit of this style of breakfast is that it doesn't take long—even with children—so we were soon ready for the off.

We drove for an hour or so and finally passed into the province of Inner Mongolia. We immediately stopped at the "Seven star lake", so called because it has seven ponds arranged like the Big Dipper (which I presume is more obvious from the air than it is from the ground). It was pretty, though: lush grasslands surrounding the ponds, swaying in the breeze; reeds rustling at the water's edge, with yellow birds hopping around on the wooden walkways that conducted you around the park; an observation tower in the middle; and a border of birch forest, which is typical of this part of China. Inevitably, there were market stalls between the car park and the entrance (just to make sure that you could not avoid walking through them) but as well as tourist grockles they stocked local produce. The dried beef was excellent and so were the dried blueberries; we also bought some strange kind of rock honey that I have never seen before. It looked like an enormous melon: the outside was grey—the vestiges of the honeycomb itself—but when broken open it was bright orange inside. The market trader smashed off lumps with a hammer to get the quantity that you wanted, and then broke it up into little pieces inside the bag. It had a slightly odd aftertaste—almost like some kind of medicine—but it was very popular with Annabelle and Elizabeth.

An hour and a half was enough and we headed on up the highway. The countryside was predominantly rolling green grassy hills, with a smattering of lakes and birch forests. Historically, birch forests have formed an important basis of north Chinese economy and culture (although generally more to the east, in Heilongjiang, than in Inner Mongolia). In many ways, the Oroqen people in Heilongjiang used to live like the First

Nations around the Great Lakes—constructing birch bark canoes and snowshoes, and living largely by hunting game in the woods. We stopped at a beautiful birch forest with a tourist trail where you could walk a short circuit and read Chinese poems posted en route. This is a very Chinese activity. You will often go to a tourist spot and find an ancient poem reproduced for your contemplation and erudition. Chinese children spend many hours rote-learning classical poems in school, so Lily recognizes many of these verses. Hence, she had been motivated to see Mongolia by such artistic descriptions of the swaying swathes of green grass. I have to tell you that, apart from the lake locality, we saw no swaying swathes of green grass in Inner Mongolia. We saw thousands of square miles of sandy soil covered in very sparse and sickly grass. I suspect that the poet may have been taking a very large amount of artistic licence in the verbal landscape that he painted. I confess that the Chinese poetry proffered at these moments leaves me largely untouched. It tends to be terse and dominated by description (a bit like the Japanese haiku but a little longer and less rigid): I think that you are supposed to be carried away into the scene and meditate on the profound meaning of nature. (I am told that there are other styles of Chinese poetry—and obviously much longer works with multiple verses—but I guess that they are not as suitable for posting beside tourist attractions.) From my perspective, the primary attraction of the poetry placards was that Annabelle wanted to read them and could basically do so without assistance (although Lily was there to help with the odd character and the interpretation). Progress!

By lunchtime we approached the town where we were to spend the night. Just outside town was a huge plain where Emperor Kangxi—regarded as the greatest Qing Emperor—assembled his army in 1696 in order to fight the Mongols (technically the Dzungar Khanate, which was the most powerful Mongol successor state after they lost control of China to the Ming dynasty and retreated north). This successful campaign led to the annexation of areas of Inner Mongolia to the Chinese Empire. Kangxi fielded two armies—one led by himself and the other by his uncle—totalling around 80,000 men and they joined forces at this location.

We also passed a showground going into the town and Lily noted the phone number so that she could check out the show times. The Mongolians are famous for lamb and we were keen to sample the local roast (which even comes with roasted potatoes!) but we saved that treat for the evening because we wanted a quick lunch before the afternoon disappeared. So we settled for pork and dandelion dumplings and some kind of lamb and yellow flower dumplings. Over lunch, Lily arranged for us to see a Mongolian cultural show at the showground we had passed coming into town. They were having shows every evening but would also put on an afternoon show if there were sufficient demand. Lily arranged for us to see the show that afternoon, and go horse riding afterwards. This infuriated the driver. He had wanted to take us to another venue 10 km away where they also put on Mongolian cultural shows and took people riding. This was more expensive—precisely because the drivers get kickbacks from the show organizers. Hence he was angry because he was missing out on maybe a day's pay from inducing us to buy overpriced show tickets. Of course, this scam is completely normal in China; I am sure that the drivers do not even consider it to be a scam, but simply part of their standard remuneration. Lily's entrepreneurial activity created quite a lot of bad feeling, which was an unfortunate start to our trip and created difficulties in the long run.

The showground just outside town was very unusual. It had been an army camp until very recently and was the place where the military came to practice for the May Day march past in Tiananmen Square. As a result, the camp had a replica of the Forbidden City gatehouse, which fronts onto Tiananmen Square and serves as the podium for Party Officials to take the salute. The showground had repurposed this building—which is at least 30 m long—as a grandstand to watch the horsemanship displays in the adjacent field. There was also an interesting display about the military's preparation for the May Day parade. Apparently, the soldiers line up on parade and there are metal posts at both ends of each rank (row) of soldiers. They run numerous white string lines between the posts at different heights and these are the guidelines for every soldier to correctly position his body. That is, they all have to have their chin on the topmost string; they all have to lift the toe of their boot to the bottommost string; and so on. Apparently, they also do marching practice on the spot, in front of a string line, while wearing ankle weights: this makes sure that they have enough precision and thigh muscle to goosestep correctly at all times. There were also photos of harrowed troops doing the same thing in the pouring rain, and with wasps on their faces, just to make sure that they were prepared for every eventuality on the Big Day. It is good to know that China's defence is in such safe hands.

We had not realized that "sufficient demand" for an afternoon show was six people! So we discovered on arrival that we were the entire audience for that afternoon's performance. It was a surreal experience. It felt like my Wuyi trip all over again—as if they had accidentally mistaken us for visiting royalty. We were greeted by about a dozen people in Mongolian dress, half of them women. They were predictably thrilled to meet our children. We were treated to a traditional Mongolian welcome: this involves the gift of a silk scarf and the presentation of a cup of very strong alcohol; you dab some alcohol on your forehead, flick some up in the air and some onto the ground, and then drink the rest (I just about managed for the sake of diplomacy, being teetotal). There were Mongolian outfits available for the entertainment of visitors, so the girls were led away by the giggling women to do some dressing up—trying on many outfits and having many photos taken while I examined the military display. After a while, they had gathered together the entertainers and we were conducted to the concert area, where about 20 people were waiting on stage to regale us with Mongolian singing and dancing. So we sat on a little row of seats while a trio of musicians played traditional tunes on their "morin khuur" (an unusual instrument, a bit like a violin, that I found quite sonorous and also powerful—unlike the Chinese erhu, whose sound I also like but is rather quiet). Then a trio of Mongolian singers each performed a song (Mongolians from the country Mongolia, not the Chinese province of Inner Mongolia), including the winner of the Mongolian version of "The Voice". They were all very powerful singers and the Mongolian style is unique and striking. Finally, a troupe of dancers stomped and twirled. It was wonderful and we all really enjoyed it, and did our very best to show our appreciation.

As soon as the show finished, a couple of hostesses conducted us to a nearby yurt. We sat cross-legged at a low table while some snacks and Mongolian milk tea were laid out for us. If you like English builders' tea (plenty of full fat milk and sugar added to every mug), then you will like Mongolian milk tea. Despite coming from a family of builders (or maybe because of it?), I don't like builders' tea and never touch the stuff. But I was sufficiently inured to it as a boy that I can down a few mugs out of politeness. (It may never have occurred to you that you need to be polite to builders, but it always helps if you want to get them onside to finish the job on time!) There were some nice wheat biscuits on offer, as well some that were much too sweet for the average palate. Suitably fortified, our hostesses took us on a short walk—past a couple of lazing camels and a horse who was rolling in a dust patch—to a Mani stone mound at the top of the hill. You see these commonly in Tibet. Technically, a Mani stone has a mantra inscribed on it ("Om Mani Padme Hum"), although it may also have other sutras or images of deities. Once a Mani stone mound starts, believers will deposit another stone on top whenever they pass it to bring good fortune—hence they grow continuously. They are often additionally decorated with colourful Tibetan prayer flags. The Mongolians mostly follow Lamaist Buddhism, which came to them via Tibetan monks in the fourteenth century: after Genghis Khan forced the Tibetans to submit to his authority—which they wisely chose to do, rather than being conquered and slaughtered—Tibetan Buddhism became the religion of choice at the Mongol court and hence spread widely and deeply amongst the Mongolians. There were some monks monitoring the Mani stone mound (sitting behind a table in a little tent to one side) and as we approached they gave us prayer scarves and guided us clockwise around the stack of stones; we tied our scarves to a corner of the circumvallating rail, put our hands together and bowed towards the mound, and then retreated respectfully. Our hostesses were already waiting to usher us down to the Tiananmen gate for our private show of Mongolian horsemanship.

We stood on the (replica) bridge that crossed the moat to the (imaginary) Forbidden City, about 10 m from the action. A long strip of wood chips ran across the field in front of us, roped off, with two targets facing us. Six riders in Mongolian dress appeared on horseback at one end. One after the other, they raced from one end to the other doing tricks: lying prone across the saddle; hanging off one side, with one foot in the stirrup and the other on the floor; doing a shoulder stand on the neck of the horse. Then they threw down some red scarves and galloped along, leaning out of their saddles to pick them up from the floor. Finally, they galloped along while standing in the stirrups and shooting arrows into the targets. I have to say that the targets were very close to the strip. If Mongol warriors really had to get that close to their target to hit it, then I would have thought that they would have been knocked off by the enemy's lance before they could let fly. In any case, I was shortly to understand much better what it is like to ride a horse moving at speed.

After our wonderful welcome at the showground, we drove down the hill to the historical campground where horse riding was available to tourists. We hired six horses for an hour for 60 RMB each. However, the "horse riding" was limited to being led along on a horse by its keeper; if you wanted to ride free then you had to pay another 90 RMB. We paid our 360 RMB for the group and headed to the corral to mount up. The girls had all ridden horses before and happily scrambled up onto the horses (whose stirrups were a bit long for them, as you might expect). Personally, my only experience of riding a horse was once round a sand box on William, the sedate steed of my friend Susannah. Since I was now required to mount a horse in front of twenty tourists and twenty Mongolian horsemen—who were all very keenly watching the behaviour of this odd bunch of blond tourists—I was rather glad of this minimal experience at this point. With luck, I would at least be able to get out of the corral without humiliating myself (such as mounting one side of the horse and immediately falling off the other, à la Mr. Bean). Annabelle and Elizabeth mounted first and were immediately led out of the corral by their keeper—much to Lucy's angst, as she had to wait several minutes to mount her own horse and the two children were out of sight by then. We eventually all got mounted and headed after them at walking pace. After a few minutes, we caught up with the children and all stopped for a confab. The girls and Lucy were adamant that this was far too tame and that we should pay extra to ride free, since this was more tame than pony trekking (sneer). Personally, I was perfectly happy being more tame than pony trekking—but if they wanted to ride free, then they could go right ahead and I would happily wait for them. During this conversation, my horse decided that it was bored and started heading back down the trail—with me still on board—and people started yelling at me to pull back on the reins to stop him. That is all very well if you know what pulling back on the reins means, and if you are not concerned that the horse may take offence and throw you off. (Obviously, none of us were wearing riding helmets because we were doing this in China, not the USA.) I dutifully pulled back on the reins and the horse did eventually deign to stop, although rather reluctantly and he took advantage of the first sign of any relaxation to head for home again.

Lucy badgered and bothered me until I also agreed to ride free, very much against my better judgment. Now, I can tell you that I rarely go against my better judgment. I may do things that seem crazy to other people—actually, I think that I quite often do things that seem crazy to other people—but I am very good at predicting the outcome and I can see that it is going to work for me (even though other people might not be satisfied with that way of working). From my perspective, my judgment is pretty sound and I am rarely persuadable to go against it. And with darn good reason. Having agreed that we would all ride free, the Mongolian horse keepers—a couple of whom were mounted—set off up a nearby hill, with our horses automatically following. I am sure that this was at a very modest pace to an experienced horseman—trotting or something—but I am not an experienced horseman and it seemed fairly fast to me. My first dilemma was what to do with my testicles. Every time I bounced up and down (i.e. every couple of seconds) I gave myself a nasty squeeze. I am sure that professional horsemen have a technique for avoiding this—after all, they wear those very tight trousers when they ride—but no one had told me what it was. Losing the long term use of my regalia would scarcely be a tragedy, since I cannot afford any more children anyway, but I feared that I might either fall of the horse in my discomfort or vomit, if the provocation continued long enough. I was jolly glad to get to the crest of that hill, where they stopped to admire the view and I stopped simply to enjoy the stillness. Sadly, the stop was all too brief and we set off again back down the hill. I adopted a posture with a rounded back (which seemed to be how the Mongolians were riding) and shifted the weight back towards my tailbone. This successfully solved the testicle-crushing problem but now I had a sore backside problem. (I discovered when I showered that night that I actually had welts on my rear end; it was sore and scabby for days—even sitting in the car was painful.) Boy, was I glad to get off that horse. I am sure that horse riding can be wonderful if you learn how to do it. But the main learning point on this occasion was that I should never neglect my better judgment.

We nipped back into town and returned to our earlier restaurant for dinner. Lily cleverly phoned ahead and ordered the roast lamb, so it was almost ready when we arrived (obviously, it takes a while to roast a joint of meat). The Mongolians are a simple folk who regard chopsticks as an unnecessary extravagance: they just lop the lamb into lumps and you pick it up with your fingers and gnaw the meat off the bones. It is ideal for children (for my children, at least, who seem to get worse at using eating implements every year—it is like living with three Benjamin Buttons). If you don't like fat and gristle (which the Chinese love—they regard it as the best bit), then it involves a lot of spitting stuff out, but that is perfectly socially acceptable. The lamb was nice, and so was the roast potato (which was sliced thin and came out a bit more like crispy potato gratin than English roast potatoes). It was a seriously satisfying supper.

The driving next day took longer than planned. In fact, all the driving legs took longer than planned. I suspect that the tour agent systematically understates driving time to persuade you to take the tour. You might drive four hours to see something (two there and two back) and have four hours at the attraction; but you wouldn't drive six hours in order to have two hours at the attraction. So the agents just tell you that the driving will take four hours, rather than six. But it was an interesting drive. It started through green rolling hills, like the western end of the Pyrenees. Lily expressed surprise that it appeared completely empty and I suggested that it was probably used by migratory flocks of sheep, rather like the *Mesta* in mediaeval Spain, because the grass was not lush enough to support permanent flocks. Sure enough, we saw a shepherd shortly afterwards, leading his flock along the rolling ridge. After an hour, we descended a beautiful escarpment, with little valleys folded into the ridge on either side of the road sheltering copses of trees and green meadows. By the time we reached the bottom, the land was parched and brown. Lily had been napping during the drive and commented on the fact that it was all green when she nodded off and all brown when she awoke, and it is true that the change was quite sudden. We were soon driving alongside hills of soft rock and sand with deep clefts due to water erosion. We had chosen to come this way because we were crossing the Xar Moron river valley. This was supposedly the most impressive canyon in Inner Mongolia (although it hardly compares to the Grand Canyon, frankly—it is just a broad valley) and was the ancestral home of the Khitan. They were a nomadic tribe who occupied northern China in 907 CE and founded the Liao dynasty, making Beijing their southern capital (referring to it as Nanjing, which means "southern capital").

Once across the river, we headed up the valley on a long, flat road. Beside us, they were putting the finishing touches to a new highway, which will presumably make future travel a lot faster. It was surprising how much work was being done by hand. For example, the embankments were being covered in concrete hexagons to hold back the soil until shrubs could be established to do the job (standard motorway construction technology); but they were all being laid by hand! A lorry was driving along slowly with kerb stones that were being carefully unloaded by hand—one every foot, carefully placed on the diagonal until someone came along to bed them in. Labour is cheap in China—but so is machinery, so it is not obvious that you would want to do so much work by hand. I wonder to what extent these are make-work projects, as well as infrastructure projects.

After another hour, we turned off the main road onto an unmade road and headed across the grassland. We were now getting close to the southern end of Dali Lake, our objective for the day. We had chosen it because it has remnants of volcanic activity (i.e. it is geologically interesting), as well as being a key stopover for migrating birds and a major water source for the parched plains. Although the plains looked green, you could see close up that the grass was very thin and the supporting soil was mostly sand. In fact, the southern end of Dali Lake has seen extensive desertification over the last 30 years from overgrazing, and we thought that it would be an interesting educational experience for the children to see it. The plain was dotted with flocks of sheep and associated yurts, with ATVs and a few trucks parked outside. It struck me as quite a tough life and you could see why the younger generation would migrate to the cities if they could. We were about to feel the unhappiness of the local inhabitants when we witnessed our first act of Chinese civil disobedience. The local herders had blocked the road with a log and were standing around threateningly to stop all the traffic. We soon found ourselves sitting in a queue of about a dozen cars and trucks, waiting for someone to see reason. Since roads were few and far between, there was no question of taking an alternative route: we just had to wait for the situation to be resolved. A few cars gave up and turned around, heading back the way that they had come. Our driver phoned our hotel—which was on the other side of the blockade—to ask them to intercede with the pickets. It was actually perfectly possible to circumvent the blockade: simply choose a point where there was no ditch running beside the road, cross onto the prairie and head parallel to the road until you could cross back. A couple of cars did this and men on motorbikes took off after them, yelling angrily and kicking up clouds of dust in their faces. Soon a truck did the same thing, which was the beginning of the end. After about a half-hour, the men lifted the blockade and we were allowed on our way. Apparently, the locals were upset because the road was unmetalled, which meant that the passing traffic created clouds of dust. I can see that this would be very annoying if you lived there. The only way that the locals felt that they could get their message across is to repeatedly block the road until something gets done about it.

We stopped for a quick lunch at the place where we were to stay that night and headed straight off to the nearby lake. Some aspects of Dali Lake are very nice: it is pretty, surrounded by steep hills that give way to grassland (in the north) or desert (in the south). Once we entered the park, we took a long boardwalk across reeds to get to the southern shore. The reed area was alive with flowers and dragonflies and birds—and very few mosquitoes. In fact, we have not really been bothered at all by mosquitoes in China. Of course, there are some mosquitoes and we have had a few bites; but not more than you would get if you were out and about in England. Certainly, many fewer than you would encounter in the US, which is generally a very buggy place. It is true that we visited Yunnan and Hainan in January, and we have mostly stayed in the north in the summer; but I still expected a lot more mosquitoes. For example, horses tend to attract insects (horse flies and so on) and we were not at all bothered by them when we were riding.

The shoreline of Dali Lake was a bit disappointing. The water was thick with green algae and we decided not to let the children swim (although we did later see a few hardy—or foolhardy—Chinese adults paddling). The sand was black and presumably volcanic. We considered getting a motorboat to the north shore, partly for the fun of it and partly because the park museum is there. It would have been nice to see a presentation about the geology and biology of the park, and some of the main areas where the birds flock. But the boatmen were clearly not interested in taking us, even though they had no other customers. First, they said that the posted price was only valid for a full boat; this was obviously not going to happen because there were essentially no other tourists, so they wanted us to pay for the empty seats. Second, they would wait for us at the north end for only 40 minutes (hardly enough time to see anything). Third, the trip was an hour each way (hardly worth it for a 40-minute stopover). I am never quite sure how these things work in China. Are these guys running their own boat service and just very lazy? Or are they running the service for the park and therefore paid regardless of the number of customers served? And if they are running the service on behalf of the park, then are they allowed to jack up the prices whenever they want?

People in China often seem to prefer to have no customers at a high price than to have six customers at the posted price. We face this often with taxi drivers. They refuse to put on the meter and demand to charge us double for a short trip. We refuse and they then drive away to look for another fare. This may make sense if there is huge demand for cabs but my impression is that a lot of these guys sit around for a long while waiting for another pickup (e.g. they go and join the back of the rank at a very quiet railway station). I don't really understand this mentality. They could take us at the posted price and still get back in time to join the back of the rank and get another fare. I am always reminded of a cab that we took in Boston one day. We got talking to the driver and it turned out that it was his uncle's cab but he was using it for a week while his uncle was on vacation. He himself had taken a week of vacation from his regular job and was spending his vacation driving a cab to earn extra money—just because the opportunity was available to him through a family connection. This is a very American and (to some extent) British attitude: let's make money, let's do it now. Many Chinese drivers don't seem to be interested unless they can gouge you: they would rather do nothing.

In any case, the children were happy. We let them play for an hour or more in the black volcanic sand and they dug to their hearts' content and got filthy and wet. Then we walked back up the boardwalk and took the electric bus up the big hill that backed the shoreline. The view was magnificent, despite the two German wind turbines cycling slowly on the summit. The lake stretched out for miles in front of us and the area afflicted by desertification stretched out for miles behind us. On the rim of the lake were several horseshoe-shaped hills that were the remnants of volcanic cones. A large flat area lay off to our right, separating our hill from the first volcanic cone. We learned later that a "river" flows into the lake here: its breadth is 50 cm at the widest point, 6 cm at the narrowest and averages 10 cm! When water resources are so scarce, I suppose that the bar to qualify as a river is rather low.

The girls were super excited to be spending the night in yurts. This is a common arrangement for tourists in Inner Mongolia and yurt camps are springing up like mushrooms in anticipation of a tourist tornado (I assume that the improved highway is expected to bring many more visitors). These yurts are "pitched" on a round concrete base, complete with plumbing and electricity, and have uPVC windows and doors. They are generously sized for a double room, complete with an en suite shower room. Although the white walls and roof are fabric, this is the limit of similarity with yurts of Genghis Khan's era. When we had arranged with the tour agent to sleep in yurts next to a lake, this was not exactly what we had in mind: but—this being China, rather than Switzerland or Norway—we should have guessed that it would all be industrialized, rather than cluster of artisanal dwellings. There were about 50 yurts packed cheek by jowl in neat columns and rows, with more in a campground across the street. I suppose that this is what it was like when the Mongol hordes gathered, but with fewer horses and less dust.

Given the lack of local water resources, I really fear the impact of opening up Inner Mongolia to mass tourism. Unless they are going to import water by tanker lorry—which would itself be an environmental disaster—they must surely exhaust local supplies very quickly because there is just no major water source within hundreds (perhaps thousands) of miles. It is dry from Dali to Beijing, 500 km to the south, and greater Beijing itself is desperately short of water. Hence they recently reversed the Grand Canal so as to send water 1000 km north from the Yangtze River, and built another waterway to take water directly from the Han River all the way to Beijing city. (I should point out that moving water is a political statement in China, as well as a productivity improvement. The Chinese have undertaken grand water projects since ancient times—the Dujiangyan Canal was built in 256 BCE and is still in use today—and this demonstrates that the emperor or great leader is a visionary who can tame the land for the benefit of the people. Hence the Three Gorges Dam is more than just a power station: it is a power statement.)

Dali Lake is in the far west of the huge Hexigten Geopark (1750 km^2). The following day we headed east to a mountainous Nature Park with interesting rock formations. We initially followed an "A" road (a decent road but not a motorway) and then turned up a twisty valley. It was very pretty, though arid, and reminded me of parts of the Italian Alps; it was dotted with hamlets whose residents were farming the fertile land alongside the mountain torrent, mostly planting maize and keeping horses and a few cattle on the hillsides. As we wound higher the road became ever more twisty and the surface became gravel. We crossed the col at the head of the valley and admired the grand view behind and before us before plunging down into the next valley. The driver drove well, although I would still have preferred to have been piloting myself around all those hairpin bends. Eventually, we popped out onto a main road and soon climbed up to the entrance to the mountain park that we were seeking.

The area was very scenic: a scattering of beautiful granite peaks decorated with lush vegetation on their flanks, rising up to high and very long grass-covered ridges. The rock was obviously very old because the granite peaks were quite small (i.e. severely eroded): this takes a long time because granite is one of the hardest rocks. Since it was very hot, and we were a bit pushed for time, we paid to take the chair lift to the top of the ridge. There were several rock outcrops around the top of the chairlift that you could imagine into various shapes (the kneeling monk, the rabbit, Guan Yu and so on), which were all suitably signposted and which provided entertainment for the children. We walked a few hundred metres from the top of the chair lift to the bus stop and bought tickets to be whizzed several kilometres along the rolling green ridge to its far end. There, you take a metal walkway perched on top of the rocky crest and advance several hundred metres more to the final outcrop. The views were spectacular on all sides—we were soaring high above the broad valley that stretched out flat for miles, far below us. The emptiness of it all was inspiring: Inner Mongolia occupies many thousands of square kilometres and very few people live there. You have the impression that you could walk or ride across the rolling hills and ridges for hundreds of miles without meeting a single soul.

That evening, we were slated to stay at a swanky hotel at the "Sand Lake". Due to more road construction work, we knew that this was going to be a three-hour drive, and the driver was understandably keen to arrive before nightfall. So we headed back to the chairlift and down to the car as swiftly as possible. We quickly picked up the main road in the valley—which was a brand new dual carriageway—and made good speed for about 15 minutes. Then we got to a barrier blocking the main road, manned by two middle-aged ladies in dresses, tights, court shoes and road mending attire (fluorescent jackets and hats). They refused to allow us access—even though the car ahead had just joined the carriageway. Although the road was usable, it was currently open only to people with a special permit. Since we had an out-of-town licence plate, the ladies were definitely not interested in doing us any favours. So we diverted onto an unmade road that ran parallel to the new highway and shadowed it for miles at high speed, coveting the smooth and speedy ride enjoyed just a few metres away by the lucky few allowed to use it. We ran alongside a beautiful river valley for some time; the river itself was shallow and split into twisting channels between stony strands, while horses grazed on lush meadows bordering the water. After following a big bite of unmade road, we were back to blacktop (as Amy Winehouse would have it), being able to cross back onto the new highway and continue our journey.

After some time we suddenly switched again to an unmade road and grass gave way to desert—a bit like arriving at the beach on the south coast of England, where meadows are suddenly supplanted by dune grass. We carefully skirted a man herding camels down the road and passed enclosures of horses and camels on either side as we pushed further into the desert. The sun sank below high dunes on our left as we approached the hotel. It was a great hotel, sited on an oasis. The main building contained the restaurant and shops and so on. A grassy area running down from the hotel to the reeds at the edge of the oasis was dotted with conical white tents with yellow lanterns inside, like a scene from *The Four Feathers*; it was really magical. Apparently, these luxury tents are places for the drivers to stay when they bring customers to the hotel (like us). The rooms for the paying guests were built on stilts at the edge of the oasis, slightly further round where the hillside ran down steeply into the reeds. It was marketed as a "glass hotel" because the end wall of each room, which looks out over the oasis, was entirely glass. In fact, these hotel rooms were 20 ft. shipping containers converted into accommodation, which was actually a lot better than it sounds; they were bolted side by side in blocks of ten, with wooden walkways connecting them to the shore and wooden balconies added on the lakeside. They were sprayed camouflage colours and really blended in with their surroundings. Apparently, living in shipping containers is a common occurrence in China: many migrants to Beijing cannot afford accommodation there, so they doss in disused shipping containers on the outskirts of the city, with no running water or electricity. I believe that in World War 2 this was used as punishment in Japanese prisoner-of-war camps (putting non-cooperative prisoners into small corrugated iron boxes in blistering heat and humidity), but this is now considered to be housing in Beijing (at least for a certain class of people).

One of the things to do at the Sand Lake hotel is see the sunrise: you can walk up to a viewing platform on one of the dunes around 4 a.m. to get the best views. Lily determined to do this but we did not want to leave the children. Instead we watched the sun rise over the dunes from the comfort of our bed; saw Lily silhouetted on the summit; and recognized her walking down the dunes by both the red jacket and her gait. We sat on the balcony over the reeds in the cool morning air and listened to the dawn chorus as the sky lightened. It was very nice.

The children had done no swimming since we arrived in China, since pools are not so easy to find and are notoriously crowded. So the next day we let them have their heads and play in the pool for whole morning. The driver was insistent that we had to leave by noon and that it would take five hours to drive to Beijing. This was actually a bit cheeky because we had paid for his services for the whole day, and the day does not normally consist of just five hours' driving. In fact, we could not see how he was going to get back to Beijing in five hours—and we were right because it took six (even though we stopped for only five minutes en route to refill with fuel). This timing was a problem—and, I suspect, not entirely accidental. Beijing traffic is kept under control by limiting the number of vehicles on the roads. Hence, Beijing residents have to win a lottery to get the right to own a car. But what about out-of-towners, such as people visiting relatives or those arriving by taxi from another town? First, you must have a permit to enter central Beijing (i.e. any area within the fourth ring road); second, you can enter only between certain hours. After six o'clock, the taxi driver's permit would not be valid. In fact, we had a suspicion that his permit was anyway fake (as Lily later confirmed). He had collected us early on a Saturday morning, when his permit was unlikely to be checked. But returning us during rush hour on a Wednesday could result in his papers being checked and potentially big trouble. So he stopped the car just outside the fourth ring road and basically dumped us in the street, with three children and a pile of luggage. We then had to call a local taxi (not so easy, since we needed a seven seater) and pay our own way home. Obviously, from our driver's perspective, it was better to arrive after 6 p.m. and have an excuse to dump us: he would not want to have driven faster and then have the added hassle (and risk) of taking us all the way home. This is the kind of service you get if you go through a tour agency in China, and if you upset the driver by not allowing him to collect kickbacks from the local attractions.

We were very happy to get home. It was nice to sleep in our own beds and eat our own food, and have a couple of days to wash everything and repack before heading off on our next adventure. I had been continuing my campaign to get Lucy and the children to pack "light", to which Lucy had reluctantly conformed. My persistence paid a pretty dividend when we repacked for our trip to the west, as Lucy actually agreed to dump some of the stuff that we had schlepped to Inner Mongolia and not used (such as boots and rain trousers). So we ended up with less luggage on the longer trip than on the shorter one, which was a real boon as far as I was concerned. I will fill you in on our Journey to the West in a future letter. But I am going to send this one now before it gets too stale!

OK, I hope to see you again soon, when we will all be back in England. And I can thank Susannah and William properly for saving my blushes in Inner Mongolia!

Very best wishes,

Liam.

Letter 13

"School's Out for Summer, School's Out for…"
8 June 2016

Dear Tim,

The girls' semester finished on 30 June—an occurrence that caused us considerable confusion. We were originally told that the semester would finish on 13 July. Then we were told, around 14 June, that the semester would finish on 7 July (i.e. a week earlier). Then we were told, around 21 June, that there would be no more classes after the girls' end-of-year tests on 30 June. What? So, with basically a week's notice, the school just lopped two weeks off the end of the semester. It is lucky that we had nothing else planned for those two weeks—work, for example—and that were just sitting around waiting to do some extra childcare. If this happened in the US, then parents would be in revolt (rightly so)—and probably threatening to sue the school—but Chinese parents just shrug their shoulders and accept this kind of arbitrary action without a murmur. (We asked various parents about scheduling for the semester and discovered they were as surprised as us by the sudden shift in dates. Of course, most of those families have grandparents on hand to provide childcare—indeed, this is often a key reason to return to China from the US, where many of them previously had academic careers—so it is easier for them to cover shock shortfalls in childcare.) In fact, Elizabeth's kindergarten had already terminated their timetable on 24 June—which was another working week *de facto* destroyed by having a five-year-old at home. Ironically, in Elizabeth's case we had the opposite annoyance. The term officially finished on 24 June, but it turned out that classes ran for an extra week for those who wanted to bring in their children each morning. We would certainly have exercised this option—since Annabelle and Catherine had to go to school every morning anyway—but there was no way that Elizabeth was going to accept an additional week of kindergarten if it were voluntary. If we had known in advance, then we would simply have told her that kindergarten finished on 30 June! Most annoyingly, Annabelle and Catherine were still required to be in school on 8 July for class prize giving—an event that would last about 90 minutes, and to which the parents were not invited. So we were not even free agents after 30 June: we were being held in limbo, at the school's whim, until they deigned to release us.

We understood that Annabelle and Catherine were slated to have end-of-year tests for the last two days. In the event, only Annabelle took any tests, since Catherine's year apparently do not have them. The school takes these tests quite seriously. Although they are marked by teachers in the school, they are not marked by your child's teachers and they are common tests for all schools in Beijing. Since we have been told by several people that the girls' elementary school is the second best in the country, I suppose that there is some kind of school benchmarking going on. The children take tests every two weeks during the semester, every time they complete a unit of the course, so they are rather used to them. The test set-up is interesting. On the last two days, the children had to go to school at the normal time and sit a test from 8 to 9:30 a.m. Then they came home for the rest of the day. Obviously, this would never happen in the UK—the children would stay at school for the rest of the day—and it effectively meant an extra two days of unanticipated childcare for us.

There is a parallel here with the dreaded Gaokao—the high school leaving exam that Chinese high school students take in order to rank them and allocate university places. I recently learned that the Gaokao consists of only four exams: 2 hours each for mathematics and English and 2 ½ hours each for Chinese and science. This lack of examining is mind-boggling. Suppose that you were to take four A-levels in the

UK. You would typically have two exams of three hours (i.e. a total of 24 hours of exams, rather than 9 hours as in China). You would imagine that in 24 hours you could test the knowledge and understanding of candidates fairly thoroughly and achieve a fair grading. But how can you test someone's knowledge of "science" in only 150 minutes? This partly explains why there is such a premium on rote learning large numbers of facts in the Chinese system. There is no opportunity to test understanding: in the exam, you need to regurgitate the largest number of facts possible in a short time to show what a superlative scientist you are. Notice also that there is basically no place for the arts, humanities or social sciences in this curriculum. Parts of China (such as Shanghai and Hong Kong) rank very highly on international educational comparisons (the PISA tables) in mathematics and language ability. But that is virtually *all* they learn—so they should be good at it. Graduates of the Chinese education system may speak excellent English and Chinese, be marvellous mathematicians and have a broad (if shallow) scientific understanding. But they do not know much else, and their ignorance of historical or cultural or socio-economic issues—such as the rise of Islamic fundamentalism or global warming or conservation—is absolutely alarming.

Just to give an example, at one tourist attraction we saw a reconstruction of a Chinese opium den from the nineteenth century. The explanatory board noted (in Mandarin) that 70 per cent of the Chinese population of 25 million in 1850 was addicted to opium, as part of a British plot to cause the breakup of the Chinese Empire. Our well-educated Chinese friend took these figures and explanation entirely at face value. Obviously, if you are frequently fed—and dutifully digest—this kind of xenophobic rhetoric then you eventually believe it to be true. But anyone having a modicum of knowledge of their own history would immediately smell a rat. I asked my friend if this was really the population of China in 1850—pointing out that the UK population was around 21 million in 1850—and she confessed that she had no clue. The Chinese population was actually around 450 million, not 25 million. It is also obvious to anyone who considers the case for a moment that 70 per cent of the population cannot have been drug addicts: there would be insufficient agricultural workers to feed everyone, let alone man the military and the government; and since around 40 per cent of the population were children, it implies that all the adults and a third of the children, too, were addicts. So the board was obviously garbage. In fact, academic research suggests that there were 4–12 million opium addicts (based on the amount of opium imported and the amount that you need to become an addict), which is only 1–3 per cent of the population (rather than 70 per cent). For comparison, it is estimated that around 1 per cent of the UK population are drug addicts (consisting of 200,000 people in treatment and an estimated 300,000 other users of opiates or crack cocaine); and around 3 per cent of the US population use opiates or cocaine for nonmedical purposes.

Someone schooled in critical thinking would also realize that the geopolitical claim is wrong: the last thing that British wanted to do was break up the Chinese Empire. A break-up would have reduced trade—rather than increasing it, which is what the British so dearly desired. Hence, the British supported the Chinese Emperor against the quasi-Christian Taiping Rebellion in the 1850s and were instrumental in turning the tide against the so-called Hongwu Emperor; if the British had instead supported the Taipings, then the Qing Emperor would almost certainly have been overthrown and the country would have descended into chaos and civil war (which is supposedly what the British desired, according to the explanatory board). I do not wish to act as an apologist for British drug policy in 1850, but the whole narration was extremely inaccurate, twisted and flawed. But the education system in China would not equip someone to realize this, which is very concerning for the rest of the world. The Chinese people are fed a constant diet of stories and supposed analysis showing that the whole world is trying to undermine China and keep it divided and in poverty—as they have been doing for hundreds of years—and that this is the only reason that China is not the richest, most advanced and successful nation in the world. Outside observers might consider this narrative to be paranoid and xenophobic.

In any case, Annabelle dutifully took her school exams. This was a relatively big deal for her because her teacher had decided when she first arrived that she should not take the regular timed tests in class. We are not sure if this was to save her blushes, or to avoid demotivating her, or simply because the teacher thought that she was too slow (which may well have been true). So Annabelle did all the regular tests but was not required to complete them in class—she was instead allowed to finish them in the evening as extra homework (lucky girl!). Her final exam was thus a revelation, in the literal sense, because we had no idea how she would perform. In the event, she got 80/100—which seems very respectable to me. Of course, Annabelle has had to make up more ground than Catherine and Elizabeth, in terms of learning Chinese: Annabelle started learning when she was four years old, whereas Catherine was three and Elizabeth around two. So Annabelle had to make up four years of missed work in four years. (That is, between the ages of four and eight she had to learn as much as her Chinese schoolmates had learned between zero and eight—including getting her ear attuned to the "tones" that are used in Mandarin to distinguish words that sound otherwise identical. Chinese children start to pick up this skill even prior to leaving the womb. In fact, when babies are born they have many connections—synapses—in their brain that are waiting to be used. If they are not used in the early years, then they die and it becomes much harder to absorb information that would have been processed by these synapses, such as speech inflections used in various languages. This is one reason that it is easier for children to learn languages than adults: their brains are more plastic than adults' brains and they physically adapt to the sounds that they hear.) So we were very happy and proud of Annabelle's performance. Importantly, she was content with her score and not traumatized by the examination experience—which is fortunate because she is going to have to take a lot more exams in her life (albeit easier ones than those, hopefully!).

Catherine had already finished her semester on a high. She regularly got 99/100 on her timed tests. To give some idea of the spread of marks, 95 or above is generally "in the box" (where "in the box" apparently means that you are in the top ten in the class, to which other students are supposed to aspire). But this series of 99s was driving Catherine crazy because her best friend in the class always got 100 and Catherine is very competitive. (This friend happened to be the best student in the class, so she was a tough act to follow. She had lived in the US for some time and spoke excellent English, which is one reason why it was easy for Catherine to become friends with her from the outset. Somewhat by chance, we had also set up regular homework dates and play dates for the two of them, which I guess made her an obvious comparator in Catherine's mind.)

Catherine was also driven to despair because a couple of times she had a mark deducted for things that were wrong, but in a way that she would not have known. For example, the teacher says a word and the children have to write the corresponding characters. But there are many homonyms in Chinese, so Catherine would write down a correct character for the sound but it would not be the character required and a mark would be deducted—a bit like distinguishing "farther" from "father" in an English aural test. It seems that you are supposed to know which one is in the teacher's mind based on work that you have done recently. (A Chinese friend told me that this is a lesson for life in China—it is very important to be able to guess what is really in your bosses mind when he asks something, in order that you can gave the answer that he requires! This is especially true if you work for the government.) In any case, this made Catherine even more desperate to get 100. Fortunately, she managed to get full marks in her last two tests, and her catharsis was complete.

After the girls had taken their tests, we took them all to the local toy shop (which is at the end of our street) and allowed them to buy whatever they wanted as a reward. They had been passing it regularly and ogling various cuddly toys. Annabelle wanted a huge, blue cuddly fish (consistent with her obsession with sea creatures); Catherine wanted a huge cuddly Totoro (some kind of Japanese cartoon character that I have never run across myself, but which is apparently a smash hit in East Asia); and Elizabeth wanted a cuddly teddy bear in a dress. So they each attained their heart's desire and we were able to tell them how proud of them we are—which is absolutely true. Of all the troubles that you might expect in transitioning to China, settling the children into school would be top of the trauma list. But, in fact, that proved to be the least problematic aspect of the whole adventure. I always thought that they would be able to cope academically if they put in enough hard graft—they have been learning Chinese for a number of years, they are bright, they have good support at home—although I thought that the intensity might make them miserable. (In the beginning, they were predictably unhappy about the amount of homework but they soon knuckled down and got used to it.) I was actually more worried about the social aspects of our sojourn—having to make new friends, in a foreign language, and adapting to a new social system. But they took it all in their stride and I am really proud of them for that. I am not at all convinced that I could have switched systems so seamlessly if I had been asked to do it as a seven-year-old.

Elizabeth did not have any tests because she was in the last year of kindergarten, which does not have them. In fact, Chinese kindergarten is much less academic than either English or French kindergarten. Whereas children in England would be learning to read and write at age five, the Chinese children learn virtually no characters or pinyin (the system of writing Chinese sounds using the Western alphabet). Chinese children start to learn pinyin before they start to learn characters (at least, they do in formal education—they may pick up characters from seeing them in the street before they learn the pinyin for them) and pinyin continues to be important because the Chinese use it to send text messages and also type characters in a word processing programme. (You type the pinyin for the sound and the computer suggests a character corresponding to the sound that you have written. It starts with the most commonly chosen one and, if that is incorrect, then you can cycle through a collection of characters that correspond to the sound until you find the character that you want.) The lack of formal academic training for Elizabeth was a bit baffling. There is a great gap between kindergarten and grade one, in terms of academic level, and it is not obvious to us how this chasm can be crossed. Speaking to another parent whose child just finished kindergarten, we discovered that she was about to send her child to summer school to prepare her for first grade—because she had not yet learned the characters or pinyin that she would need next year! But surely not all Chinese families can afford this kind of fillip? Children and parents must find first grade full of drudgery, and desperately stressful, when they start.

Falling behind seems to be a systemic problem in Chinese schools. A friend was telling me that her brothers were having trouble keeping up in middle school. The school makes no effort to assist them: the onus is on them to take extra classes outside school (more on which in a moment) in order to regain lost ground and get back with the group. The cliché that a convoy sails at the speed of the slowest ship seems not to apply in China: if you are too slow, then you get torpedoed. This may make sense for the Chinese for several reasons. First, they simply do not have the educational resources that we have in the West: class sizes are large and they do not have enough staff to devote extra attention to children who are falling behind. Second, the Chinese have 1.4 billion people. They are looking for the brightest and the best to lead their businesses and university research departments—but they have very many able candidates from whom to choose. They will always be able to find someone who is a smart self-starter and does not need to be molly-coddled. If a hundred other, similar candidates never fulfil their potential, then this is not necessarily a constraint on Chinese growth (even though it may condemn those people to a much lower standard of living and levels of life satisfaction). In the West, we have far fewer labour resources—and we are much more concerned with social equality—so we want to maximize the potential of every individual. But this is an entirely different ethos to the one that reigns supreme in China. They basically regard schooling as a screening mechanism (can I find the brightest people?), rather than a means of improving people's education (can I make the most of every person?). In the long run, I think that the Western system will prove superior. From an economic perspective, it must be better to raise everyone's productivity—even those who are not gifted—and get them usefully employed, rather than just concentrate on a few and consign the rest to the scrap heap. And it is also going to lead to far fewer social problems.

The other thing that is brutal about Chinese middle school is the hours. From Monday to Friday they are in school from 8 a.m. to 5 p.m. *and* 7 p.m. to 10 p.m. They then come in to school on Saturday mornings (8 a.m. to noon) *and* Sunday evenings (7 p.m. to 10 p.m.). This should certainly reduce problems of teenage delinquency: they are locked up for most the week and must be exhausted for the remaining hours. Given this schedule, when are suffering students supposed to take extra classes in order to regain lost ground and get with the group? Their brains must be addled already by the end of the working week.

Elizabeth had an end-of-year test of a different kind to her sisters. Her kindergarten puts on a show at the end of the school year. The boys in her class were going to do some kind of kung fu display and the girls were going to do drumming. This involved each girl standing behind a large drum and then beating it in time to some backing music—not beating continuously, but starting and stopping at certain points and making certain arm movements in between, and so on. It seemed to be super stressful for Elizabeth to master all the moves to this performance: one morning she was in tears before school at the thought that she would have to do drumming that day. Of course, Chinese children spend a lot of time working on coordinated (regimented?) movement. For example, every morning, when they go out to raise the flag, they subsequently stand in lines and run through a series of kung fu moves in time to music blasted out from loudspeakers. Then they do coordinated exercises (jumping jacks and stretching and so on). From their earliest experiences, they are accustomed to following cues from a group leader and taking collective action. This is really not something that we drill into children in the West: in fact, it is the exact opposite, since we mostly stress individual expression. If you think about school drama classes, for example, the teacher tells the children to show sadness or joy or some other emotion, and the emphasis is on each child finding their own form of expression; copying other peoples' forms is frowned upon. In any case, Lucy and Lily had expended some effort to help Elizabeth get up to speed with her drumming. We got a video from the teacher of the best girl in the class drumming to the background music; and we bought a drum of the kind that they would be using; and then Elizabeth practised at home so that she knew the moves better. Importantly, this made her much happier about the whole endeavour and she came to look forward to her show.

The spectacle was scheduled for Saturday morning in the main theatre of the university, which is a grand building—a very modern design with a sweeping wooden interior. We had not realized that it would be such a big budget event. Each kindergarten class performed a song and dance routine (sometimes two, with boys and girls performing separately) and most of them took China's ethnic minorities as their theme. For example, we had girls with pots on their heads doing a "water dance" that was reminiscent of Xishuangbanna (down near the border with Thailand, where they have a water festival); and there were several sets from Xinjiang in western China (where we were to be headed in a few days). Elizabeth's class was the first to perform. They were dressed in vaguely Middle Eastern-style outfits—tight red tops that showed the tummy, yellow waistcoats and matching pyjama trousers—that were supposed to be evoke western China. (It really seemed more reminiscent of Egypt than Xinjiang, where the Muslim population is rather conservative and would never dress in such revealing outfits. But I guess that we should give the school credit for attempting to be inclusive and celebrate minority culture.) The set was backed by a *son et lumière* projected onto a massive screen behind the performers, with all kinds of landscapes and fireworks accompanying the girls' drumming. The Chinese really love this kind of technology—and, indeed, almost any other kind of new technology! We had already seen a lot of it at the *Impressions* shows. We had also seen a shopping mall in east Beijing where the ceiling in the entrance hall was one huge screen—maybe 30 m by 10 m—showing a scrolling image of an ancient Chinese painting: it was almost like a modern counterpart to the Sistine Chapel. The show was very loud (typical of Chinese public performances) and energetic and went without a hitch, so we were very happy for Elizabeth and her teachers. We were then treated to myriad other marvellous performances, full of colourful costumes and surprisingly slick dancing (given that we are talking about kindergarten children—you would never see something so well coordinated in a Western kindergarten show).

After the show, all the children and parents went off to a grand lunch at one of the university restaurants, for which we had purchased tickets. The food was plentiful and very good. Teachers were given tokens of appreciation and made tearful speeches about how much they would miss the children. (The graduating classes were going off to different schools in the autumn: some children would go to completely different schools; some would stay at the university school, but the upper school was anyway completely separate from the kindergarten.) Apparently, it is normal (required?) to be emotional and extrovert at these events if you are Chinese, rather than maintaining a stiff upper lip as we would in Britain. We then watched a video that had been prepared by one of the parents—featuring extracts of events and activities that the children had done during the year, interspersed with video clips offering thanks and best wishes from parents and children. Naturally, this was all very slickly produced, as I guess it would be in a middle-class Western school with tech-savvy parents. Elizabeth was also very happy to receive various gifts from her classmates. (Elizabeth had already given gifts to her classmates. On the last day of school, Elizabeth, Catherine and Annabelle had given an English book to every child in each of their classes. We had taken a substantial stock of storybooks with us to China because we wanted the girls to keep up their English reading. But it seemed ridiculous to bring the books all the way back and we had always intended to give them away to Chinese children. All the children in elementary school learn English and many have additional after-school English lessons foisted on them. Maybe some additional age-appropriate books will make learning English seem desirable for the children, rather than drudgery forced upon them by Tiger Mothers.)

This was also our opportunity to say thank you to the parents who had welcomed us to China. We had actually seen a few of the families socially at weekends and they were mostly drawn from Elizabeth's class: she seems to be more gregarious than my other daughters, and we had also had the opportunity to break the ice with some of the parents on our army adventure. We are typical Europeans: if we want to be sociable, then we tend to invite people to lunch or dinner. Hence, we had hosted several lunches and cooked and chatted while the children played. The Chinese are more like typical Americans: if they want to be sociable, then they tend to suggest going out somewhere to lunch or dinner. So we had had several trips to parks or the zoo, followed by lunch at a restaurant. I am not sure why this cultural difference arises—whether, for example, it is due to the size of peoples' apartments or the fact that it is complicated for them to cook a big meal (bearing in mind that Chinese meals typically have many dishes, whereas Western meals tends to have only two or three).

After Elizabeth's Saturday show, we headed off on the Sunday for an adventure in Inner Mongolia (more on which elsewhere). But we had to be back for the following Friday so that Annabelle and Catherine could attend their school prize giving. This was an occasion for them to receive various gifts from their classmates. The Chinese definitely agree with Pliny the Younger that "it is shameful to be outdone in affection". Annabelle was very happy on that day because she got her test scores (80/100). Catherine was also happy because she was rewarded for her "jiang piao". Her class teacher gave out these little paper tokens every day for good behaviour or good work; each child could earn up to three per day. If you accumulated 50 tokens through the year, then you were eligible for a certificate, and Catherine had crossed that threshold in her first semester. She also got an award for having the best attitude in PE. (They do PE every day, lined up outside and doing jumping jacks and other exercises on the spot—there is no room for anything that requires more space, as they are crammed into a small courtyard! It is interesting that they give the PE award for effort, rather than achievement: this probably makes sense as a motivation device but, of course, runs absolutely counter to the way that they allocate awards for academic achievement.) I can vouch that Catherine has a very good attitude almost 100 per cent of the time: she will try her very best at everything, and do it with good grace and a cooperative spirit. Not surprisingly, therefore, Catherine's teacher really liked her. (Lest I appear to be bragging, or looking at life through rose-tinted spectacles, I should point out that my other daughters are more "normal", like me! I think that Elizabeth is quite a handful at school—just a little too energetic and wild—and Annabelle is rather self-contained. Catherine seems to have found just the right balance, and if her sisters are lucky or wise, then they will find it too.) Catherine had earlier been elected "Class learning bean" (which I think means "model pupil") and Annabelle had been elected "Class kindness ambassador" (which I guess means that she enjoyed at least some measure of popularity) and "Class model teacher" (an election surely swung by her all-singing and all-dancing PowerPoint presentation about the Roald Dahl book *The BFG*). There were lots of positions up for election in Annabelle's class—maybe 20 posts in a class of 32—so many people were elected to something but it was not universal. As well as being happy for the children, I was also relieved that we had made a good impression. It is possible that we will want to go back to Beijing in the future to continue our research and their education, and might imagine that this would be easier to arrange if we have made a good impression the first time around.

In order to say a proper goodbye and thank you to Annabelle's and Catherine's new school friends, Lucy and Lily arranged to take a group of them to the cinema. They hired a minibus and collected our girls and ten other children from the school at 9:30 a.m. (just after prize giving) and took them to a 10 o'clock showing of *Finding Dory*, followed by lunch at Pizza Hut. In fact, some of the parents had trouble collecting their children at lunchtime (not surprisingly—after all, some parents do have to work during school vacation…) and we brought a few of them home afterwards until they could be collected later. Everyone had fun and we felt that our time in Beijing was best ended with a bang, rather than a whimper. Of course, Boston is the centre of the academic universe and so it is quite likely that we will see at least some of these children again in future years. Various parents have links to universities in Boston (they did their PhDs or postdocs there, or worked there, or have co-authors there) and they have an obvious incentive to spend a sabbatical there to benefit both themselves and their children's English education. I had done my best to encourage this line of thinking during our time in Beijing, and helped with the odd research proposal for funding sabbaticals in the US. It is also the case that Chinese children frequent US summer camps (at least, if they come from the right socio-economic class). There are no summer camps in China, so finding a solution for minding the children is a challenge unless you can park them with grandparents. One strategy is to send them to US summer camp, which has the additional benefit of improving their English. So it is entirely possible that our children may see their Chinese school friends in the US in the summer in the future. Many academics visit Boston over the summer and put their children into local summer camps while they are working with co-authors, and so on.

After the end of school, we felt as liberated as the children. School was a lot of work for everyone, not just the kids. For example, the pressure is on to help them complete their homework every night, ready for class next day; mostly, Lily dealt with this but everything still has to be juggled around this requirement every evening. And sudden requirements can land on you at any moment—such as needing to provide an art set by Thursday because Annabelle is going on a school trip, or needing white shoes for a dance event tomorrow (where the hell am I going to find white shoes at 5 p.m., and what about my plans to cook dinner?). And there was a constant flow of messages on the WeChat board that had to be monitored and occasionally dealt with. So the old Alice Cooper song seemed particularly appropriate and was going around in my head for weeks afterwards (I believe that the Germans call this kind of catchy tune an "ear worm", which is very apt): "School's out for summer! School's out for-ever!" Now it was time to reward our children with some of the travel adventures that we had promised them before we left Boston—in particular, our Journey to the West. I will update you in that in due course.

Anyway, I am going to end this letter here. I had intended to send it to you while you still had time to enjoy it in a quiet café on your idyllic island, but I have already blown that deadline. I hope that you have a lovely weekend, and that we will be able to meet somewhere sometime soon.

Love to everyone,

Liam.

Letter 14

Journey to the West, Part 1

15 June 2016

Dear Erik,

It is high time that I brought you up to date on our continuing Chinese adventures. You will see that there have been a lot of adventures, so it has been hard to find the time to write about them! If you have a very rainy weekend, then you might just muster the time and stamina required to read all about it.

As soon as Annabelle and Catherine had wrapped up the school year with their class prize giving, we headed off on our long-awaited Journey to the West on the trail of Tang Seng. For a thousand years (roughly 300 CE to 1300 CE), the Silk Road was a conduit for Buddhism to flow into China. Thus, it was dotted with monasteries and temples and grottoes created by Buddhist monks, financed by local dignitaries who made a fortune from facilitating the Silk Road trade. Therefore, some of the most important cultural relics in China can be found in this vast and remote area, which was intermittently under Chinese control until definitively annexed in the late nineteenth century. A wonderful account of this place—and the international scramble to uncover its cultural treasures in the late nineteenth century—can be found in the book by Peter Hopkirk, *Foreign Devils on the Silk Road*. Lucy and I wanted to see these unique historical sites, so our trek to the West was for our benefit as well as that of the children.

Since the school semester had ceased surprisingly soon, we were left scrambling to schedule our stopovers. The widespread economic wisdom is that China has overinvested in infrastructure and needs to rebalance towards consumption. Personally, I have not experienced a lot of excess infrastructure in China. True, the new highways out in the provinces are not used very intensively. But the Beijing metro is packed all hours of the day and night; it is not more full than the London Underground at rush hour but it seems to be rush hour at all times and they clearly require extra capacity. And trains seem to be full all the time, too, judging by how hard it is to get tickets. We had intended to take the overnight train on Friday from Beijing to Yinchuan, which is the capital of Ningxia province and about a 12-hour train ride away—long enough for a good night's sleep and arriving early enough to get in a full day of sightseeing. But we had to go by plane on Saturday morning instead because there were no train tickets left. By hook and by crook, we just about managed to book the tickets that we needed on the other trains on our long journey: it took Lily the best part of a day, and multiple attempts, to do this. For example, sometimes you book a ticket on the website and then get an email an hour later saying that the booking failed for some reason, or that there are actually no tickets left. Then you have to try to rebook the same tickets or find an alternative train. If you have already successfully booked the next leg of the journey, then this is obviously super-stressful. We also have the problem that we get six tickets on a sleeper train but they are spread across multiple carriages or cabins: this is obviously no good to us because we have three small children and cannot split the group. So then we have to try to rebook and get a different set of tickets, which is a bit like trying to draw four aces from a deck of cards. Being foreigners, we are not able to have our tickets delivered; instead, we have to go to the train station in person with our passports to collect them. In the end, the only ticket not booked was the one-hour bullet train trip from Lanzhou to Xining, which departs about 50 times per day. This turned out to be fortunate, but more on that later.

We got up around 6 a.m. to get our early flight to Yinchuan, so that we would have near enough a whole day there. En route, we discovered another issue with Chinese travel infrastructure. Apps are used universally in China to book taxis; there are several apps in operation, although Didi has about 85 per cent of the market (hence Uber sold out to them recently because they were losing $1 billion per year trying to compete). The problem is that you cannot book a journey on the app until you have completed the previous one. Having booked a car to take us to Beijing airport, we rushed through departures (being a bit short of time) and bundled onto the plane. But then we had no internet access to book a car for our arrival in Yinchuan. This would be no problem in Beijing because you can easily get a car at almost any time; but Yinchuan is a much smaller city and it is much more problematic, especially if you need a seven-seater car (rather than a regular four-seater). We simply couldn't manage to find a car when we arrived at Yinchuan airport, despite spending about an hour trying. Eventually, Lily managed to book a car and driver for the day through the car hire desk at the airport. But this took almost an hour because they did not have anyone onsite, either; and it was significantly more expensive (naturally, since you also have to pay the agency fee). Fortunately, we did not lose much time during this procedure because the airline had lost our luggage on the short hop from Beijing and it took about an hour for them to track it down (it had been accidentally left in Beijing) and arrange for it to be delivered to us later in the day. This was not an auspicious start to our trip.

Yinchuan was the capital of the Western Xia dynasty for 200 years, until its annihilation by the Mongols in 1227 CE (more on this later). But between the airport and the city I had planned for us to stop at Shuidonggou, a vast historical site inhabited since the Stone Age. It is presumably a propitious position: located on the Yellow River, where it crosses the plain at the foot of the Helan Mountains, it has shelter, water, game to hunt and land to farm. In fact, "Shuidonggou" translates as "WaterCaveFurrow", which successfully summarizes all its attractions. (I should say that the Yellow River—which is really very brown—is immensely long. It starts in Qinghai, on the Tibetan plateau, and meanders 5500 km to meet the Yellow Sea slightly south of Beijing. We would meet the Yellow River again on our trip, many miles from Shuidonggou.) The Shuidonggou museum has a great display of artefacts and nice narrative boards about the history of excavation in the area, which stretches back to French archaeologists in the 1920s. It also has a unique presentation, the like of which I have never seen elsewhere. There is a dedicated auditorium—seating maybe 200 people—that is decorated like a Stone-Age settlement. Front and centre is a life-sized diorama (like a stage, but with dummies instead of actors) featuring a couple of cave dwellers looking out from their lair across the grassy plains, where animals graze in the distance. The sides and rear of the auditorium are decked out with rock walls and trees; the seats are an erratic series of fake rock terraces. The show lasts about 15 minutes; there is a narration (in Mandarin) about life in the Stone Age—complete with thunder and lightning, and families and animals and fire projected vividly into the diorama. It was really excellent—especially for children, for whom museums about the Stone Age are typically rather dry. The Chinese are really into technology and they use it very well in museums and shows.

The other reason that the museum might be dry is that it is situated in a desert. I guess that the area was more verdant 10,000 years ago—with all that water run-off from glaciers formed in the Ice Age—and more densely populated by game. In fact, the Chinese Government has been trying to reverse the process of desertification on the other side of Yinchuan. But it may be a little late for Shuidonggou, where the plain has primarily a sandy and gravelly surface that is baked by a merciless sun; it was around 38°C on the day that we visited. Of course, the aridity helps to preserve ancient relics. The occupation of Shuidonggou and adjacent areas has been quite continuous through human history. One of the main tourist attractions is a Ming dynasty fort, where we would end our tour. But immediately following the museum about the Stone Age, we took an electric bus to a nearby cluster of mud huts with thatched roofs. This is where the earliest archaeologists studying the site stayed during their excavations in the 1920s, lodging with local people, and these huts continued to be occupied until the end of the 1960s. It is odd to think that my elder brother could have been born in one of these huts, had a quirk of geography relocated our family from Chatham to China. The huts were constructed half in the ground, which I guess keeps them cooler in the stifling summers; and they had oven-type beds (i.e. ones that you can light fires inside) that we had seen in the Minorities Village back in Beijing, so as to warm them in the winter (when the mercury falls to minus fifteen). I think it is fair to say that China still possessed an enormous potential for economic growth in the late 1960s.

Slightly further on, the park staff had set up an amazing archaeology station for children. First, the girls were able to make their own ancient tools. There were stacks of stones and an instructor helped the girls select suitable ones and knap them into spearheads. Then they made fire with a bow, using it to spin a stick, like a drill bit, on a plank of wood until the friction created enough heat to ignite a small bundle of wool clippings. This was surprisingly successful and only took a couple of minutes—although I am guessing that this is easier in a sun-baked Shuidonggou than a wet Wolverhampton. Then we moved to an area that had been divided into square metres using string lines—standard archaeology practice—and the girls were able to excavate a plot to find a stone implement, which was evidently very exciting.

After the archaeology station, we walked up to a section of the Great Wall. Ningxia province (technically, autonomous area) borders Inner Mongolia: hence sections of the Great Wall are built along its boundary. This section was fairly long and in good condition. Since the wall was such an enormous undertaking, it ran through very varied terrain—mountains, deserts, plains, even across lakes—and had to be built from materials that were locally available. So some of the wall was stone and much of it was rammed earth, as at Shuidonggou. To see an earthen wall still standing tall after 2000 years out in the elements is pretty impressive. Who would have thought that you could make such massive and enduring monuments out of mud? Our entry ticket allowed us to take several forms of transport (ox cart, boat, donkey cart, camel train) to the next major attraction, the Ming fort.

I had read in the guidebook that the Ming fortress was underground. But I did not exactly believe this because it seemed so odd. First, what is the point of building a fortress underground? Won't your enemies just walk straight over it and head off over the horizon? It is not as if the ground was strewn with barbed wire—like the trenches of the World War 1—because barbed wire hadn't even been invented. Second, why would you go to all that effort? It is not as if the barbarian hordes had heavy artillery that they could use to pound your defences, so why bother to hide your positions under the earth? I never really got a satisfactory or complete answer to these questions, although there are several plausible explanations. For one thing, it is beastly hot in that location for long periods. The fortress was actually hewn into solid rock, which meant that it was quite cool (good for storing people and provisions). The sandstone would also have been relatively easy to work (sandstone being one of the softer rocks) and self-supporting (i.e. no need to bring in timber to shore up the walls and roof). Also, the fort guarded a gate. Although the barbarians were banished to the north side of the wall, there was a lot of trade undertaken in times of peace (which was most of the time, in reality). The Mongolians would bring horses and sheep to trade for Chinese manufactured goods. The gate would open to admit Mongol merchants and the caravan could park in a narrow defile between two sandstone walls. The merchants were effectively trapped and could not use their position either to sneak off into China or mount a surprise attack. The fort was excavated in the sandstone crag on one side, with gun loops and so on overlooking the defile, so I suppose that this meant that the Ming soldiers could keep a watchful eye on the merchants while they were trading.

We passed through a doorway and worked our way forwards into the fort, braving a host of booby traps: pits full of sharpened stakes to spear the unwary (as revealed by glass plates in the floor); nets full of rocks ready to drop onto people's heads; stocks of hand grenades (consisting of ceramic balls filled with gunpowder and slow match). We even saw the General's bedroom—complete with emergency escape tunnel hidden in the back of a cupboard, in case the fortress were overrun. We exited down a dark and narrow passageway that was not for the fainthearted (as stated clearly on a board beside the opening). One of the girls felt something brush her leg and, when she looked down, said: "There's an arm!". The light on Lily's phone went on—followed immediately by a shriek and Lily leaping three paces backwards! This completely unnerved the girls and they all started shrieking and wailing; I was amazed that a rubber arm on a spring could give anyone such a fright. I doubt that the Mongols would have been so easily deterred. Exiting the fort brought us back into the sunshine, up on top of the sandstone crag and we headed across the dusty parade ground to walk under the wall for the last time and take a ride back to the car park. Our driver dutifully met us there and drove us to the hotel.

Since the driver and his car were both perfectly nice, we arranged for him to drive us around for the next two days as well. Our first port of call on the morrow was the ancient rock carvings of the Helan Shan at the Rock Carvings Conservation Park about 20 km northwest of Yinchuan. The oldest rock carvings date back 10,000 years, although there are also some more recent additions to the site—some from the Western Xia dynasty (around 1000 CE) and some from the Ming dynasty soldiers (around 1500 CE) who guarded the frontier against the Mongols. In any other location, rock carvings from 1000 CE would seem old, but here they seem almost like modern graffiti! (Actually, they are still very nice to see. They are mostly quite distinctive representations of Buddha because the Western Xia had a particular take on Buddhist worship in which the Buddha was supposed to be present always in your heart. This is represented in a special symbolic way in many of the carvings. It is one of the few remnants of the Western Xia culture than outlived the Mongol conquest.) The drive out to the Helan Shan was pleasant enough, through the desert that they are on the process of reclaiming through tree planting (although it still looks fairly desertified to the untrained eye).

When you find the park, you first pass the World Rock Art Museum. As the name implies, this museum has pictures and replicas of rock art from around the world (Viking runes, Egyptian glyphs and so on). Some of these replicas are set in concrete on the long broadwalk that carries you from the car park to the museum. It is interesting to be able to compare rock art from similar dates around the world; juxtaposing them (albeit replicas) was a genius idea and makes the rather small museum much more worthwhile to view. Some of the rock art at Helan Shan is carved into slabs and huge immovable blocks. But much of it—and there are *6000* pieces—were bashed into smaller boulders. The museum houses many examples of mountain goats and hunters with bows and arrows, and so on, which you can examine very close up. Naturally, there are also some "get pregnant soon" stones, with pictures of stick men and women copulating in the hopes of raising local fertility rates. There is also a carving of goats inside a square, which is taken to be some of the earliest evidence of pastoralism (i.e. the domestication of livestock)—the square being a pen to keep in the ovines. There is a nice part of the museum given over to children's education where they can paint and do other artistic enterprises. An educator appeared a few minutes later and demonstrated how to ink up a brush, cover a carving in special paper, and then blacken the paper with the brush while leaving the incised lines visible in relief. Then the girls were able to choose their own rock carving—there were a dozen or so scattered on the floor—and lift their own print. Our children (and children more generally) are very lucky that they are able to do these kinds of things these days—learning how anthropologists and museum curators work, and doing it themselves. When I was a child, museums tended to be very dry places aimed at adult erudition and reaching out to children was not part of the mantra.

After the museum came a tour of the narrow, steep-sided valley nearby, where thousands of rock carvings can be seen *in situ*. A rocky river bed, mostly dry at the time of our visit, filled the valley floor. In fact, there was a sudden downpour—about 20 cm of rain in seven hours—a few weeks after our visit, which did serious damage to the site: 1500 rock carvings were washed away as the token river turned into a raging torrent. Park staff are still looking to recover the pieces, scouring the river bed downstream for dislodged boulders. The first artworks that you see are the largish Western Xia Buddha carvings, incised into a slab with an overhanging top (and therefore better protected from the elements). As you walk up the valley you see smaller and fainter inscriptions of hunters with bows, mountain goats and such—so many that you soon stop counting. You take a very short track up the flank of the valley to see the *pièce de résistance*—a sun with a face (rather like a child would draw) that is thousands of years old. It is the park poster child and you can easily find photos of it online. It presumably represents some kind of sun god, but we cannot really know. At the head of the valley is a tall, narrow waterfall that feeds the small stream trickling down the valley; presumably, this became a wide, gushing waterfall that overwhelmed the valley during the recent downpour (it obviously drains a considerable area of the massif higher up). We descended the other side of the valley, where there are many more carvings. Most of these are ancient but they include a really extensive inscription set down on the order of the local Ming general about 500 years ago, detailing his command of the area. As you leave the valley, and head back towards the bus, you walk along a pathway lined with boulders covered in archaic carvings. On the one hand, you think:

"Wow, it is so irresponsible to just leave these ancient artifacts lying around beside the path." On the other hand, what else are they going to do with 6000 boulders? Put them in an aircraft hangar? This way, at least, they lie where they have always lain and people can appreciate them in their natural environment.

Our plan for the afternoon was to visit a famous film studio that is situated between Helan Shan and Yinchuan. Now, most children would say: "Cool! I want to go to a real film studio." Whereas my children said: "Oh, that sounds boring. Why on earth would we want to go there?" I should have just left them at the museum. In any case, off we went to the film studio and it happily turned out to be far more fun than they were expecting. Of course, the film studio was very busy—it being a major tourist attraction and a summertime Sunday—and everyone came armed to take photos because they were expecting to see lots of weird and wonderful things. My children just happened to be an unexpected bonus. So we were about to step into photo hell: we had to keep moving, otherwise we were surrounded in an instant. It was like avoiding mosquitos at dusk next to a forest lake.

The film studio had several distinct *quartiers*: Ming dynasty town, Qing dynasty town, rural village and so on. Of course, these were all packed cheek by jowl into a surprisingly small space, as so often with film studios: the back of one town was the front of another, and so on. The enceinte that enclosed all the *quartiers* was made to look like a desert fort on the outside, adding another ambience to the mélange. They were actually filming in two parts of the complex while it was open to the public: a few areas were roped off, but the tourists were welcome to stand and stare at the actors—just a few yards away—as they delivered their lines. I would have thought that the disruption and crowd noise would have ruined the take, but apparently not. You certainly cannot say that the location was underutilized, since it was multitasking as a film set and a tourist attraction at the same time! Walking through the giant gateway, we found ourselves entering a Ming dynasty town. In the courtyard of a traditional house, a couple of old ladies (in period costume, of course) were spinning wool, like something out of Snow White. They were very happy to let our children try, and they were soon surrounded by about 30 people taking photos. The girls went off to hide in a nearby wagon (complete with plastic horse) but this was ineffective so we took to our heels, passed through a temple (inhabited by some evil-doer with a big selection of chopping implements) and jumped through a hole in the wall into the Qing town (a bit like a surreal prison escape).

We then went to witness a period wedding. Of course, red is the traditional colour for Chinese brides (since red is a symbol for prosperity and good fortune); no one would ever marry in white because that is the colour of death and mourning. The bride appeared already attired, along with the gentleman officiating and a retinue of female followers. A cloth ball was tossed to the assembled audience and the man who caught it quickly found himself married again (I am not sure what his wife thought about that). Opposite the building where the wedding took place was the local bordello, so I squeezed inside to get a feel for the local ladies. There was an enormous bed downstairs (almost like a small stage) covered in cushions where the ladies would recline to look alluring. Then there was a series of small bedrooms upstairs where the paramours passed their personal appraisals. The walls were decorated with ancient Chinese pornography—pen and ink drawings of couples copulating in callisthenic positions. (Amusingly, visitors under the age of 18 were banned from the brothel. Heaven forbid that any teenager should be corrupted by a pen and ink drawing! In fact, I think that they are all too busy watching "salacious banana eating" on the internet. This is a craze in which teenage Chinese girls broadcast themselves eating bananas in a seductive way and Chinese men log on to watch. The Government has just banned it, on the basis that it is corrupting Chinese morals.)

Leaving the walled town, we headed across the film lot to find the local farm. This is the place where *Red Sorghum* was made, an important film in Chinese cinematic history and an important film in the life of Zhang Yimou—he who directs all those *Impressions* shows around China—because it was his breakthrough work in 1987. Based on Mo Yan's Nobel Prize-winning novel from 1986, it centres on a woman trying to run a rural distillery during the Japanese occupation. You can see for yourself the farms and the distillery where all the action happens. Even if you are not an aficionado of *Red Sorghum*, it is still interesting to peek inside a period distillery (albeit a fake one) and see how things worked. We were all getting tired by this stage and headed back to the car—just in time. It started to rain as we left the car park and it was soon hammering down. This is scarcely what we expected when we prepared our desert periplus but at least there was no possibility of the children getting sunburnt. It was a bit hairy having to watch the drive back to Yinchuan, though: our driver was OK but it is obvious that the locals do not get to practice driving in the rain very much.

The rain was still threatening the next day but we went off to visit the Western Xia tombs that lie just outside Yinchuan. When you see pictures of the Western Xia tombs, they look like giant mud beehives. However, this is because the earthen mounds used to be housed inside fancy buildings, surrounding by huge walled courtyards with gatehouses and so on, rather like the ancient tombs near Xi'an. But this was all razed by the Mongols and only the mounds are left. They are pockmarked because originally the mounds had niches in them with Buddha statues. The museum and display at the tomb complex is very interesting, which is useful because the mounds themselves are not that striking or enlightening. The smallish museum has various artefacts that have been uncovered (seals, swords and so on) and several very nice models of the tomb (showing how it extends underground and so on) and of the tomb complex (which filled the entire valley before it was all razed). This gives you a much better idea of how impressive it was. As is often the case in China, the museum also contains an extensive display of university research related to the Western Xia: there are photos of researchers who have studied the period, off-prints of academic articles carefully arranged in cases, and books standing tall and proud on display. You would never see this in a Western museum because it is far too dry and bookish; it is interesting that in China it is considered appropriate to acknowledge the academics who have devoted their life to unearthing the artefacts and information, as well as seeing the history itself.

Next to the museum are two courtyards containing nice plantings and large masonry models of Western Xia pagodas. In the surrounding buildings, created in traditional Chinese style, it is a bit like Madame Tussauds but with historical scenes from the Western Xia. The explanation boards are very interesting, recounting how the Western Xia state came to be created after the fall of the Tang dynasty and how Kublai Khan annihilated it as a prelude to conquering the whole of China. (Kublai Khan eradicated the Western Xia in homage to his grandfather, Genghis; then, once he had conquered the rest of China and made himself emperor, he backdated his dynasty to make Genghis the first emperor of the Yuan dynasty as a further token of respect.)

We then walked to the nearby earthen mounds, which were quite atmospheric—the mounds standing on a dusty plain, the mountains rising behind and the threatening cloud gathering on the peaks. A persistent rain started falling as we left the mounds. We had anyway planned to spend the afternoon visiting the two museums in town, and a famous pagoda located in a temple complex. Unfortunately, we had not realized that they would all be closed because it was a Monday! (Many museums and attractions are closed on a Monday in China, so better to check ahead before showing up somewhere…). Given the rain, the afternoon was literally a washout. So we decided to head back to the hotel and have an easy afternoon—as if that would be possible with young children. Annabelle lay on the bed in our room and read a book while Lucy and I dealt with email. Meanwhile, the other two were playing in the room next door—getting wilder, and wilder, and…. Eventually, Lucy went to find out what they were up to and came back to report that they had torn the doorframe off the wall. What? They are Catherine and Elizabeth, not the Who and the Rolling Stones. I marched next door, feeling the pressure building inside me like Krakatoa. Catherine had seemingly slipped the security chain on the door and Elizabeth had attempted to exit—tearing the frame off the wall in the process. They were hiding by the time I arrived, so I gave them a verbal dressing down across the king size bed. Having examined the damage, I may say that the construction quality was a significant part of the problem. If a five-year-old can burst through the security chain on a hotel door from the *inside* (i.e. by pulling on the door handle, not by shoulder-charging the door from the outside), then it suggests that the security chain isn't very secure. Closer inspection revealed that the chain was just screwed to the architrave around the doorframe; and the architrave was stuck to the wall with a few squirts of silicone. Hence, the architrave had just popped off the wall when the door was opened with the chain engaged. I pushed the architrave back into place and it stood there, as proudly and uselessly as it had before. We left it at that and everyone seemed happy. But I would advise you to not put too much faith in Chinese security chains.

The next morning we got up bright and early to take the train to Zhongwei, about two hours away on the edge of the Tengger Desert. Many Chinese towns have two railway stations—one for the old, slow train line and one for the new, high speed train line. The new stations are typically a long way (perhaps 20 km) from the city, so it is more like taking a plane than a train: you have to take a long taxi ride to get to the station and this involves leaving a margin for error in case there is traffic, as if you were going to the airport. You also have to pass through intensive security screening. We took our taxi early enough for the street cleaners to be circulating in Yinchuan. This cheered the girls up greatly because Chinese street cleaning trucks play Disney's theme song, "It's a small world", as they scrub away the scum that has accumulated in the streets overnight. I am sure that Disney is thrilled to lend its corporate image to that particular activity, and doubtless earns a hefty royalty fee from the license to use their intellectual property.

Zhongwei is becoming known as a hotspot for hip, outdoor tourism as disposable incomes rise and young adults delay having children. You can take trips into the desert (camping, camel rides, horse rides) and indulge in other "sports" such as sand surfing and river rafting; it is the kind of place where young people go to hang out with friends and horse around—especially at the Sharpatou Amusement Park, which is on the escarpment at the edge of the desert and overlooks the Yellow River. We wanted to take the children out on camels and camp in the desert—something that you cannot do in many other places in the world with any degree of safety, these days—and we had managed to arrange this through a tour agent-cum-local guide. He collected us from the train station and we dumped our baggage at his office. With an hour to kill, we then scooted along the street to see an unusual Buddhist/Daoist Temple. It was very quiet and very pretty. There was an extensive park just inside the gate, with a lake and magnificent mature trees. Sitting around the lake were several elderly Daoist fortune tellers, looking suitably sage in black pyjama outfits and long black beards. Having paid a small sum, you find your fortune by shaking a pot of sticks until one of them pops out. You then read it and the fortune teller interprets it for you. Your fortune is invariably bad, and you can then pay the fortune tellers more money to intercede and make it better. Come to think of it, they sound very much like Western politicians.

The other awesome aspect of this temple is that it has its own private Hell. That is, the cellar is a network of passages with small side rooms; each of these is decked out with a diorama displaying the dismemberment of dead sinners by demons and devils. So those guilty of lying are portrayed as having their tongues ripped out; some are having their eyes put out; others are having their guts pulled out and so on. It is very dark in these subterranean vaults and difficult to find your way around, especially when you have to duck as much as I did (practically doubled-over at points); then you suddenly stumble into a side room and it lights up, to the accompaniment of howling winds and the screams of tortured sinners as they gradually turn on the spit above a fire, or similar. As an educated Western adult atheist, I cannot honestly say that I found this particularly frightening—not so much Stephen King as stunningly kitsch. Interestingly, Lily initially refused to go down and look—Lucy and I went on our own—and she then plucked up the courage after I reported back and agreed to guide her. In general, I have found that Chinese people take tombs and the afterlife a lot more seriously than we do, even though most of them are nominally not religious after 70 years of Communism. We didn't take the children down because we weren't sure they had recovered from their Ming fort experience! I assume that this was the original purpose of the Hell—to scare small children and keep them on the straight and narrow (a job that the Party has now taken on itself). The high point of the Hell tour is ascending to a room full of Buddha statues, where relaxing music is played and you can imagine yourself in Heaven. This is just in case you were in any doubt as to which Home you should be aiming for in the afterlife.

Around one o'clock, we bundled into a minibus with our baggage and headed off to the Tengger. We got to a kind of transfer station at the edge of the desert, where regular road vehicles can go no further and you must off-load to an off-road vehicle. Here we hit our first snag. The deal with the tour agent-cum-guide was that he would take us camping in the desert (providing transport and tents and sleeping bags and water and an evening meal and so on). At this location, it was also possible for us to pay to do various activities—ride camels for half an hour, take a spin on an ATV, drive a dune buggy, do archery or rifle shooting—and the most economical way to do this was buying an all-inclusive ticket. But we did not want to do most of these activities and preferred to pay only for the camel ride. But we were then told that the vehicle ride into the desert (i.e. to the campsite) was provided only if you bought an inclusive ticket for all the available activities. So either we had to cough up or the camping trip was off. This is just typical of China. We had not agreed in advance to buy this all-inclusive ticket—but he had promised to take us camping (and we had paid for that already). But he was not going to fulfil his part of the bargain unless we spent extra money buying the tickets sold by his business associates. At the point you are dumped on the edge of the desert with three small children, so you don't really have much alternative but to agree.

We mounted the old open-top Chinese army truck that was waiting, a six-wheeler that was obviously designed for this kind of work. It was fitted out with individual seats with seatbelts, which the young Chinese (of whom there were a few onboard) were buckling up. This suggested to me that it was going to be a bumpy ride, since the Chinese never normally wear seatbelts. The driver put on goggles and pulled his bandana up over his mouth. I made sure that the children were strapped down, tied on their hats and put on their sunglasses. Then the lorry took off along a track over the dunes like a freestyle rollercoaster—shooting up one side, levitating across the summit and speeding down the reverse slope. The luggage looked like it was part of a space movie, when they show those slow-mo shots of objects spinning through the space station in zero gravity. Our gyrations elicited screams and groans from many of the passengers, although I wasn't particularly concerned by our cavorting: slopes seem much steeper in a vehicle than they actually are, and you are unlikely to crash as long as you keep heading straight up or straight down. After joyriding around for a while, the lorry halted at a line of camels lying patiently in the desert. This was our cue to dismount and take a camel ride, to be followed by sand sledding and riding ATVs (as per the all-inclusive ticket).

Then the guide led us off on foot up a nearby dune, which was fairly easy-going and not too hot due to the cloud cover. When we crested the dune we were greeted by an entirely new and surprising vista: a small and very blue lake lay beneath us on our right, with a tiny hut at one end. We strolled down to the lake and ate a snack that the guide prepared—including watermelon, of course, since the Chinese consume this at every opportunity. (Although a friend told me that a feature of watermelons—in contrast to most other fruit—is that the fluid they secrete is essentially unfiltered. So polluted water provides poisonous watermelons. With the state of the water supply in China, this information made servings of watermelon considerably less appealing.) The children begged us to swim in the lake. This presented something of a dilemma. There was quite a lot of trash around the edge of the lake—plastic bottles and bags—that had been left by previous campers. This is very common in China, where the ethical call for environmental conservation (and the folk wisdom of not defecating on your own doorstep) has yet to resonate widely. The guide and his son were none too particular about bagging their own litter, even though they presumably use this site regularly; there were also black plastic bags full of rubbish dumped behind the hut. But the water looked clean and it seemed unlikely that it was seriously polluted by human activity—such as pesticides or fertilizer run-off, since we were in the middle of the desert—so we permitted the children to paddle. After all, swimming in your own oasis in the evening sunshine is an opportunity out of the ordinary—one that they will likely never repeat in their lifetimes.

As we were eating dinner—picking over the dismembered carcass of a scrawny chicken that had been boiled with potatoes into a vaguely decent soup—another party of people arrived just over the dune in a neighbouring depression. The Chinese concept of visiting the wilderness is to show up by the hundred in trucks, laden with essentials such as super stereo sound systems (with supplementary sub-woofers, no doubt), and party loudly late into the night. With karaoke. As night fell, our neighbours fired up their music station and warmed up their voices (or strangled their cats—it was hard to tell which). Our guide had thoughtfully brought along his own karaoke equipment, primed for a wild night out, and asked if we wanted to let loose. Apparently, Lily had always wanted to have a go at campsite karaoke and regaled us with a ballad or two. Her conclusion was that "it was more difficult than you might think". Honestly, it was not more difficult than *I* might think—which is exactly why I stayed as far away as possible from the microphone. Unfortunately, the Dark Side was just getting started and they blasted away at us for some time. Our guide had popped over to see them and they had enquired if we wanted to pool resources for a campfire, to which the answer was obviously "no" (with me and Lucy not speaking Mandarin, not liking karaoke, and hoping to have a relatively early night). So the guide kindly proceeded with Plan A, which was to have a small campfire of our own, and the children had great fun.

The big banks of grey cloud, visible all afternoon on the distant mountains, had finally rolled over our location. The wind was starting to get up as we went to bed. It was very hot in the tent. The two tent doors were all mesh—basically big mosquito nets—which probably make sense if it is only ever used in the desert in the summer. The flysheet was a regular nylon fabric. Since we were so hot and the doors were anyway made of mesh, the only way to cool the tent further was to unzip both sides of the flysheet to get a through draught. This was enough to make life bearable—in the beginning, at least. As the night wore on, the wind mounted. Sand started blowing in through my side of the flysheet, penetrating the mesh door and landing on my legs and turning them into personalized sand dunes. In the morning I had to dig myself out, and felt like I had just spent the day at the beach (even though it was only seven o'clock in the morning). Score two for British weather (after our similar experience at the Xia Tombs).

The lorry dropped us back at the transfer station, which had the aura of a disused army base. There were rows of buildings—made to look like yurts—along three sides, surrounding a paved parade ground overgrown with weeds. It was damp and blustery. In principle, we were able to shoot rifles or bows (we had paid for this as part of our bundled ticket) but only archery seemed to be on offer. We were the only people in evidence. An uninterested attendant brought two bows—for the six of us—and a couple of quiverfulls of arrows and left them on a table. We then helped the children fire them at the target boards. Naturally, there was no child-size equipment, so this was quite an effort for both adults and children. Lucy and I then went into the range to collect the arrows, which was dangerous work as the ground was covered in shards of shattered green glass: presumably, the best fun you can have at this particular tourist trap is shooting beer bottles. After a while, the children had had enough and Lucy and I had a go ourselves. By that time, the guide was bored and soon came back to round us up for our next stopover.

At this point, we divided forces. A minivan showed up with two tour guides and a Chinese couple who were evidently holidaymakers. Lily was cold and bailed out of the rest of that day's activities—which did not look promising, it is true—and went into Zhongwei with our guide to find a hotel and take a shower. We bundled into the van with the Chinese couple and headed off to a nearby ranch where you can ride horses and indulge in other entertainments (a "dude ranch", in American parlance). This was really our first experience of being part of a Chinese tour group, which is a truly unique phenomenon. We soon arrived at the entrance to the ranch and one tour guide went to buy tickets while the other waited in the van. This was already quite interesting. Basically, the second person seemed surplus to requirements. We were either driving along or parked to buy tickets; one man could easily have performed both functions, since they never occur simultaneously. Like many operations in China, they were strikingly overstaffed. Having entered the ranch, our first stop was at the horse riding, where you could pay 100 RMB to take a short ride round a circuit with a horse keeper. This was rather overpriced compared to Inner Mongolia, but Lucy and the children went anyway since this was the main point of coming to the ranch. While this was happening, the Chinese couple had to wait for us (since—like me—they apparently had no inclination to ride). The tour guide then hustled us onto an electric tour bus that whisked us away to the next drop-off, a two-storey stopover with a restaurant on the ground floor and a viewing platform above. Here, you could gaze out over the misty and drizzly desert, past the fake camels, and watch your loved ones pay 100 RMB to drive around a short circuit in a dune buggy. Since we had done that the previous day—and we could see that the cost of this was going to mount up faster than a Mongol warrior—we just settled for the view. The Chinese couple did the same. And so it went on until the fed-up guide shepherded us all back to the park entrance. Not so much a dude ranch as a dud ranch.

The lunch location would have been hard to find, had you not known its whereabouts. I assume that it was run by a relative of one of the tour guides, who wanted to bring in some business for the family. It was a modern, nondescript house from the outside, in a secluded area off the main road; but in the back it had a room used for dining, a couple of adjoining bedrooms and some mahjong tables. I guess it is mainly used for illegal gambling parties and hosting loose women. That said, the food was inexpensive and surprisingly good and plentiful. Our first challenge was to choose from the Mandarin menu, which only Annabelle amongst us was equipped to interpret. However, either dishes were described in poetic terms or Annabelle was not finding quite the right translation. We ended up ordering the "Farmer's Big Event Dish", and that was the most normal-sounding option! Apart from the fact that the toilet was so foul that I wouldn't let the rest of the family go inside, purely for safety reasons, it was really an enjoyable interlude. Suitably fortified, we head off to the afternoon's adventures in Sharpatou.

We arrived at the park and the guide insisted on mediating to buy our tickets from the kiosk (even though we were standing right next to him in the queue and paying for them directly—it is not as if anything was included in our package). Following the powwow about what we wanted, we paid and entered the park—whereupon the tour guide proceeded to frog march us around. Through the able translation services of our children, we asked if we could just head off and agree to meet back at the entrance at a certain time (which is obviously what you would do if you were part of a Western tour group going to an amusement park). No deal. We had to move together as a tour group the whole time. We all had to go to the same things at the same time and—if we did not wish to participate—wait patiently for the other members of the group. How bizarre. It seems to be a system conceived to minimize the pleasure of the people who are paying and maximize the power of the tour guide. Obviously, I wouldn't put myself in this situation a second time but it was an interesting cultural insight: I will never look at Chinese tour groups in the same way again. It is like taking a holiday run by the army. If this is the only way that Chinese people can go on "holiday", then it is very sad for them!

We took a five-minute powerboat ride up the Yellow River to the far end of the park, a chair lift to the top of the sand escarpment and then a walk along the promenade running the length of the ridge. We were hurried and harried by our tour guide—keep up, look there, stop here for photos—with the only let-up being when he needed to stop for a cigarette. On the top of the escarpment was a sandy plateau where you could take a tour bus to see the desert and indulge in the usual cocktail of overpriced activities. Our tour guide frog marched us to the bus stop—no stopping, please!—and prepared to purchase tickets. At this point, we said that we did not want to go on the bus and we would wait happily for the others at the nearby souvenir stalls. The tour guide was not impressed. At this point, the Chinese couple said that they did not really want to go on the bus, either. We assured them that we were really happy to wait for them and do some shopping while they toured the plateau. And they assured us that they really didn't want to tour the plateau. Hooray! Within an hour, we had inspired a mutiny. The tour guide harrumphed and immediately reversed course, striding back to the promenade on the ridge (no time to lose, obviously). At this point, we were extorted for some more money: the chair lift up the ridge is included in your entry ticket but the descent is not. So you can pay to sled down, pay to take the chair lift down or walk down a steep (and fairly high) sandbank. Lucy and the elder girls opted to walk (or run) down the sandy slope. I was rather bored with getting covered in sand, so I opted to pay to take Elizabeth down on the chair lift. We schlepped the stuff for the others (shoes and socks and so on) and met them at the bottom.

Our final activity was to take a sheepskin raft back down the river to the park entrance. This is apparently a traditional way to travel on the Yellow River. The scalps are kept complete in the skinning process; having sheered the sheep, you sew up the anus and ankles and neck hole and grease the outside. Then you blow it up like a balloon and you have a very sheep-shaped flotation aid. Now tie about twenty of these underneath a bamboo frame and you have a raft. Necessity is the mother of invention: if all you have to work with are sheep and bamboo, then I guess that this is an ideal approach to constructing a raft. You wouldn't get a lot of cargo on it, though. There was just about enough buoyancy for four passengers (sitting very carefully in the middle, back to back) and a boatman. He guided us gently downstream to the dock with his paddle.

We found a wedding party on the quayside, a gaggle of girls giggling and taking photos. Naturally, they all wanted to have their photos taken with our children. And, for once, our children wanted to have their photos taken with the ladies—who were all turned out in traditional Ningxia dress (sheer robes in very bright colours, wearing small, sequined air hostess hats with long veils). Once we had extricated ourselves, we headed towards the exit. But our children had already decided that they wanted to buy to their own Ningxia hats. A stall just inside the entrance had a one with a blue veil and one with a red veil and Annabelle was able to negotiate a good price (20 RMB each). This meant that we needed only a yellow one for Elizabeth. They had scoped out the stalls on the way in and found that the one just outside the entrance had yellow. Unfortunately, the vendor at the entrance was a tough bargainer and refused to take less than 40 RMB. Annabelle told her (with real outrage) that this was much too expensive and that they were only 20 RMB inside. The lady was annoyed by this (she immediately asked who was selling them for that price) but nonetheless refused to come down in price. This presented a problem: we did not want to go back to the stall that had them for 20 RMB because they did not have yellow, but Lucy refused to be ripped off for 20 RMB (as a matter of principle). Elizabeth was verging on meltdown at the unfairness of it all (as a Quebecoise friend of ours so aptly put it, "There is no injustice so great as that felt in the heart of a child").

Annabelle saved the day. She spotted some yellow ones at a stall a bit further along and took off with her sisters to strike a bargain. As Elizabeth stood in tears, Annabelle explained that they had bought their hats inside for 20 RMB each but the lady on the other stall was demanding 40 RMB, which was much too much. The lady complimented Annabelle on her Mandarin and her keen negotiating skills and agreed to sell her one for 25 RMB. I was really proud of Annabelle: learning to negotiate is a life skill (up there with driving, swimming and first aid—basic things that every adult should be able to do), and she can do it in Chinese, to boot. I would recommend anyone to take Annabelle to the market with them if they want a good deal! I was also proud that Annabelle had taken it upon herself to help her youngest sister, which is not generally the case. The tour guide was rather annoyed by all this delay (five minutes, at the very least!) and sat in the minivan beeping the horn impatiently. I was already in the minivan, along with the Chinese couple, and none of us were in a hurry to depart—except the tour guide. In fact, when Lucy and the children got back, the Chinese couple were quite tickled when the whole escapade was explained to them. The minivan headed back to Zhongwei at top speed.

The tour guide from the first day, with whom we had originally made our bargain, reneged again on his contract. He had agreed to store our baggage at his office until 8 p.m. and then take us to the train station. But he then decided that he was not going to look after our luggage—he was going to close the office at 6 p.m.—and he was not going to take us the train station. Lily had returned Zhongwei earlier in the day and taken a hotel room so that she could have a shower and a place to work (she was preparing for some exams) and she ended up minding the luggage. We later made our own way to the station in two taxis to get the overnight train to Lanzhou.

Being an organizational genius, I had booked a hotel opposite the train station in Lanzhou and we were literally able to walk across the street and into the lobby when we rolled into town at 5:30 a.m. Given my situation—I had a terrible stomach bug and had spent the whole night in the train toilet—this was (almost literally) a life-saver. I have found that Chinese hotels are very happy to check you into your room ridiculously early, as long as they have one free. And so it was in Lanzhou. We were unable to get a room anywhere near our children (which was an advantage in my mind, but very stressful for Lucy) but we were able to check in at first light and have a nap before starting the day proper.

When we travelled around China in January—before finally arriving in Beijing at the start of the semester—we had similarly taken the overnight train from Lijiang to Kunming. This was the week that a belt of snow had descended across China, reaching places (such as Kunming) that hadn't seen snow for decades. So we arrived in Kunming with loads of luggage at 6:30 a.m. on a freezing cold morning. We were extremely happy that they agreed to let us check into the hotel immediately, so we at least had somewhere to shelter and sort ourselves out. In fact, we soon realized that we had checked into a room with no heating. Kunming, of course, is in the balmy south of China, where they never get cold weather. Or snow. Except that day, when it covered the palm trees. Having eaten (in an attempt to generate heat from the inside), we headed off to Carrefour and bought a room heater (in order to generate heat on the outside). Then we installed it in the hotel room and had it going full blast for the rest of the day and all night. Unfortunately, it was a rather large hotel room—being a family room—with a mezzanine, and it was impossible to effectively heat all of it. I should have bought two heaters! But we at least avoided hypothermia and the next day we were able to move rooms, up to the top floor, where they had heating (hurrah!). Interestingly, the hotel staff had impressively failed to master the hotel infrastructure: they had trouble making up the bill, trouble charging a credit card machine, trouble providing room cards that worked consistently…. I will say that the Byzantine nature of the system made their life unnecessarily difficult. To give but one example, you needed to hand in a paper ticket at the restaurant to get breakfast (they couldn't just tick your name off a list, as in a normal hotel). This created a huge scrum of people at the desk every morning trying to get paper tickets at the same time as another scrum of people was trying to check out and make their train or plane. This created a lobby full of very stressed guests and staff. Still, they let us check into our rooms in our hour of need, and for that we are eternally grateful.

There is not that much to do in Lanzhou, so we had planned to visit Bing Ling Si—the Temple of a Thousand Buddhas—about 130 km away. This is a major historical and cultural site where almost a thousand Buddhas have been carved into the rock over the last 1700 years. It is set in a truly magnificent location—a narrow valley that opens onto a long lake hemmed in by cliffs that plunge hundreds of metres, almost vertically, into the water. Its remoteness has meant that it has avoided the destruction visited upon many other major cultural sites. Unfortunately, it is correspondingly difficult and time consuming to reach. We hired a car and driver for the day, expecting a two-hour journey each way. Unfortunately, the guidebook was woefully inaccurate on this occasion—the writer had obviously never done the journey himself.

The traffic in Lanzhou is dreadful. In fact, I would say that traffic in most Chinese cities is dreadful, not just in Beijing. A decade or more ago, when I heard that China was looking to emulate the US and become a "Great Car Economy", I thought that this was a foolish idea: with 1.4 billion people, this was obviously going to be an environmental catastrophe. I am not thinking of the "environment" here purely in terms of CO_2 emissions: I am thinking of the environment in terms of the localities where people live. If 1.4 billion people are going to own cars, then the congestion and noise and road maintenance is going to be an appalling burden on everyone. Instead of allowing people (indeed, prompting people) to become addicted to cars, I thought that the Chinese government should have pushed for a Swiss-style solution to transportation: make public transport quick and universal and cheap, and encourage people to continue to use bicycles (to which they were already accustomed). If rich people insist on private transport, then make private ownership penally expensive (as in Norway) and add more private hire cars (but keep the price very high and use the tax revenue subsidize the public transport). Of course, China wanted to emulate the US because it was the world's leading economy—China just has to have everything that the US has. But the US was already choking on its own congestion (with only one fifth of China's population) and trying to improve its public transport system as an alternative.

Now China is indeed catching the US and every conurbation is chock a block with traffic. At this point, some might counter that China is aware of this problem and pushing public transport vigorously—creating new train networks and metro systems, rationing the use of cars through licence plate lotteries and so on. This is all true but China still lags far behind in terms of public transport per head of population (whether you measure it in terms of track built or freight moved or passenger miles travelled). In any case, my point is more fundamental. Chinese people now aspire to own cars—not only for convenience but for social câché—whereas it would be better if they aspired to use public transport, as in Norway or Switzerland. Having adjusted people's aspirations towards cars, it will be very difficult to adjust it back and car numbers are rising precipitously. Hence, it now takes an hour to queue your way out of Lanzhou, even though it is not many miles; and hence you cannot possibly get to Bing Ling Si in two hours.

In our case, progress was slower because the driver had an accident as we were going out of town. There was a place where various lanes were merging and someone pulled into our lane without warning (or looking, presumably); our vehicle braked hard but bashed the obtruder's front wing. Lily seemed to think that this was our driver's fault—if people are ahead of you then they have the right to pull into your lane—although it would clearly be the fault of the other driver in any country in which I have driven. The lack of lane discipline in China is alarming: they wander from one lane to another without warning (or thinking, seemingly) all the time. The only predictable aspect of other drivers' behaviour in China is that it is unpredictable. China is like Florida or Germany, in that no one is allowed to move once they have had an accident: the cars must stop and wait for the police to arrive. Obviously, this causes traffic chaos (since several lanes of the highway are then blocked) and it can take the police quite some time to arrive. We waited for a while with no sign of being able to move again, so Lily phoned the car company and asked if they could send another car. In truth, I was quite enjoying being stationary; I was exhausted after a night spent emptying my insides into a hole in the train floor, and still feeling intermittently queasy (despite my anti-nausea pill). I sat in the back of the car in the sunshine and dozed off, oblivious to the traffic struggling its way around us. Before the company got around to sending another car, we finally got the all clear to move and continued on our way, with an hour delay to our travel plans. We were initially on a new highway—which was largely empty, as all the new intercity highways seem to be—and enjoyed pretty views of the mountains running alongside us. They were very colourful sandstone, parched but heavily eroded by water like parts of the American West; we crossed several wide, dry riverbeds.

Then we started our ascent into the mountains. It was beautiful. Stunning. It was not rocky or rugged, like the Alps or the Rockies. Rather, it was rolling green uplands, like parts of the Pyrenees, but really quite high (the valleys were very deep down below us). It went on for miles and stretched as far as the eye could see. The amazing thing was that it was all farmed. Every hillside was carved into a thousand curling terraces, faithfully following the contours of every hill. How many millions of man-hours must it have taken to create all those terraces? How can it possibly have been economic? Only if labour was worth nothing. It is honestly hard to see how it can be economic to farm it today, even though the terraces already exist. They are so remote, and so awkward to work, that you would think that the value of the produce must scarcely cover the cost of bringing in the seed and fertilizer and then carrying out the produce. As we neared Bing Ling Si, I saw an old woman with a bent back, out harvesting a tiny terrace of wheat with a sickle. It was like something out of the eighteenth century. (By the nineteenth century, the English had ceased to use the sickle: it had been replaced by the scythe because it is so much more efficient.) Even if you are going to harvest by hand, then one little old lady working on her own is hardly the way to do it; in the nineteenth century it was done by gangs of men and women working together—men scything, women binding the sheaves. As it stands, Chinese agriculture must surely end with the generation that is now dying off. Clearly, no young person is going to want to work like that and they must surely have better prospects to be productive in the cities. Terraces are inherently inefficient because they cannot be worked with big machinery—so how can farmers there ever produce grain or potatoes as cheaply as farmers in the Midwest or on the Russian steppes or in Australia? Only if they are protected by big tariffs.

The closer we got to Bing Ling Si, the worse the road became. The last 10 km was a dirt track, heavily potholed and negotiable only at walking pace. It was a relief to arrive—especially since it was now 2 p.m., four hours after we had started our journey! No one was really keen to spend three hours driving back to Lanzhou so we agreed that instead we would take a boat to the end of the lake and the driver would collect us there. He would set off straightaway, which would give him plenty of time to arrive before us. We would then have a 90-minute drive back to Lanzhou. Lily negotiated with the boatman that he would take us all to the end of the lake for 200 RMB, which was a very good price. We then headed off to explore before the place closed at 5:30 p.m. Entry tickets are 120 RMB per person but this does not include access to the most spectacular part, the "Big Buddha", which costs another 300 RMB each! As with everything else that we visited in China, my view was: "We are only ever going be here once, so we might as well do the whole thing and have no regrets", so we coughed up a small fortune (cash, of course—most tourist places in China don't accept credit cards, even Chinese ones) and continued on our way.

Above and behind the head of the Big Buddha, many other statues were carved in the Ming dynasty, or earlier; you access these grottoes by climbing a crazy wooden staircase that winds up through several platforms and across several walkways hanging from the rock face. I think it was the inspiration for an Indian Jones movie, or two. You must be at least seven years old to be allowed to ascend this staircase, whereas Elizabeth is only five and nominally excluded—which was upsetting for her and also unnecessary (she is a very good climber and would have no trouble at all with a set of stairs, albeit a steep and idiosyncratic set). We just hoped that we could somehow sneak her up in the mêlée when the time came—not least because otherwise one of the adults would have to stay with her and also miss out on viewing the statues. Lucy told me afterwards that her greatest fear was not whether we would be allowed up, but whether the scaffolding would support us all until we made it back down! Apparently, one such temple in Datong—another very famous Buddhist cultural centre that we had wanted to visit from Beijing, but not found time—had had a scaffolding collapse and people were killed.

The first site to see was up on the hillside. We wound our way up a set of steep stone steps and found a wizened old man—grey pyjama suit, long grey wispy beard, weather-beaten face—minding a tiny temple hewn into the rock face. There was a highly decorated ancient Buddha statue inside, around 1500 years old, with incense burning and offerings made. It was similar to some of the temples that we had seen on the rock face in Kunming, but there were fewer visitors here and you really felt that you had stepped back in time. The children were frightened of the old man, I guess because he looked old and wrinkled and different; they had been similarly frightened of Yang Yang's grandmother when they met her on our Wuyi trip. It was a real shame because, in both cases, the old folk were extremely friendly and pleased to see us: the old man hobbled into the temple and brought out three plums, one for each girl, which they were too frightened to take until we cajoled them into doing so. We descended back down into the valley and continued along the valley floor. There were clearly many statues carved in niches in the rock above us: they have been given doors to protect them from the elements and were not open to tourists. We were able to see some of the statues that were lower down, those within touching distance being protected by Perspex screens.

The niches increased in frequency until we reached the massive Buddha carved into the rock face, standing (actually sitting) almost 30 m tall. This is the Maitreya Buddha (or "Future Buddha") who is generally depicted as seated; he has attained complete enlightenment and will arrive to enlighten the world when the word has been almost forgotten. The statue is a cheat in the sense that the upper part (torso and head) is carved into the rock while the lower part is made of clay, which obviously necessitated a lot less work. In fact, many of these ancient Buddhist statues are carved into the rock only very roughly. That is, they are carved in a stone that is easy to shape but does not give a smooth surface; so the statue is then covered in clay to create its finer features and painted to maximize its visual impact. This approach stands in stark contrast to Western traditions—such as Greek and Roman statuary, or cathedral carvings—where the finished work is carved directly into the finest stone. Sculptures based on that approach exist in China—such as the Leshan Buddha—but are less common. In fact, amongst the statuary that we have seen in China, there are many lions, dragons and so on that are finished directly in stone but I have never seen such a statue of a person. In Europe, we have countless busts of rich Romans—just check out the Vatican Museum—and idealized individuals standing in fountains and arbours from the eighteenth century, as well medieval lords lying on their tombs in cathedrals. Were all such statues destroyed in China during the tumultuous wars of the twentieth century and the Cultural Revolution? Or was there never a tradition of carving statues of people, such as generals, lords and emperors?

At the Big Buddha, the guard climbed the eccentric staircase ahead of us and opened each locked trapdoor that permitted entry to the next level (this is starting to sound like a computer game). We were able to walk around the base of the Buddha—which was already rather high above the path—and Lily was able to touch the Buddha's foot. Apparently, touching the Buddha's foot is supposed to give good luck, if you are Chinese, and Lily needed this because she had some exams in the offing. She should have got a lot of luck, given the size of that foot. I commented that if she failed her exam, then she could always come back and break Buddha's legs (that was the East End gangster in me coming out). Interestingly, Lily commented that this was a very Western worldview. A Chinese person would say that they had failed their exam because they had not touched the Buddha's foot enough, and would rush around and find more Buddha's feet to touch in order to secure the requisite amount of good fortune. The Western view would obviously be that touching the Buddha's foot doesn't work and you should try something different (such as revising more, or getting a different tutor). I thought that this was an interesting cultural contrast. Then it was onward and upwards until we reached the dizzying heights of the Buddha's head and the statues above it. The most amazing part was not the statues *per se* but the associated paintwork (on and around the statues) that was 500 years old—much of it still bright and intricate and complete.

Having feasted our eyes for as long as we wished—effectively on our own private tour—we descended the devilish staircase back to the main path. It is lucky that there were no outsized snakes to supplement those ladders, or we could have found ourselves at the bottom far too fast. We crossed the footbridge at the head of the valley and walked back down the far side, where there were a few more grottoes to see. In particular, there is a large reclining Buddha statue. The reclining effigies represent the point at which the Buddha ascended to Nirvana (I think that "died" would be a more prosaic interpretation). This was a very fine and carefully painted one. It was getting towards closing time at Bing Ling Si and I was happy that we had managed to see everything in the couple of hours that were available to us.

It was now time to take the boat trip down the river and meet our driver. This was not straightforward. The boatman was willing to take us for the price previously agreed—but only if the boat were full. Since the boat would obviously not be full—we would need to find five other people to fill it and most tourists had already departed—we were going to be gouged for some more money. In the end, Lily negotiated that he would take us for 360 RMB (i.e. double the agreed price) and drop us less far down the lake. Our driver would then have to drive 20 minutes back up the lakeshore to collect us. From our perspective, it made little difference in terms of time (20 minutes more driving, 15 minutes less boating) but was more costly, since we were paying mileage on the car as well as the extra boat fee. In any case, we had little choice and everything ran smoothly. The boat was small but enclosed and quite speedy, so the trip was not cold or wet; and we had wonderful views of the sheer cliffs as we wound our way into the wider part of the lake. If money were no object, then this would be the way to see Bing Ling Si—an inspiring drive to arrive and a beautiful boat trip back. By contrast, if money *is* an object, then it makes you gulp to spend that much in a single day.

The most interesting aspect of Lanzhou is its historic waterwheels. There are several parks in Lanzhou where you can see reconstructed waterwheels in operation, raising water from the Yellow River, so next day we went off to find one. The area is arid and agriculture arises from irrigation. There is plenty of water available in the Yellow River, but how do you get it onto the fields? In ancient times, they constructed mighty waterwheels—maybe 10 m tall—beside the river. Cleverly, each wheel has two components. There is the standard paddle part that makes the wheel go round—you see this on any mill used to grind grain, for example, where the power of the wheel is being harnessed to turn a driveshaft. But attached to each paddle is a pot (a bamboo pipe, really) set at an angle. As the wheel turns, these pots pick up river water and are pushed up into the sky by the paddles below them; as they near the top of the wheel, the angled pipes pour out their water into a chute next to the wheel, from where it is led out through piping onto the land. So the power of the wheel is used directly to lift water out of the river; and it attains such a height that it creates a head of water that can be used to push the water far out into the fields. (It works a bit like a water tower that serves towns on hilltops, for example.) Old pictures of Lanzhou show many such waterwheels constructed beside the river.

The waterwheel park was very nice, and we sat there and savoured our ice creams—which had been somewhat difficult to find. The Chinese are rather ambivalent about ice cream: the traditional view is that it is unhealthy to put cold things into your stomach, so ice cream must be bad for you. (In the West, we know that ice cream is bad for you, but I don't think that altering our stomach temperature is a key consideration!) It is a bit strange to hear a young Chinese person tell you this very earnestly when they explain that they don't eat ice cream. Although ice cream is available on every street corner in Beijing, it is often scarce out in the provinces. So stock up while you can, that's what we say! We then walked the length of the pedestrianized shopping precinct to pick up a taxi to our hotel, which was on the far side of the central shopping district. If five aliens had landed from Mars, then I don't think that they could have received more stares than us.

Lily had to leave us for a few days but before doing so had kindly gone to collect the next day's train tickets to Xining. It was lucky that we had not collected these earlier because Lily discovered at this point that our train had been cancelled. This was due to flooding, of which there had been a lot in China around that time. But—rather puzzlingly—the earlier and later trains were not cancelled, just the one that we had booked. Now, it was very unhelpful of the train company not to tell us that our train was cancelled (bearing in mind that they require your email address and phone number when you book the tickets, like an airline). It was also very unhelpful that the ticket lady told Lily about the cancellation only after she had issued the tickets (i.e. she happily printed off tickets to a train that she knew was cancelled and then told the customer that they would not be able to use them). Lily then had to return the tickets and get a refund, which made the lady very grumpy. If we had had to do this ourselves, then it would have been super confusing and who knows what time we would have ended up getting a train? Lily came to find me at the hotel so that we could queue up together to buy new tickets, on a train that was actually running. By the time we arrived, the queue was snaking out the door—there were hundreds of people crammed into a very hot hall trying to buy train tickets. We eventually made it to the front and rebooked on a train that was actually quite convenient, so no damage was done: we were lucky. We got up bright and early next morning and made our way without incident to Xining, enjoying the spectacular mountain scenery as the track took us up to the Tibetan plateau. In fact, Xining is on the mainline from Beijing to Lhasa and sits at 2300 m above sea level. If you are going to Lhasa, then it is recommended that you stop in Xining to get at least slightly acclimatized to the altitude: otherwise, disembarking in Lhasa at 3650 m (almost the same height as the Aiguille du Midi on the Mont Blanc massif) is really a serious shock to the cardiovascular system. In fact, the train crosses a col at 5100 m (higher than any mountain in western Europe) and there is supplemental oxygen in every seat to stop passengers getting altitude sickness en route!

I am going to sign off here. If this missive gets any longer, then it won't be "unputdownable" as much as "unpickupable". And your printer will probably run out of ink.

OK, more from me soon with our further adventures.

Very best wishes,

Liam.

Letter 15

The Journey to the West, Part 2
22 June 2016

Dear Erik,

Let me continue with my story. The first challenge in Xining was to get to the hotel. We headed for the taxi rank and declined offers from black taxis touting for business; I prefer to take a regular, metered taxi whenever possible. Having reached the front of the queue and loaded up, the taxi started off without putting on the meter. Annabelle complained about this (naturally, your eight-year-old would know the relevant Mandarin vocabulary for demanding that the taxi driver switch on the meter—this is an everyday necessity in China). The taxi driver then told us that they don't use the meter from the station, which was obviously untrue. He said that, anyway, since we were five (rather than four) he would not do the trip for less than 40 RMB. I have been known to put my foot down in this situation—initially metaphorically, and then literally as we get dumped in the street and have to walk home (more on which in a later letter). But, given the hassle of being deposited in the street with luggage and three children and then having to find another taxi, and since we were being gouged for only a small amount of money—about 20 MB—we agreed to pay it.

Hotels in Xining are super expensive—about two or three times the price of similar hotels in Lanzhou, or anywhere else that we had stayed in

China. They seem to have a real shortage of accommodation. Hence, I had ended up booking a fairly swanky "international standard" hotel. This had the advantage that the staff spoke English and were competent. Checking into the hotel still took quite a while because the competence of the staff meant that they were careful to dot all the i's and cross all the t's. For example, they photocopied the children's passports as well as ours (most hotels don't bother). But it was a very nice hotel and conveniently located in the city centre. We immediately went to the main market, just next door, to get some lunch. Having done a circuit of the market, none of the eating options looked very upmarket—which was a shame because I was desperately hoping to avoid picking up another stomach bug! But we homed in on a noodle shop where you could buy one of the local specialities, mian pian, and squeezed onto a table. ("Mian" is the word for flour and so mian tiao are regular noodles because they are "long flour". "Pian" means sheet and thus mian pian is "sheet flour"—although it really looks like chopped up fettuccine, rather than lasagne.)

We then took the bus to the nearby Qinghai Provincial Museum. The museum building is grandiose (modern, with stone pillars stretching to the sky beside the grand entrance) and it fronts onto a huge square that is new but still rather Stalinist—acres of white stone slabs (which were absolutely blinding in bright sunshine) and formal lines of trees. The Qinghai Museum is unusual—and very interesting to me—because it is largely a "living museum". So there are displays of traditional local objects (pots, jewellery, clothing, carpets and so on) but they are all new; and beside each object are photo boards showing how that particular object was made by a local craftsman using techniques that have remained unchanged for hundreds, or maybe thousands, of years. It is the next best thing to visiting the craftsman's workshop in person to see him creating his art, which would hardly be practical. I can see why you would want this in a museum: not only is it a celebration of local craft tradition, it is an important document of a dying breed. These artisanal producers cannot conceivably compete with mass manufacturers (in terms or price or quality) and as Chinese markets open up internally (thanks to a better highway system, for example) these workshops will be driven to extinction. They will die with the current generation, not least because their children will have brighter futures as computer programmers than ceramic potters. There were also photo boards and dioramas showing cultural events of the local people (celebrating marriages and so on), which were very colourful and interesting to see. Again, you wonder how long these sacraments will survive the onslaught of homogenization.

We have visited numerous provincial museums in China and they have all been excellent, far above expectations. For example, I don't think that we have seen a museum that doesn't display objects that are at least 5000 years old—the ubiquity of truly ancient relics in China is simply mind-boggling. The Qinghai Museum was no exception to this rule. Having examined the half of the museum concerned with contemporary craftsmen, we crossed the staircase to look at the historical half. The halls were arranged chronologically. We began with local stone tools and pottery that was 5000 years old and then progressed to comparable material that was "only" 3000 years old: interestingly, the more recent implements were clearly more refined—even though you don't naturally think of the Stone Age as being a period of technological improvement. There was an accompanying display of human remains and some reconstructed dwellings. Thereafter, you get into the Bronze Age and there were pins and tools and weapons on display. In ancient times, the Qinghai people were outside the orbit of China. But as you get towards the year 0 CE, Han Chinese influences make an appearance, in both technological and artistic terms. Later—around the time of the Tang dynasty—the area fell under the control of the Chinese Empire and there are many more remnants (weapons, coins, ornaments) that you would see elsewhere in China. The display ends with suits of Ming armour and Qing military hardware. Although it is a simplistic way to display history—purely in a linear, chronological order—it worked because you could see the economic and cultural development of the region as it became incorporated into China proper.

We then headed off on foot to the Temple of the Golden Stupa. As the name implies, this particular temple is distinguished by the Golden Stupa that sits in the middle of the courtyard. The temple is less touristy than most that you will visit. It is not at all large or grand—in fact, it is tucked into a row of buildings down a backstreet—and for that reason seems more authentic. The courtyard is formed by a two-storey structure with wooden balconies on the upper level. The decoration on the doorways and shutters on the lower level was luscious—not gaudy or eye-catching, but rather small and precise, with birds and fish and other animals carefully carved and coloured. The back of the courtyard housed a hall with various statues of Buddha and the Arhats, together with beautifully embroidered garments. There was virtually no one in the temple when we visited but there were several disabled people slumped around the entrance, begging for alms. In fact, a shocking feature of Xining was just how many disabled or horribly disfigured beggars there were. On several afternoons, a young man positioned himself on the street corner near our hotel, trying to make money by singing along to a music box. He was fit and healthy-looking, and even handsome—except for the fact that he had no arms. I have no idea if he was born that way or lost them in an accident, although the latter seems most likely because his torso looked like it had been used to doing manual labour. But how is a man to earn a living with no arms? I saw him packing up his kit one evening—which was no mean feat, when all he had to use was his feet. Obviously, he can't wear shoes because he is using his feet like hands and that must be tough when the snow comes. The beggar in the gateway of the temple was an older man with smashed legs and a couple of walking sticks to help him hobble around. I gave him some money on the way out, which seemed to surprise him. The temple was completely free for us to walk around (it not being a tourist attraction) and I felt that the least I could do was help support the needy locals who gathered there in hope of help. The beggars in Oxford or Cambridge, or Paris or Toulouse, are just not in the same league as the ones you find in China. The latter definitely make me feel that I should do something, while the former mostly make me feel that they should do something.

That evening, we fed the children Western food for a bit of variety, since there were options available. PizzaHut is an intriguing experience in China. We have been there several times in Beijing because there is one near our apartment, and they have never yet got our order right. The interesting issue is why. For one thing, the staff do not recognize any of the dishes. There is a picture of each dish in the menu and words nearby: but the staff do not know which words go with which picture because they have never eaten any of the food. So, even if you point to the picture, there is a half chance that they will bring you the dish described by some other set of words. Hence, the children ordered spaghetti bolognaise and they brought us lasagne (after a very long wait). The other issue is that the Chinese like to share dinner dishes—so they order a number of them and all partake. They do this in PizzaHut just as they do in Chinese restaurants. This means that the staff have no expectation about how many dishes you will order—whereas it is obvious to a Westerner that you want one main course per person. So we order three plates of spaghetti bolognaise and they bring us one—after all, wouldn't the five of you just share one and then order some other dishes? So having waited half an hour for spaghetti bolognaise, and been given a lasagne, we sent it back and emphasized that we wanted spaghetti bolognaise. Half an hour later, a spaghetti bolognaise duly appeared—but only one. So we insisted that we wanted three, and after another half hour another one showed up. By this time, Lucy and I had already finished our main courses and we had shared out the two bolognaises between the three children (since they were all very hungry at this point) and we simply couldn't be bothered to pursue the third bolognaise. We finally got back to the hotel at bedtime, having spent two and a half hours trying to get a dinner in PizzaHut; it was comfortably the worst service that we have experienced anywhere in the world. It just goes to show how difficult it is to take a fairly basic concept (a pizza restaurant) and make it work in a different culture, where assumptions about eating patterns are so different.

We headed off next morning to Jiayuguan by train (which was 15 minutes late, as usual). Nowadays, Jiayuguan is in the middle of nowhere: it is at the western end of the Hexi (pronounced "Hershey"!) Corridor, a strip of desert running east–west between the Tibetan massif (on its southern side) and the Gobi Desert (on its northern side). The Hexi Corridor connects the Chinese lowlands in the east with Xinjiang and central Asia in the west; hence, Jiayuguan is now just a nondescript stop on a long highway or railway journey. However, historically it was the western end of the Great Wall. It is easy to see how the Great Wall has an eastern end—it continues all the way to the ocean—but it is hard to see how it can have a western end. After all, why can't an invader just go around it? When you have been to Jiayuguan, you can understand much better. The Tibetan plateau rises abruptly from the desert floor, around 15 km south of Jiayuguan.

Snow-capped mountains are clearly visible—even at the height of summer—and that section of the escarpment (created by the 800 km-long chain of the Qilian Mountains) rises steeply to 5547 m. You could obviously walk around the end of the Great Wall and traverse the face of the escarpment to get into China proper (assuming that the Chinese border patrols did not pick you up, of course); but there is no way that you could take an army that way. So the Great Wall is really anchored to the Tibetan plateau and—all the time that the Tibetan plateau is free from invasion—Chinese defences are complete.

Jiayuguan remained the limit of the Chinese Empire for hundreds of years. Imperial control extended into Xinjiang in some periods: for example, it did during part of the Tang dynasty, when military garrisons ran further out along the Silk Road; and the Qing dynasty finally subjugated the Uyghurs permanently in the late nineteenth century and created the province of Xinjiang. (We were to see more historical evidence of this later.) But Jiayuguan was regarded as the end of the civilized world for long periods and the outer gate of the fort was known as the "Gate of Conciliation": people who displeased the emperor were ordered to remove themselves beyond the Gate of Conciliation until a reconciliation was reached and they were allowed back (if they were still alive at that point).

The bullet train journey from Xining to Jiayuguan, which lasted about five hours, was both scenic and interesting. The first part crosses the Tibetan plateau, which is big and flat and green, as you might expect, with big mountains in the distance. You can see herds of yak grazing. The line then descends from the plateau through a series of tunnels, so you do not get much of a view until you get down into the Hexi Corridor. Then the background on your left is filled by the Qilian Mountains, rising suddenly from the plain, while the foreground is full of irrigated and cultivated farmland scattered with small settlements. It is green but hardly verdant. Later, strange polytunnels start to appear: they have a two-metre mud wall on one side (always the north side) and around the ends; then curved metal struts provide a skeleton for plastic sheeting to stretch from the top of the mud wall down to the ground on the south side. I suppose that this design makes the most of the sun—which obviously circles to the south—while blocking out the bitter northern winds in the winter. It also costs only about half as much to make as a full greenhouse! Later, agriculture gives up altogether and you are really back into the desert—grey and gravelly, harsh and parched. The land was littered with small white dots and it took me some time to realize that they were tombstones. There are no set burial places in that area. Why would there be? It is not as if they are short of space, or have other uses for the land. So they are scattered far and wide, seemingly wherever someone wanted to set one down. It was slightly eerie. As we got closer to Jiayuguan, there were some more irrigated settlements where small plots were being intensively cultivated; I am not sure what was being grown, but there were some magnificent patches of purple blooms, and some others with striking orange flowers.

When we arrived in Jiayuguan, the classic comedy of errors came into play again with Chinese taxis. Lily ordered a car to collect us from the train station: but there are two train stations in Jiayuguan and the car went to the wrong one, which was quite a long way away, so scratch that one. She then tried to order a taxi to the correct station but there were no seven-seater cars available and no smaller cars would take us. So, having walked all around the very large station forecourt, we ended up getting two cabs from the taxi rank. (Lugging all our baggage up and down stairs and all around the various station exits, and back again, was hot work on a day when it was 33°C—especially given that there are no escalators and all the roads that are open to traffic are a long way from the station entrance, for security reasons.) We were glad to get to the hotel, and even more glad to discover a very good hot pot restaurant next door.

Although it was 3 p.m. when we returned to the hotel and got ready to roll, I really wanted to go and see the Wei Jin Tombs about 10 km east of Jiayuguan. We managed to get a car and head out there and squeeze them in before bedtime, and I was extremely glad that we did because they are really exceptional. There are around 1700 tombs dating from around 200 CE, when Jiayuguan was the outpost of empire—the last stop before leaving Chinese civilization and setting off into the wilds. It was thus an important city on the Silk Road. The Wei Jin tombs were constructed 10 m underground, having one to three chambers and vaulted ceilings made entirely of brickwork. The bricks were laid without cement, so it is simply their close fit and the weight of the earth on top that holds everything together. It is the decoration on the bricks that is so extraordinary.

Many of them are painted, and the colours are as vivid now as they were 1800 years ago. We descended into a tomb with three vaults that belonged to a medium ranked civil servant. The painted bricks in the first vault depict life in Jiayuguan, in the second they portray family life and in the third they revolve around the burial itself. The bricks show people engaged in agriculture (ploughing with oxen and a surprisingly advanced plough) and trade (leading camels along the Silk Road). They show cooking at home (baking bread and preparing a boar for cooking). And they have motifs about the afterlife. They constitute a unique historical document of life on the frontier in ancient times. The small museum at the site contains some really nice artefacts, including a beautiful painted casket made from massive wood. Everything was preserved like new because of the dry climate. The site and the display were not large but the quality was outstanding—I have never seen anything like it, and I was really glad that I went.

On the way home we stopped to see an ancient ruined town, Yemawan Bao Yizhi, with tumbledown city walls made of rammed earth that still stood 7 m high in places. It was surrounded by trees and small agricultural plots—probably as it was 2000 years ago—and was very atmospheric. On the opposite side of the road was a well-known local watermelon seller, which was far more interesting to Lily and the children. When we walked back to see them, they told us excitedly how they had gone out into the field and picked their very own watermelon, which the woman had then cut up for them to eat. We trotted along the track to see for ourselves—never having seen watermelon growing in the field—and it is quite interesting. I had not realized that they grow on vines that spread across the ground. Next to the track was a corrugated iron box on stilts (the words "shack" or "hovel" would be much too grand) with a duvet and personal items inside, indicating that someone was living there (whether full time, or only for the watermelon harvest, was unclear to me). I spotted something else rather striking as we were getting back in the car: a lorry drove past, watering the road. The local roads are very dusty—being located in the middle of a desert—so they send lorries out to spray the roads the water to keep the dust down! Can this possibly be a sensible use of the scarcest and most precious local resource? And since it is frequently 40°C, how long will the roads remain damp (and thus less dusty)?

The main attractions in Jiayuguan are a section of the Great Wall (called "the overhanging wall" because it climbs a very steep hillside) and the Jiayuguan fort. The wall was visually similar to the section that we had visited at the Juyonguan Pass near Beijing. The main point of interest is the stream running down the hillside that forms occasional pools. Of course, this stream was of substantial strategic significance in such a parched landscape, so the Chinese had carefully built the wall between the stream and the barbarians to provide water for their own troops and deny it to the enemy. We soon headed off to the fort, where the conservation of water was even clearer. The fort sits atop a crag (at least, the ground falls away vertically on one side, even as the other faces out over the flat, featureless desert). At the bottom of the crag—on the "civilized" side of the wall—is a substantial lake, which must have been a real resource in earlier times.

By this time, it was very hot and you could feel that the sun was dangerously powerful; we were trying to find shade as we moved along. The first display as you enter the fort's outer courtyard is a series of photo boards showing various parts of the Great Wall at the earliest possible date (i.e. reproducing the oldest photograph that historians have been able to locate) matched with more modern images of the same view (typically from around the year 2000, and then again today). So, for example, parts of the Great Wall were photographed around 1920 by Royal Navy Officers on a day trip, when they were based in Beijing to liaise with a local warlord. It is striking how much of the wall was still standing in 1920. Later photos, from the 1970s, show how much damage had been done during the World War 2 and the civil war that followed: the wall had become a pile of ruins. Then it was restored in the 1990s and today looks more complete than it had even in 1920. The way that some parts of the wall have been allowed to deteriorate is criminal. A photo from around 1990 shows one particular gatehouse still standing tall—deserted and derelict but complete and intact. Then a photo from around 1995 shows that someone had removed the carved keystone from above the doorway, which obviously led the masonry above to fracture and slump dangerously into the doorway itself. Someone stealing a stone worth a few RMB has ruined a historic monument. At the very least, the wall will have to be carefully stabilized and rebuilt (which will obviously cost thousands of RMB) and it will never be the original piece of architecture that had stood solidly for several hundred years. We can only hope that the rising standard of living in China, and increasing consciousness of the importance of cultural heritage, will stop this kind of wanton destruction.

A show was starting as we entered the main courtyard. There was Chinese dancing, all kinds of acrobatics, martial arts by a group of Shaolin monks (which is probably the single most famous school of martial arts in the world) and a short historical play. The children loved it. Certainly, much of it was very unusual and clever. For example, two men presented an act based on spinning very large ceramic flowerpots on their heads. I know, I know: this sounds totally ridiculous and bizarre—but it was amazingly skilful. The pots were at least two feet high and must have weighed a couple of kilos each. The men tossed them up onto their foreheads (imparting spin at the same time) and then threw them to each other (forehead to forehead) and all kinds of other stuff. I do wonder how people fall into this kind of career. Did someone really say to their child: "I have got just the thing for you, boy. If you go away and practice spinning pots on your head for hours on end, then a future filled with fame and fortune awaits!" What was the fallback plan in case of failure? A business repairing broken ceramics? There was a troupe of girls doing rhythmic gymnastics with Diablos: after all, anyone can toss a Diablo up in the air and catch it, but few can perform somersaults while it is airborne—and even fewer can do it synchronized with several other acrobats. Then we had girls spinning multiple plates on long sticks; a dozen people riding a single bicycle; and so on, and so on. Given the heat, I was exhausted just watching it all.

The inner courtyard was surrounded by a very high wall, maybe 10 m tall. It was obviously going to have wonderful views—largely unchanged since the Ming dynasty—so we marched off to take a tour of the battlements. Interestingly, the ramparts were gained by a ramp in the corner of the courtyard, rather than a staircase. Given its width, I assume that horses and carts were used to haul ammunition to the top. Everything in China is on an industrial scale, including siege warfare! I don't recall any European castles or fortresses having such ramps. The views were indeed striking: the desert was strikingly sterile, the mountains moody and magnificent (clad in cloud), the lake lush and lucid. But it is also true that it was brutally hot up on the parapet and we were happy to get back down!

The final fraction of the fort was the barbican. Chinese forts, or city walls, commonly have both an inner and outer gate with a walled (fortified) courtyard in between. It acts like the airlock on a spaceship. Caravans coming from the barbarian side of the wall are confined to the barbican (i.e. contained in the walled courtyard between the two gates) while they are searched for illicit substances. If they are cleared, then the inner gate can be opened to allow onward travel; if not, then arrows can be rained down upon them from the walls around the barbican and the intruders can be slaughtered. We went out through the barbican and the Gate of Conciliation to face the empty expanse of the endless desert, stretching 2000 km across the Taklamakan to Kashgar. The name Taklamakan means "abandoned place", which seems apt, and the desert is the same size as Germany. Not only is it very dry and hot in summer, it is also very dry and cold in winter (getting down to −20°C). Faced with crossing the Taklamakan to find an uncertain future amongst barbarian tribes, I think that you would do your very best to be reconciled with the Chinese emperor. I told the children that if they were naughty in future, then I would send them out through the Gate of Conciliation. Sadly, I don't think that they believed me.

After a hot and tiring day, we headed back to the hotel for an early night—especially since we had to be up early to get the train to Dunhuang. It would obviously have been a good idea for the driver, too, because he forgot to show up the next morning at 6:30 a.m. Hence, we had a frantic 15 minutes flagging down taxis to take us to the train station—since we needed at least two taxis to fit the six of us and all our luggage. Fortunately, we were departing from the in-town train station, rather than the out-of-town train station, so it was relatively close to the hotel and we got there in time.

The train trip to Dunhuang was long, leaving at 7 o'clock and arriving at half past noon. This is partly because it is a long way and partly because the train settled into a very stately pace—a big, old-fashioned animal, with sleeper compartments and a restaurant car that swayed across the desert like a caravan of camels. Outside, the flat grey gravel gradually gave way to undulating grey-brown sand. To save some time when we arrived, we decided to lunch in the restaurant car, which was an interesting experience. We arrived at 11:25 a.m. to find that lunch was served from 11:30 a.m. The staff were just finishing their own lunch; then they lined up and were given a talking to by the boss. This is standard in Chinese restaurants: you always see this at hotel breakfast if you arrive at the very beginning or the very end. I am not quite sure what they say, but it usually ends up with some kind of group chant. Once the staff had started work, a young man kindly came over to our table and went through the menu with us and we ordered several dishes. He then came back to tell us that only two out of twelve dishes were available, so we ordered one of each of them to try, together with some rice. The dishes were OK, so we ordered some more about ten minutes later—to be told that there was none left. So we ordered some more rice—to be told that there was none of that, either. This is obviously totally unbelievable (how can you run out of rice in a Chinese restaurant?) so the chef presumably couldn't be bothered to do any more cooking. There was about one other occupied table in the restaurant car, so the restaurant car effectively caters only to the train staff.

Although we were travelling in the morning, we had booked a sleeper compartment. This meant that we did not have to compete for carriage space with other travellers (a pretty fierce competition on most Chinese trains) and did not have to have people staring at us and taking photos for five hours, which gets a bit much. I am always amazed what a stir we make when we travel—even me, and I am not much to look at. I was waiting for the lift in the lobby of the Xining hotel and the door opened to reveal a Chinese couple and their daughter (maybe six years old?) on their way out: the little girl's eyes widened and she literally gasped when she saw me. When I walked along the train companionway en route to Dunhuang a little boy stared at me open-mouthed. Of course, the girls have to have their photos taken with the train staff on every trip. When they are not around, people demand to have their photos taken with me—even on the rainy day in Zhongwei, when I was wearing dark glasses and a wide-brimmed hat, and had a rain jacket pulled up around my neck: I was surprised that they could even see that I was a westerner, so little of my flesh was exposed. I always tell the girls afterwards that, while they were gallivanting, I was busy doing their job for them—being a poster child for international peace and goodwill. At first, they flatly refused to believe that anyone would want to have their photo taken with me (oh, the arrogance of youth!) and now they are just nonplused by my exemplary exertions.

When we arrived it was raining hard and blowing a gale—hardly the weather that we had been expecting in Dunhuang at this time of year. Apparently, it was the first rain they had seen for two months. Happily, we had booked at a luxury hotel and they sent a car to collect us, complete with a driver armed with umbrellas. In fact, the hotel was really part of the experience of this stopover. It was modern but designed to look like a desert fort; located on the edge of town, its rooftop restaurant looked out over endless dunes. The rooms were decorated in a central Asian style—Persian carpets laid over stone tiled floors, furniture made of wizened wood, quilted cushions with geometric patterns. It was very cosy and the children were overjoyed—cosseted like khan's on a court tour. We scheduled only one day in Dunhuang because trains are infrequent (one per day to Jiayuguan) and the main attractions are the oasis and the Mogao Grottoes, which we thought we could cover in a day. Since we had tickets for next morning for the Grottoes, we were basically committed to going to the oasis on our first afternoon. So, as the rain eased off, we headed out to find the Crescent Moon Lake.

The Crescent Moon Lake looks spectacular and idyllic in photos that you find on the web: a sliver of blue bordered by trees and surrounded by soaring dunes. You can imagine yourself stumbling into this desert oasis, its lucid waters saving you from certain death by desiccation. The photos are physically accurate (the location really does look like that) but they somehow managed to take those shots without 10,000 tourists *in situ*. When we arrived at the park entrance—which is some way from the lake and on the other side of a large dune, so that you cannot see the lake—the place was running alive with tour groups. We dutifully queued up and bought tickets before heading inside. There was a camel corral next to the entrance, where hundreds of tourists were mounting up and being led off into the desert in continuous, sinuous lines—the head of one camel tied to the saddle of the one in front by a short rope to form a train of 100 camels that wound its way off between the nearby dunes, with another such train in sight ahead and more passing in the opposite direction bound for home. Wild it was not. We headed off on foot up the valley that curved to the right, which has the lake at the head of it. It would have been nice to walk up one of the adjacent dunes but access is denied: they are all roped off and you are allowed to walk only in specified areas.

In order to gain the ridge and take in the view, we cut up the very high dune on our left (which was permitted, and being pioneered by pearls of prior pedestrians strung out all the way to the distant crest). The rain had compacted the sand and if you were careful, then you could climb it without collapsing the crust, which made your ascent quick and easy. As it dried, and as it became more trafficked, the crust broke and you found yourself in soft sand, sinking a half-a-step down for each step up; this was obviously a lot more tiring. But we made it up onto the ridge after a while and enjoyed very fine views—down into the oasis below us on one side, and out across the high dunes and mountains of the Taklamakan on the other. The middle distance—beyond the sandy bowl with its oasis in the bottom—was filled with the flat, sprawling town of Dunhuang. It was unnaturally green and obviously benefits from a lot of irrigation. The Crescent Moon Lake is actually shrinking quite rapidly; it is forecast that it will disappear entirely in about 20 years' time. Considerable damage was done during the Cultural Revolution, when it was used as a water source for irrigation. I could imagine that the Chinese government will end up reversing this policy: in order to perpetuate the oasis, and prevent the embarrassment of allowing a cultural icon to expire, they will end up pumping water back into it.

The Mogao Grottoes are, of course, the real reason that everyone comes to Dunhuang: they constitute a cultural and historical relic of global significance. Not only are they ancient works of art of amazing quality (despite various depredations during the last 500 years), they also chart the spread of Buddhism from India to China and reveal the interface of two great ancient civilizations. Tours are tightly controlled. They sell only 2000 tickets per day in order to guard the grottoes from degradation. Just think about thousands of people entering the cool caverns—even the humidity from the breath of so many people could create enough condensation to damage the frescoes. So I absolutely understand the need to manage the masses. However, the booking system is bizarre and

Byzantine. There is a ticket allocation for Chinese tourists and an additional allocation for foreigners. The first oddity is that the website is *only* in Chinese—so unless they have excellent Mandarin, or else go through a tour guide, foreigners cannot actually purchase the tickets that are reserved for them. This would explain why there were plenty of tickets still available for foreigners when we wanted to visit. We used our secret weapon—Lily—to buy our tickets for us. But the next problem is that Lily was eligible to buy *only* Chinese tickets because she is a Chinese national—and all the Chinese tickets were sold out (they sell out months in advance). So she could kindly coordinate our trip to the caves but could not visit herself because there were no tickets left.

This was clearly ridiculous—especially given that there were unused foreign tickets—so we cooked up an alternative tactic. In principle, children do not need to buy tickets to see the grottoes, so we just booked an extra (adult) ticket using Annabelle's passport (this being China, you have to give all your personal details, including passport or ID card number, to buy a ticket and you cannot get one without having such a number to enter). This tactic was risky: if they actually checked the tickets against the passports, then they would obviously spot that Lily looked nothing like Annabelle and we would be ejected. However, we decided to risk it: how could we condemn Lily to sit out the session and not see her own heritage? When we arrived in Dunhuang, we called via the ticket office on the way to the hotel to collect our order and discovered that children actually *do* need tickets but they are free—you just have to show up at the entrance half an hour early to claim your child tickets from the kiosk in order to tag along with your accompanying adult. Unless, that is, you are foreign: foreign children have to pay for their tickets. So we prepared to show up early next morning to buy the relevant tickets.

Mogao visits are managed through a welcome centre located on the edge of Dunhuang. Once you enter the centre, you see a short film about the Silk Road—which was, of course, the reason for Dunhuang's existence, and the source of wealth of local worthies who paid for the grottoes to be created. You then see a second short film about the grottoes themselves—such as how designs and styles in different subterranes reflect the fashions prevalent at different stages (bearing in mind that the grottoes were created over a thousand years, so artistic and political ideas altered considerably). Following the films, you are crowded onto coaches and carried on a 20-minute ride to the caves. Arriving at the welcome centre for the grottoes, we discovered that the place was overrun with tourists, with long lines at every kiosk. Failing to book a *bona fide* tour ticket *ex ante*, you can buy an "emergency ticket" on the day: this enables you to see only six caves, rather than enjoy a more extensive tour, and involves a lot of lining up at the kiosks and at the caves. Amongst the multitudes, managing to locate the correct kiosk to collect the children's tickets was difficult. Thank goodness we had Lily with us: not only was she able to get information fast by interrogating people but she has sharp elbows and was able to get quickly to the front of the correct queue. (I did not feel guilty about this. Most of the people queuing were waiting for emergency tickets and did not have a deadline, whereas we had to stay with our tour group.) Having attained the head of the queue, we faced an unexpected problem: they demanded the details of the children's documents to dispense their tickets. But Annabelle was already in the computer system as having purchased a ticket, so they would not sell us a child ticket for her. Eventually, Lily managed to persuade the woman that it must be some kind of mistake (ahem) and we got three children's tickets to complement our three adult tickets. So we were cleared to tour and sprinted across the courtyard to the welcome centre entrance, now in danger of missing our tour because everything had taken so long. Being late turned out to our advantage: the staff checked that the number of tickets tallied with the number of passports and waved us through (rather than matching each ticket to each passport—as they normally would—and thereby spotting that we had two tickets with Annabelle's passport number and none with Lily's!). I think that we got the rub of the green there, and I wouldn't recommend this as a sound strategy to anyone else. Even the most straightforward task—such as purchasing a tourist ticket—turns out to be very stressful in China, even if you are fluent in Mandarin.

When you arrive at the grottoes you wait for a guide, which can take a while if you are in the foreign contingent because the Anglophone guides are a bit scarce. Still, it was pleasant enough—you sit beneath the trees in a little park and admire the hundreds of little doors decorating the rock wall that faces you. To your left are the main caves with the Buddha statues; to your right are the caves where monks and artisans lived. Some of the doors are at ground level, and some are ten metres up the rock face, accessed nowadays by concrete walkways and staircases. The rock face is about 40 m tall at its highest point and the mid-section is dominated by a fantastic seven-storey wooden façade that opens into the largest temple. We chatted to the other foreigners who were waiting with us; naturally, they were not a random selection of Westerners. There was an academic couple from Boston (where else in the US?); a young(ish) couple from London; an English ex pat working in China; a young German backpacker who was working his way across central Asia (and whom I had spotted at the Jiayuguan Fort two days before). After a while our glamorous tour guide arrived—crisp white blouse, black slacks and shoes and gloves and parasol, shades to hold hair in place—and we headed off to see six or so caves with our small group.

It is interesting to see the different styles of Buddha statues. For example, early statues (fourth century) tend to have long, narrow faces—just as Buddha was being portrayed in India around that time; but the standard for later statues (eighth century) is rounder faces and moustaches, which were popular in the Tang dynasty—so they are mimicking more local tastes. Several sites have ceilings covered with identical images of a thousand Buddhas (according to the scriptures, the holy cycle will be complete when a thousand Buddhas have descended to earth—the Buddha that we typically think of in the West, who lived around 450 BCE, is only the fourth Buddha in the line of a thousand). On a few of these images, gold leaf is visible on the halo around the Buddha's head: but what you have to realize is that originally all thousand Buddhas had gold halos! Also, the pigments on most of the faces are now black due to oxidation but they were originally pink or peach. It must have been an amazing sight in all its glory. And the reflective ceiling must have made the temple very bright inside, even if candles were the only source of light. One way in which the grottoes have been degraded is by the garrisoning of captured Russian troops there in the 1920s (they were interned by the Chinese after they fled across the border during the Russian civil war). The Russians peeled off the gold leaf with penknives, since it could be sold; and they made fires in the caves to cook their food, so the ceilings are soot-blackened.

Of course, there were also depredations by British, French, German, American and Japanese orientalists, such as Sir Aurel Stein. They came to Mogao before World War 1 and lifted (cut away) some of the frescoes and sent them back to their home countries, where some of them can still be seen on display in places such as the British Museum. The Chinese are very upset about this and remind you about it at every historic monument you visit in western China. In fact, at the Flaming Mountains exhibition centre near Turpan (more on which later) there is a real Rogue's Gallery! They have created bronze statues of the foreign adventurers and listed next to them the items that they took from various locations along the Silk Road. An apologist might point out that the removal of these objects was undertaken in a desire to document, understand and share this unique cultural heritage. By contrast, depredations by other historical actors were undertaken with the sole intention of destroying the cultural heritage. Notably, the Thousand Buddha ceilings in the grottoes of Bezeklik (more on which later) were scoured with mud, and the statues had their faces hacked off, by local Muslims in order to profane them: they could not tolerate the worship any god except Allah and also view images as blasphemous. This happened hundreds of years before the Western adventurers showed up and took some of the undamaged frescoes. Later, the Red Guards damaged or destroyed many historical sites during the Cultural Revolution (although not the Mogao Grottoes) in order to show their contempt for the past and focus on building the future. Interestingly, this gets no mention on any of the narrative boards or tours to which you may be treated.

Two of the grottoes house huge Buddha statues, perhaps the most impressive spectacles because they have been less damaged by time and vandals. Cave 96 features a statue of a Maitreya Buddha that is 35 m high—all carved inside a cavern that was created by the sculptors themselves as they worked. It gives you a crick neck just to look up at it. And cave 158 contains a reclining Buddha that is 16 m long with many (maybe 100?) life-sized figures carved into the wall behind, gazing down on the Buddha as he ascends to Nirvana. Like Bing Ling Si, the statues are roughed out in stone and then smeared with mud to make a smooth surface for painting. The whole complex is absolutely unique and we were really lucky to have the opportunity to see it.

We were in for a long journey to our next stopover, since we had to retrace our steps to Jiayuguan and then take the overnight train along the mainline to Turpan. The train transported us across great tracts of desert through the night, leaving behind the province of Gansu and finally entering Xinjiang. We arrived around 9 a.m. and it was already very hot. A driver was there to meet us with a seven-seater minivan—less lux than the Beijing Buicks but perfectly good enough for us. (Buick has a virtual monopoly on seven-seater cars in urban China; it is most impressive that they have made themselves the market leader, since their cars are nothing to shout about. The main alternative—decidedly down market by comparison—is something more like a minibus, with bench seats and a bumpy ride. These are popular out in the provinces.) Most of the Turpan attractions are some distance outside the city, so we headed out of the station and straight off to our first stop, the ancient city of Jiaohe.

This is a city made entirely of mud; but you would not believe just what you can make with mud unless you saw it with your own eyes. The city was founded around 100 BCE and occupied a pivotal position in the desert provinces until it was plundered by Mongol invaders in the twelfth century. For example, it was a way station on the Silk Road and the basis of a Tang prefecture in the eighth century. It was later an important administrative post for the Uyghur kingdom that occupied the area before the Mongols swept through. The city sits on a leaf-shaped plateau sandwiched between two rivers, surrounded by steep cliffs on all sides. You can see why it was such a desirable location: strategic situation on the Silk Road; easy access to water, even though it is in the middle of a desert; natural fortifications all round (supplemented by great walls and gatehouses). The whole plateau is covered in the remains of houses (many still multi-storey, despite the passage of a thousand years), temples, municipal buildings, fortifications and so on. From the park entrance, you walk up the entry ramp to the plateau—between the remnants of the ruined gatehouse on top—and then walk the streets of the old town, free to wander widely. On the far side of town, a more complete gatehouse gazes down onto the racing river and the lush vegetation that it supports. On the opposite bank, grape vines grow extravagantly and you could imagine that in ancient times the whole area was cultivated—courtesy of the abundant supply of life-giving water—to feed the town. It must have seemed miraculous to travellers trekking across the barren desert, to come across this thriving town with all the comforts of life.

Agriculture around Turpan is enabled, not by the rivers at Jiaohe, but by an extraordinary irrigation system called the karez. The karez was pioneered in Persia, where it is widespread, and seems to have spread east to China and west to Europe and North Africa. It harnesses local topography to move water to where it is needed. And the topography around Turpan is quite exceptional. Turpan is located in a huge basin (29,000 km^2) that reaches 154 m *below* sea level, making it the fourth deepest depression on the earth's surface. Yet the Tian Shan Mountains lie only 30 km north of Turpan (technically, they are the Bogda Mountains, which are an eastward extension of the Tian Shan) and these top out at 5500 m! That is a 5654 height differential over a rather short distance. For comparison, the Rocky Mountains top out at only 4800 m and Denver (at the foot of the mountains) is already 1600 m above sea level, generating a differential of only 3200 m.

If there were more precipitation (i.e. if it were close to the coast, rather than being at the centre of a huge continent); and if the sun were less punishing (i.e. if it were located at 52° north, instead of 42° north), then the Turpan basin would host a huge lake like Baikal. In fact, it boasts a vanishingly small salt lake, Ayding Lake ("Moonlight Lake"), about 20 km south of the city. This lake also has the distinction of being the hottest place ever observed in China: 50°C in July 2015. It was not that hot when we were there in July 2016: in fact, it was raining. Another desert, another rainy day: the British weather strikes again. We went there on the morning that we left Turpan, before taking the train to Urumqi. It seemed like an educational opportunity too good to miss. The area is perfectly flat to the naked eye (although it is really sloping imperceptibly down to the lake, of course) and it is covered in scrub desert. (This is actually an order of magnitude more verdant than the sand and gravel desert that stretches for hundreds of miles all around, which just shows what the presence of a little moisture can do as it migrates down through the sand and into the salt lake.) Having followed a rough road for several kilometres we paid an entry fee to the lake area (is there anything in China for which you do not have to pay?) and parked the car. The lake is just a few hundred metres in circumference and mostly surrounded by reeds, long grass and boggy soil. I was hoping to show the children some salt flats but, although there are traces of salt covering the soil, you could hardly glorify the area with the name "salt flats". The lake used to be large (up to 22 km^2 even as late as 1958) but a combination of global warming and water extraction for irrigation has shrunk it to little more than a large puddle. There is a concrete area along one edge for the obligatory photo stop, and here I lent over the water and filled a small plastic bottle from the lake—we decided that we would take it home and evaporate it to reclaim the salt, as a science experiment. (I can't say that we got that much salt from the water. Although I have not checked the salinity levels, it strikes me that the Dead Sea must be considerably more salty than Lake Ayding. So much for my business plan of reclaiming salt from the lake and selling it to the Beijing nouveau riche in preposterously overpriced little packets labelled "Silk Road Salt—from China's most ancient source, the Ayding Lake".)

Back to the karez. Rain and snow fall onto the Tian Shan and permeate the rock. If you tunnel into the mountains at the right level, then the water percolates through the rock and collects in these tunnels. You can then dig more tunnels—always sloping slightly downhill—and lead the water 20 km away from the mountains and out into the arid agricultural area. The tunnels serve to transport the water and save it from evaporation. There are thousands of these karez around Turpan, with over 5000 km of tunnels still in operation; thousands of other karez have fallen into disuse over the years. In the museum, you descend into the karez system itself and peer into the tunnels that stretch back to the Tian Shan: you can see the cold, clear water running through the bottom of the tunnels and feel the cool draft. The tunnels are around the size of a kneeling man—because that is exactly how they are dug. Vertical shafts are sunk from the surface at certain distances; these are then connected by miners driving horizontal shafts from one vertical shaft to the next, always sloping slightly downwards away from the mountain and always around the size of a kneeling miner. It must have been gruelling and frightening work. If there were a roof collapse, then the chances of rescue seem slim. The fact that this is all geologically feasible is amazing, as is the fact that someone worked out how to do it. But, more than that, it is impressive that the population possessed the requisite level of social organization and had a long enough time horizon. They were making an incredibly costly investment (how many man-years must it have taken to dig thousands of kilometres of tunnels?) that would pay them back over 2000 years. Even the Romans were not thinking that far ahead when they built their roads and aqueducts. It is quite an experience to be able to stand in those tunnels—comparable to standing in the centre of the Coliseum but, in a way, even more impressive.

We then went off to Grape Valley. This is a famous location in China. Around 8 km long and 1 km wide, they cultivate around 500 hectares of vines here and produce 80 per cent of China's grapes and raisins. There are barriers at the entrance to the valley and you have to pay to be able to drive in. This makes sense on several levels. For one thing, the valley would otherwise be overrun with tourists (and it is just an agricultural valley with slow farm carts pottering along small roads, so it is not really adapted to the mass transportation that unfettered tourism would bring). For another thing, the farmers would get no direct benefit from being overrun by tourists if entry were free. Fundamentally, Grape Valley—as the name strongly suggests—is really just a valley where they grow grapes. How interesting can that be? Maybe very interesting if you come from China (where growing grapes is apparently uncommon) but not that interesting if you come from Europe (where many regions grow grapes). But they do their best to find things to entertain the tourists who come, so I guess they should be commended for that.

At one of the tourist stops you can walk down a shady staircase that leads to the river in the valley bottom. Alongside the staircase are many raisin sellers, each selling at least a dozen different types of raisins: the variation in colour and texture and moisture was really remarkable. The fruits ranged from yellow, through orange, to black; and from small and hard to fat and juicy. The raisins arise naturally: the farmers just leave the bunches of grapes on the vine until they wither and turn into raisins, when they can be harvested. Something that was conspicuously absent was wine. Of course, Grape Valley is in a predominantly Muslim area—and Muslims cannot drink alcohol—but it was surprising to me that no one was turning some of the local grapes into wine: I am sure that people will buy it purely because it comes from Grape Valley and they want a souvenir, whatever the price and quality.

We headed off the tourist trail onto a narrow road bordered by smallholdings run by viticulturists: they each had a house and a small yard, for processing the crop, and a few hectares of vines. The vines in Turpan are trained to form long tunnels. (Think of the grapevine being an umbrella, with the trunk of the plant being the shaft of the umbrella and the cordons of the plant being the ribs of the umbrella. But instead of training a single plant to be round, like an umbrella, take a line of plants and train them into the shape of a tunnel.) To harvest the grapes, you have to walk along crouching—or doubled over—and snip off the bunches above your head. I have never seen grapes growing like this anywhere else; in my experience, viticulturists plant the vines in simple rows (like runner beans or any other commercial vine) and you walk normally along the lines to harvest the fruit. I wonder if there is something about the power of the sun that makes Grape Valley special (it is very far south, remember). I know that that Carthaginians in North Africa used to plant vines on *north*-facing slopes (rather than south-facing, as is usual) for this reason. I could imagine that training the vines like this reduces water loss (by increasing the shade) and may increase the amount of fruit (by increasing the surface area of the plant). But that is just a hypothesis; I would be interested to know the real reason.

When the driver spotted a smallholder in his yard, he stopped and jumped out. After a quick discussion, he came back to tell us that the man was happy to sell us grapes and that we could go and pick them ourselves. Obviously, all the girls were thrilled about this (it was so much more satisfying that buying bunches from a stall!) and they scurried eagerly into the smallholder's yard. The man had two young daughters of his own, who looked at our girls curiously but shyly. Then his wife appeared with several sets of scissors and all the girls went off into the vineyard enthusiastically to harvest their own grapes. This was definitely a task at which the children had a comparative advantage—no need for them to stoop—and, as with the cherries at the army base, we quickly ended up with an awful lot of grapes! This was all right because Lily had decided that she was going to mail a box of grapes to her father in Guizhou ("Gway-joe"): they often exchange fruit, with him sending her fresh pears from home while she sends him stuff from Beijing. Having packed a heavy box full of grapes, we got back on the bus and headed for home. In fact, posting grapes to her father turned out to be less straightforward than Lily had expected. We were always a bit sceptical about how well this would work—could they really get grapes from Turpan to Guizhou fast enough to keep the grapes in good condition? Lily was adamant that this would be no problem. But when she went to the office of the courier company, it turned it to be not so straightforward. The package would have to go via Beijing and therefore take a week to get to Guizhou. Even though the grapes were fresh today, a week in the post (in a very hot country) did not sound good. In the end, it was quicker for Lily to deliver them herself (for reasons to be explained later).

Early next morning, we headed east on the highway from Turpan, stopping briefly at the Flaming Mountains. These are famous from the *Journey to the West* and also from classical poets—generally bored Imperial officials based in Turpan—who wrote about the mountains. The mountains rise abruptly from the desert floor and are formed from very red sandstone that is heavily eroded by water, so fingers of rock reach vertically from the valley to the ridge above. When the evening sun shines on them—and the air shimmers with the heat haze—it looks like flames licking the mountainside. On the morning of our visit, it was 48°C. For me, the highlight of entering the (very expensive) tourist centre—apart from the air conditioning—was the Rogues' Gallery. The baddies were all lined up on one side and the goodies were all lined up on the other. So there was a row of Western archaeologists, such as Sir Aural Stein, who had taken treasures back to Western museums; and a separate row of government officials who had made the area safe for the Empire (i.e. slaughtered local tribes who objected to Imperial rule), poets, travellers and others. A series of boards at the Dunhuang hotel had described many who journeyed along the Silk Road, so I had come to realize that there were quite a number of intrepid travellers. Tang Seng was not even the first monk to travel to India to try to gain the true word of Buddhism: Fa Hsien had done so 200 years earlier. And the diplomat Zhang Qian had travelled to the western regions several times around 130 BCE to negotiate with local rulers and open up the Silk Road to trade.

Our next stop was the Thousand Buddha Caves at Bezeklik. We took the highway for a few more kilometres and then wound our way up into the mountains, which were eye-catchingly barren. There was a deep ravine running to the right of road, possibly with water in the bottom (a few scrubby trees were visible, but no actual water). The caves are incised into one of the walls of this ravine, high above the valley floor. Bezeklik is much less extensive and frequented than Mogao, and much less fully explained. We hired a guide at the entrance to walk us round, which was a good choice because there were no explanatory boards anywhere. The guide was a young, local woman with very dark hair and flashing eyes, her handsome face looking central Asian rather than Chinese. She looked very smart in her traditional outfit—a bright red dress (below the knee, covering the arms) with white tights (despite the heat) and black shoes, and her hair tied up. Obviously, the local taste in dress is quite conservative, this being a largely Muslim area. The guide spoke her local language and Mandarin, so we were glad to have Lily to translate. We were shown round five grottoes, which is all that was open to the public (like Mogoa, most of the caves are closed at any given time). There is some nice art in the grottoes but they are generally more vandalized than Mogao—the faces of the Buddhas have been deliberately scratched out and the ceilings smeared with mud by iconoclasts. A couple of sections of frescoes were cut out by Sir Aurel Stein and sent to India or England (he was financed by both Governments and split his swag between them). Each cave had a security guard sitting inside, checking their phone; it must be incredibly boring to sit there all day, in a dark cave that is mostly devoid of visitors. One grotto was guarded by a female security agent—the first that I had seen in the whole of China (although I am quite sure that the Chinese Government is an equal opportunity employer). Most of the low down frescoes were anyway behind Perspex, so you would have to be really determined if you wanted to damage them. The last cave that we entered had a light well above the door: apparently, at a certain time of day the sun streams onto a gilded Buddha statue that was situated at the very back of the cave, which must have been magnificent.

After our brief visit to Bezeklik we headed to Hami and then the valley of Tuyoq. While Turpan is famous for grapes, Hami is famous for melons. In fact, what we in the West call a Cantaloupe melon, the Chinese call a Hami melon (although I believe that those grown in Hami are actually a different cultivar). Like Turpan, Hami is also located in a great depression—indeed; some geologists consider it part of the same depression, divided into two by an "uplift" across the middle. There were certainly many trucks full of melons parked beside the highway, waiting hopefully for casual customers. Tuyoq is a verdant valley found on the far side of a range of hills to the south of the highway. Having snaked our way through the hills, we descended to Tuyoq; below and beyond the tiny town stretched a great barren plain. Tuyoq also hosts ancient Buddhist grottoes, brought to the attention of the world by the German archaeologist Von Le Coq in 1905. We drew into Tuyoq around lunchtime—which was a mistake because there was absolutely nowhere to eat there. The eatery in the town centre, next to the car park, was closed. We asked around and established that there were no others, so we snacked on biscuits that I had bought in the Flaming Mountains tourist centre and raisins that we had bought in Grape Valley. There was a covered area, with benches, in a corner of the deserted car park that seemed ideal for the occasion. A tour group were just packing up as we arrived and a Chinese family kindly offered us half a watermelon that they did not need, which we gladly accepted: it must have been at least 40°C in the shade and there wasn't even anywhere to buy water.

Someone had finally appeared in the local grocery store by the time that we finished eating and we were able to buy precious water see us through the afternoon. Then we set about exploring the town, which was truly a settlement of Biblical proportions. It consisted of a few narrow streets hemmed in by terraces of two-storey mud houses; inside the front door of each of them was a kind of partly covered courtyard onto which all the rooms opened. In each courtyard was a large bed—essentially a wooden platform with rugs on it, on which many of the inhabitants lay prone, presumably conserving their strength in the punishing midday heat. We saw this arrangement widely in Turpan: on our way to Ayding Lake, for example, shopkeepers had these divans dumped outside their stores—right on the edge of the busy main road—and spent much of the day prostrate and seemingly asleep until customers appeared. Next to some of the Tuyoq houses were small enclosures with animals scratching around inside (chickens, donkeys and so on). One narrow street led a short distance down to the valley bottom—where a karez appeared from the earth—and then another led back up the other side. The watercourse was bordered with trees and you could see that crops were stretching out to either side further down. There were alleyways branching off the lane at various points, and houses with rickety wooden balconies overhung the street. If Mary had appeared around the corner on a donkey, then I would not have been in the least bit surprised.

The signposting in the town was appalling. You start to follow directions for the caves and then the signs run out and leave you in the middle of nowhere (actually, in a little area of dead ground near the water course, looking out over a derelict lavatory block that was designed for tourists, judging by the English signage). We took a track up behind some houses until we left the village and headed higher up into the valley. Grottoes were visible on either side, above our heads where we could not see into them; lines of dusty footprints led up to the caves, so they were obviously frequented, but there seemed to be no form of organization. We spotted some Chinese tourists slogging up the other side of the valley shortly before we were stopped by a security guard and told to turn around because the caves were closed; he then crossed the bridge and accosted the Chinese tourists to turn them around, too. This was obviously a big disappointment, having driven for some hours to reach Tuyoq. The womenfolk wandered back towards the car park while I tried to find some of the other historical attractions—the ancient houses and burial mounds and so on. But the signs soon ran out for those, too, and I gave up and headed after the girls. It does not strike me that Tuyoq is a particularly rich town. You might think that they would want to cater to the tourists who are literally hammering on their doors to find food and go to the grottoes. But apparently not. I cannot see Tuyoq being lifted out of poverty any time soon.

The next morning, we ran down to Ayding Lake and back to town for lunch. I had an interesting conversation with the young man who ran the convenience store next to the restaurant. As business was slow, he came over to practice his English on us. Apparently, he had been learning English at night school because his ambition was to emigrate to Australia. Although imperfect, his English was passable and I assured him that it would be no bar to him making a new life for himself abroad. I imagine that he will face far more formidable barriers to his fulfilling his dream. Leaving aside the fact that Australia is none too welcoming to migrants these days, I am not confident that he will even be allowed to leave China.

Getting a passport in China is not as easy as in the West: for example, you apply to the police and you have to explain why you need a passport—to study abroad, or whatever. The Government is very clear that there is no discrimination in China on the basis of ethnicity or religion: but it did recently impose a regulation that anyone from Xinjiang applying for travel documents must provide a voice recording and a DNA sample. I don't have the impression that they are giving out travel papers like confetti in that part of the country.

After lunch, we crossed the street to visit the Turpan Museum for a couple of hours. Again, it was small but secreted some extraordinary stuff. I have never seen so many mummies mustered in one place. The parched plains preserve the remains of local people without the need for sophisticated medical procedures—in contrast to ancient Egypt, for example—so numerous naturally mummified corpses have been discovered from different eras in different areas. They were in outstanding condition: the skin was complete, the scalp still boasted a full head of hair and the clothing had conserved its colour. Some of the mummies were displayed in replicas of the small tombs in which they had been interred. In other cases, we had photo boards showing the archaeological digs and what the original graves looked like when they were uncovered. The artefacts were amazing. I particularly remember a rich red dress that was 2000 years old that could have been worn to a party by our eldest daughter. (I should not commit it to print, but I can tell you that we send them to school in clothes that are more run down and beaten up than that dress. It is really, really, really rare to see such well-preserved old clothing. And there were several other dresses displayed in almost as good condition.)

After a few hours, we decided to call it quits and head to the train station for our trip to Urumqi on the bullet train. The driver was waiting for us outside and ferried us far out of town to the high speed train station, which was not the one at which we had arrived. Our arrival station in town was small and old and cramped, whereas our departure station out of town was like an airport (in scale as well as style). The check-in process turned into a personal disaster for me, but a good experience for the girls.

To enter the station, we had to pass through security on steroids. In case you are not *au fait* with affairs in Xinjiang, I can tell you that there have been numerous terrorist attacks of increasing sophistication in the last few years by Uyghur separatists (who particularly like to target railway stations). I have heard that it is becoming a low-level insurgency, with terrorist training camps up in the mountains and ambushes of military and police patrols. I am led to believe that Islamic State is now active in training the Uyghur separatists, so I am sure that it will get yet more bloody and ruthless. I have also heard that the Chinese special forces are working in the area. Surreally, a squad of soldiers, in full combat gear, was sitting bolt upright on a big bank of seats in the station departure lounge—as if waiting for a train, but actually just waiting for trouble. And the x-ray inspection was unusually rigorous. Unfortunately, this meant that they decided to confiscate my Swiss Army knife, which Lucy bought me on our first Christmas together 26 years ago. It was a good knife—the Swiss Champ—and I had carried it on many adventures: from Patagonia to the North Cape, from Northern California to Turpan. But Turpan was to be the last time. It clearly made no sense to confiscate it. I had arrived from Dunhuang by train—in fact, from Beijing via several trains—and never once assaulted anyone. No one had objected at any previous security check (which is rather typical of the arbitrary—and hence unpredictable and unreasonable—enforcement of rules in China). In any case, you would need to be a real expert to kill someone with the blade of a Swiss Army knife (even the longest blade is not very long) and if you were indeed such a highly trained assassin, then I am sure that you could find easier ways to kill people.

Lily was having the same problem with her own penknife, but is not one to give up easily. She persuaded the screening agents to give her back the knives and scooted outside to find the taxi driver, who had only just pulled out of the station. Since we had employed him for three days, and tipped him handsomely, we were in his good books. So Lily gave him the knives and asked him to post them to us in Beijing. It turns out that this is impossible. No courier company will carry knives in the mail (and all packages are x-rayed, so you cannot compromise the system); China Post will not carry knives, either. This is also clearly ridiculous, since you can buy knives online and have them delivered. And, anyway, a knife in the post is hardly dangerous without a person to use it. But posting personal effects is very difficult in China, as we had discovered in February when we tried to post some clothes from Hong Kong to ourselves to Beijing. Presumably, the Government is concerned about all kinds of calamitous contraband that could corrupt the Communist system (drugs, weapons, books). So they just ban everything that cannot easily be controlled.

While we were waiting in the station, two young sisters—local lasses, judging by their looks—came and introduced themselves to our girls. They were obviously very proud to show off their English and we smiled and complimented them. A few minutes later, Lucy took our girls into the shop and bought them a small chocolate bar each (Galaxy Dove, which has an amazing market presence in China—their management must be good). The younger sister shyly followed them into the store, so Lucy bought chocolate bars for her and her elder sister, too. This was obviously quite a trophy and the two of them were very happy. A few minutes later, they came over to us with three highly decorated sequined hats, in an indigenous style, to give to our girls. Our daughters were thrilled—they love any kind of fancy dressing up—and immediately put them on. So we parted on good terms and I think that we did our best to build international peace and understanding. Shortly afterwards, the train arrived and we bundled aboard, since it was scheduled to stop for only about two minutes. It was jam-packed and we had to turf some trespassers out of our reserved seats. Sitting with our luggage squeezed around us, it was a mercy that we were on the train for only an hour. The landscape gets more mountainous as you approach Urumqi, and more moist, so we at least had nice views for the adults to adore.

Urumqi is not a natural tourist destination. Although situated in the centre of Xinjiang, it was not historically a centre for Uyghur culture: it was always a trading hub with a significant Han Chinese population and it has expanded in recent years with the influx of thousands more Han Chinese. Kashgar is really the historic centre of Uyghur culture: it is known for its central Asian style of architecture, its fine food and its vibrant markets. If time and money were no object, then we would have travelled to Kashgar. But it is a 24-hour train ride from Urumqi and flights to Kashgar are ridiculously expensive (more costly than crossing the Atlantic). And flights from Kashgar to Beijing are so infrequent and overpriced that I wonder if this is part of Government policy to restrict travel between the western border and Beijing. Urumqi undoubtedly made a more timely terminus for our trip to the West, with plentiful and inexpensive flights back to Beijing. So we planned to spend a day there, visiting the Silk Road Museum and the International Bazaar to get our final gifts, and then head to airport.

Our first problem was getting from the train station to the hotel. As usual, the taxi drivers wanted to overcharge us—200 RMB, as opposed to the market rate of 50 RMB—but they were more persistent than most. Not only did they refuse to take us for 50 RMB, but whenever another taxi stopped to talk to us the first set of drivers started yelling that we were rich and shouldn't be taken for less than 200 RMB, at which point the other drivers headed off (not wanting any trouble). Eventually, we had to walk several streets away (schlepping all our luggage) to find a taxi. Our destination—the Hotel Mercure—is indeed big and grand. It also has a lot of security. The only reason *not* to stay there, in Lucy's book, was that it was an obvious target for terrorists. The hotel apparently takes the same view, so there were two security guards at the entrance wearing flak jackets and we had to put all the baggage through an x-ray machine before we got to the hotel check-in desk. It really felt like you were staying in a war zone. Terrorism definitely does what it says on the tin in China: people have a terrible and exaggerated fear of falling victim to random acts of violence. They also believe, for example, that it is dangerous to visit the US because the Americans have a problem with terrorism. I laughed when I heard this and assured Lily that terrorism in Europe is much worse—in fact, no European country worth its salt is without a major domestic terror network! Bastille Day proved my point perfectly—particularly since one of Lily's friends was in Nice that night for the fireworks and started WeChatting updates as the attack unfolded. China is very, very safe by comparison. By the time we had checked in and occupied the rooms, it was bedtime for the children and I had become feverish. I had had a sore throat since Xining and assumed that I had picked up a cold that I would eventually throw off. But I was definitely getting worse, rather than better: freezing cold but covered in sweat, and physically exhausted. I rolled myself up in my duvet and switched off while Lucy gave the children a snack and put them to bed.

The traffic in Urumqi is as bad as everywhere else in China. The next morning we spent quite a while queuing to cross the city, and a journey that might have taken 15 minutes took about 35. We then had to pass through security (x-ray machines and so on) to get into the bazaar complex. The Uyghurs are known for knife manufacture. This is one reason why their terror attacks often feature mass stabbings: it is a kind of leitmotif so that it is obvious who is responsible. So you are not allowed to take knives into the bazaar. Of course, the main thing to buy in the Urumqi bazaar is… great, big, razor-sharp knives! There are walls full of them in every store, from the pettiest penknife to the most substantial sword. Presumably, the police view is that Uyghur terrorists are too stupid to buy a knife in the bazaar and use it to stab people—they would only come equipped with their own favoured blade.

The bazaar is based in two big buildings facing each other across a large courtyard. In fact, the big buildings are composed of several smaller buildings, like converted warehouses linked together. In England, it would be full of outlet stores and called something like "The Designer Outlet Village". In Urumqi, the interiors are arranged as a three-storey rabbit warren, packed full of small shops and stalls. One area handles mainly handbags and make-up; another is full of furs; another has a range of rugs; another stocks knick-knacks; and so on. A handsome and ornate brick tower—apparently a copy of the Bukhara Minaret in Uzbekistan—dominates the centre of the courtyard. The girls seemed to have a lot of essential shopping to do—things for themselves, things for their friends, things for their birthdays, things for souvenirs…. There was a great deal of spying, sampling, circling and settling on prices to be done. Lucy (having a Hong Kong upbringing) and Lily are both ferocious bargainers; Annabelle is on the way there, but Catherine and Elizabeth are both a bit hopeless so far. When the stallholder says that something is 120 RMB, they say things like: "But I have only got 100 RMB", at which point the stallholder's eye light up and a bargain is immediately struck. They should obviously say that they have only 50 RMB and hold out for 60 RMB or, at most, 75 RMB. Of course, the old "good cop/bad cop" routine is useful: I am invariably the bad cop and can be relied upon to say that any item is far too expensive (whatever its price) and that we should walk away. I think I am quite credible in this rôle, since I hate shopping, look sour and would like nothing more than an excuse to walk away. Another use that I have is to carry the bags and stand around the corner—so that the shopkeepers cannot see how much stuff we have already bought and just how profligate we are.

Shopping is hungry work. Happily, Xinjiang is a home of good bread and there were many kinds of flatbread on sale, sweet and savoury.

Xinjiang is also known for its seed-honey-dried fruit biscuit (similar to flapjack if you are English, or granola bar if you are American—but loaded with all kinds of seeds, rather than oats). I had bought this before in Beijing: barrow boys from central Asia stand around with cartloads of the stuff (literally—a flatbed with big blocks lined up, weighing at least 100 lbs each), slicing lumps off with a big, square blade. I had been rather disappointed that suppliers seemed to be so few and far between in Xinjiang itself! I managed to buy the remnants of a boxful in the bazaar, although it was not the best kind (no dried apricot!). With all this—as well as ice cream and water—we rejuvenated ourselves in preparation for the trek to the airport. Since we had to go back across town in rush hour traffic, we left a considerable margin for error but everything ran smoothly and we arrived at the airport in good time.

Of course, our flight was then delayed; China is renowned for its flight delays. One reason for this is that 90 per cent of the airspace is reserved for military use, so there are relatively narrow air corridors into and out of major hubs. I am sure that Chinese Air Force pilots must be very well trained, given the amount of airspace in which they have to practice. When you board a plane in China, there is always a choice of two newspapers—one in Chinese and the other in English. The English language newspaper is always the *China Daily*, which is the official mouthpiece of the Communist Party. I picked up a copy as we boarded the plane: it sometimes contains interesting information (such as reports about historical sites that have been discovered) but I mostly read it for amusement value, since you can't really take it seriously. The situation in the South China Sea has been getting a lot of coverage recently. There was a blistering editorial lambasting Japan for the recent change to its Constitution to allow its troops to be deployed overseas; and it slated Japan and the Philippines for increasing defence expenditure and thereby raising tensions in the South China Sea. What was needed was more dialogue, we are assured. Of course, it did not mention the fact that these other countries were responding to dramatic increases in China's own military budget, and the fact that it has just completed construction of one aircraft carrier and plans to build more. Another opinion piece condemned the "illegal" conclusions of UNCLOS (the United Nations Convention on the Law of the Sea), which noted that China did not have the right to claim the whole of the South China Sea and should desist from building islands on coral reefs, and the editorial vowed that China would "never accept them". Since China will never accept such conclusions, what are possibilities for this proposed dialogue? Presumably that everyone else must accept China's claims. The editorial did not actually say that the members of the UNCLOS committee were capitalist scum who would be sliced up alive and fed to ravenous dogs—that is more of a North Korean touch—but it was well on the way there.

I have never quite worked out the point of the *China Daily*. It is presumably aimed primarily at foreigners, since it is produced in English; but any foreigner who vaguely followed an independent news stream would know that the *China Daily* was propounding an extremely biased view of world events and would therefore discount virtually every word written there. In fact, the main benefit of picking up the *China Daily* on this occasion was that it offered a perfect opportunity to teach my eight-year-old about media bias and propaganda. One of the features was a very proud piece about a new amphibious plane developed by China—the largest in the world, as big as a Boeing 737. The Government states that the plane will be used for maritime surveillance and fighting forest fires, since it can scoop up water while in flight. But we already have the Canadair to do that, so why do we need to develop this new plane? The Chinese government is the only purchaser and has so far ordered a total of 12 planes, which obviously cannot possibly justify the development cost. I asked Annabelle why they created this enormous new amphibious plane and she said: "So that they can invade other people?" While I am happy to be persuaded that my daughters are smart, one could alternatively ask whom the *China Daily* thinks it is fooling. If my eight-year-old can see that the unveiling of this plane is a veiled threat to other nations who claim islands in the South China Sea, presumably any adult can see it, too.

It is good to get back home. In truth, travelling across China has been an exhausting expedition—more of an educational experience than a vacation. Mind you, I reckon that reading this letter comes a close second, given how long it has grown, so thanks for hanging in there!

Very best wishes,

Liam.

Letter 16

Huaguoshan and Guizhou
1 August 2016

Dear Tim,

We were very happy to have completed our Journey to the West. Although it was interesting, and parts of it were fun, it was also physically and mentally tiring. It was good to be home to be able to eat what we wanted, sleep when we wanted and wear what we wanted. We had also learned that we were going to have to leave China unexpectedly early, by about two weeks, owing to some work issues that had arisen in Boston. So we immediately threw ourselves into packing—getting all the non-essential items boxed up—in preparation for the Beijing Airlift. My wife and children have a boundless ambition (and an astonishing ability) to accumulate chattels, so there were many bags and boxes to be filled to the brim. Under such time pressure, we slashed our travel plans to the two essential visits that we needed to make before leaving China.

First, I had long promised Catherine that we could visit Huaguoshan ("Fruit and flower mountain") when we went to China. In a sense, this was the very beginning of the *Journey to the West* because it is the place where Sun Wukong was reputed to have been born from a stone egg. He had later fought 72 demons there and become the king of the monkeys by bravely leaping through a waterfall into the Water Curtain

Cave. At Huaguoshan Tourist Park, 750 km southeast of Beijing in Jiangsu province, you can visit real locations that correspond to the descriptions in these legends—such as a cave whose entrance lies behind a waterfall. The problem with Huaguoshan is that, although it is on the coast, it is in the middle of nowhere in terms of the transportation network. It lies roughly halfway between Beijing and Shanghai, which is only a six-hour journey on the bullet train. But Huaguoshan is not close to the high-speed rail line, so if you get off the bullet train halfway between Beijing and Shanghai, then you have *another* six-hour train ride to Huaguoshan taking the small, local train lines. The only way to get there in a sensible amount of time is to fly to the local city and hire a car, effectively making it an expensive day trip. (Actually, it is an overnighter because the flights go only late in the evening from Beijing and return late in the evening from Lianyungang. But this at least means that you get a full day in Huaguoshan.)

Second, we had promised that we would visit Lily's family in Guizhou while we were in China. We wanted to meet her family and broaden our experiences; and her father was very keen to meet our girls, and also thank us for taking good care of his daughter when she first moved to America. (Chinese people believe that the USA is the most unsafe country on earth—it is all gunfights at the OK Corral and muggings and murders on every street corner, in addition to terror attacks. So Lily's father was terrified when he discovered that his daughter had decided to go and live on the other side of the world. I think that the sight of our family on Skype—with three cute little blonde girls—was a great comfort to him.) We had intended to spend about a week in Guizhou: there are minority villages to visit, natural wonders to see (waterfalls and underground rivers) and various other historical and cultural things to experience—all of which Lily's father was keen to show us. Guizhou is very remote and mountainous, so the summer temperature is about 20–25°C every day and there is no pollution; obviously, this made it even more attractive as a tourist target. It is currently quite underdeveloped, although the high-speed train line is just arriving and in ten years' time the place will probably be overrun by noisy Chinese tour groups. Unfortunately, we just did not have a week left to us and we were limited to about four days (which was really a bit short because Lily's hometown is a four-hour drive from the closest airport, so we would automatically lose a half-day at each end). Still, it was what it was—we would just have to make the most of it.

After two days in Beijing, we took the short evening flight to Lianyungang. Beijing was hot and sticky; but Lianyungang was even hotter and positively steamy. The airport was quite small, and it was very late at night, so we had to take whatever we could get for transport—which turned out to be a regular saloon car with children piled onto the laps of me and Lucy (like little electric blankets, but more wriggly). Since we were arriving late and leaving early, I had booked a fairly functional hotel in the town centre, which was approximately halfway between the airport and Huaguoshan. It was a well-known chain hotel called the 7 Days Inn. It was awful. They obviously get a lot of complaints because they gave a fistful of keycards to the security guard and told him to show us all the available rooms, so that we could choose the least bad one. Water was running down the walls, owing to the humidity, and the hotel is obviously like that for large parts of the year because the building was falling to pieces. I mean, the ceilings were sagging between the joists because the plasterboard was so damp; there were big holes in the walls in the corridor where the plasterboard was soft and disintegrating; the paint was flaking off the walls in large areas of the bedrooms under the pressure of the water seeping through the fabric of the building. The hotel obviously makes some effort to maintain the building (large areas had clearly been repaired and repainted), but they are fighting a losing battle against the elements. The building would require to be constantly cooled and dehumidified—rather than just switching on the window AC unit when a guest enters a hotel room—in order to secure some semblance of civilization. Lucy was used to it: when she lived in Hong Kong, they used to have water running down the walls of their school classrooms, and you had to turn on hot bars in the wardrobe to stop the clothes going mouldy in the summer. Being a frigid northerner, I would not want to live like that every day for large parts of the year.

We got up fairly early—despite our previous late night—and downed the biscuits and yoghurt that passed for hotel breakfast (they gave them to us in a bag as we checked in—like a low-quality airplane meal). Then we ordered a taxi and headed for Huaguoshan, about 20 minutes away.

Even early in the morning, it was very hot and humid. We had had the idea that we would leave our visit later in the year because it would be cooler and fresher up in the mountains than elsewhere, which would make a pleasant break. But any mountain effect was more than offset by the southerly location on the coast. I was soaked with sweat (literally) by the time we had walked from the taxi to the ticket kiosk.

To navigate your way around the park you are reliant on a sketch map of the standard Chinese style. These are basically useless. Half the paths and roads are not marked, so whenever you get to a junction you are never quite sure if it is one of the ones shown on the map, and it is not clear whether you want to carry straight on or turn off. There are never any distances or times marked, either, so you cannot know whether it is really worth walking on to some visitor attraction or not. The signposts around the park are the same—usually ambiguous and never revealing the times or distances between waypoints. I suppose that Chinese tourists always take the electric bus, so they don't really care how far away anything is. We generally end up taking the bus because we have no idea how long it might take on foot. In this case, the bus was clearly better because the climate was brutal and the terrain was rugged—even though the buses were fully enclosed (i.e. like regular buses rather than golf carts) and very hot inside.

Once past the ticket barriers of Huaguoshan Park, the broad entry road leads you alongside a large lake. The stone esplanade offers ample opportunity to sit beneath the shady trees and admire the vista, which was an attractive offer in the oppressive heat. But we had monkeys to find, so we immediately boarded a bus and headed up the winding mountain road to a temple high on the hill. You can imagine that the landscape was lush, given the heat and humidity, and the park was a jumble of soaring green peaks. We soon arrived at a tourist distribution centre—a combination of bus hub, shops, chair lift station (to the top of the mountain), temple and a track up to the Monkey King's cave. We found a shady place to sit and ate a snack that we had brought—partly because we were already hungry and partly because it was easier to have everyone carry their own food and water in their stomachs than have an adult lug it all around in a rucksack. Our actions were apparently innovative: no one else had brought their own food and we were therefore an object of amazement to the other tourists as we sat and ate (and being Westerners, on top of that). It was a nice little interlude, sitting in a shady courtyard and looking out over a sweeping valley. Then we took the track up the hill and passed through a quiet temple honouring the Monkey King, before arriving at the scene of Sun Wukong's triumph and subsequent elevation to monarchy. I hesitate to admit it here, because it is bound to cause me trouble later in life when he is unmasked, but in our house Sun Wukong sits in the same category at Santa Claus: our children are convinced that he really exists, and they send him letters (at least, Catherine does). Naturally, Sun Wukong speaks only Mandarin, so this requires her to write everything in Chinese characters, which I regard as an educational benefit. Miraculously, these letters get posted off to China and Sun Wukong dutifully replies. He is the perfect pen friend if you have children who need a bit of extra motivation to master Mandarin. Hence, I felt honour bound to call on him when we were living in Beijing.

The water curtain cave was touristy but very nice. A path sneaks along the rock face from the right and slides in behind the waterfall, which wets you slightly in the process (although this was hardly noticeable, given how wet I was already). You then follow the descending passageway 10 m into the gathering gloom—slightly unnerving if you are wearing sunglasses and frightened of bumping your head on the uneven ceiling. You emerge into a large, dimly-lit chamber with a stone throne for the Monkey King on the left and some obsequious monkey statues bowing down around it. This is, of course, the perfect photo op. You then continue along the twisting passageway, through another spooky cavern with candles and alters, until you emerge onto a pleasant terrace. I was rather sorry to leave the cool cave interior and consign myself again to the heat and humidity. As part of our life-and-death struggle to stay hydrated, we bought drinks at the kiosk and enjoyed the fine views. From the terrace, there were a confusing number of paths heading off in different directions (all badly signposted in both English and Mandarin). We had decided to take the chair lift to the summit, since it seemed like the most pleasant way to travel (a man-made breeze being better than none at all). The station was somewhat lower than where we had got off the bus. Not wanting to accidentally descend too far—since that would involve walking back up again!—we mistakenly took a path that kept too high and ended up back at the cave entrance (which was not really very far above us).

The path heading towards the water curtain cave was on a stone terrace, so that on your right you looked out into the canopies of fine trees that were planted down below. There were monkeys sitting on the wall of the terrace and they were small but rather aggressive—baring their teeth if people walked too close to them, and occasionally leaping back into the trees if they felt too threatened on the terrace. The children were scared of them, which is understandable, but you should obviously not be intimidated by a small monkey—showing fear will only encourage its aggression. When one of them bared his teeth at Elizabeth, I gave it a steely stare and walked towards it until it retreated to a respectful distance. Then I found some seedy biscuit in my bag and the girls put it on top of the wall and stepped back, whereupon the monkey streaked in and swiped it in a second. After a while the monkeys tired of us and headed back into the trees, at which point we were allowed to retrace our steps and head down towards the chair lift station. Annabelle—being slow to finish any kind of food—made the mistake of walking down with a half-eaten apple in her hand. A monkey raced past her along the top of the wall—coming from behind—and knocked it straight out of her hand, swooping down to swipe it and make off on the other side of the path. What a cheeky monkey! Annabelle screeched in surprise, although no harm was done. You would think that the girls would learn a lesson from that but later on another monkey stole Catherine's bottle of orange drink—running up behind her and snatching it right out of her hand. She was mugged by a monkey!

The chair lift to summit was almost deserted. True, the bus was cheaper but the chair lift was only about 30 RMB and it had very nice views, and it felt good to get some air. From the top station we walked about 100 m to the bus drop-off area and, from there, we followed a short path to the very top of the mountain. The path was shaded by trees and passed through a fancy stone gazebo on its way to the open ground of the summit. The top was very picturesque and culminated in a gentle rocky knoll that presented an ideal photo opportunity (assuming that you could get a clean shot of your kin between the surges of sequential tourist groups—patience was key). Having attained our two key objectives—the Monkey King's cave and the park summit—it was not obvious what to do next, especially in view of the withering weather. Back down in the wooded valley there were supposed to be 72 caves—the homes of 72 monsters whom Sun Wukong recruited to his army—together with the remnants of the stone egg from which the Monkey King himself was emerged. So we decided to head back down on the chair lift, descend through Sun Wukong's cave once again, and then pursue the path the short distance down to the caves.

The 72 caves were not immediately apparent because they are not exactly caves. They are more like large, assorted clefts and crevices scattered between jumbled boulders on the hillside—like the grottos created by a retreating glacier, when it leaves behind huge stone blocks stacked haphazardly (a good example being the Polar Caves in New Hampshire). The caves were also partially screened by the undergrowth covering the slope. Paths led up and down the detritus—running around freestanding rocks, threading through narrow passageways and dallying on slabby daises. Unless you have small children to entertain, you could probably give this part of the park a miss; but it provided us with hours of entertainment (just think of it—even at one minute per cave, it is pretty good value…). Finally, we found the *pièce de résistance*: the stone egg, now cracked in two, from which Sun Wukong was born. In a sense, this was the place where the *Journey to the West* began—given that Sun Wukong was a demon who was born long before Xuanzang came into the world, let alone decided to go to India in search of the true word of Buddha. Almost at the end of our time in China, we had finally reached the beginning of our own journey into Chinese language and culture. Any parent can tell you that putting a child in front of a cartoon will keep them quiet for ages, no matter what language it is in. So our children have spent many hours watching the animated adventures of Xuanzang and Sun Wukong, gradually absorbing Mandarin in the process, as if by osmosis. Especially in the beginning, when it was most challenging for the children, it was a wonderful way to open their minds to Mandarin and the Middle Kingdom. Now they are totally conversant and it is just a question of continuing to build, rather than facing the forbidding challenge of erecting an enormous edifice from the very foundations.

The journey back to Beijing was largely uneventful. Lily negotiated with a driver at the taxi stand until he agreed to load all six of us into his cab and run us back into Lianyungang. The flight was scheduled to leave quite late, and we wanted to have happy children on the plane, so we fed them at McDonalds. This had the added advantage of assured hygiene, in terms of a place to wash hands and use the bathroom (which is not at all guaranteed in a local eatery). Then it was a car to the airport and the flight to Beijing, arriving after midnight. Obviously, the children fell asleep on the plane and were not best pleased about being woken in the middle of the night, but they are getting much better with all the practice! Nonetheless, we were all very happy to be back in "cool" Beijing and tumbling into our own beds. We were not to enjoy that luxury for very long. The next day—Friday—we had to unpack and repack. Then on Saturday we had to get up brutally early to catch a flight to Guizhou.

It is hard to reach Lily's hometown of Liupanshui. Although many other provinces are further from Beijing, Guizhou is the least developed province in China. It is mountainous and not much happens there except some mining; the roads have historically been poor—as have the people—and the high-speed rail line is only just opening. In fact, the Government has been investing substantial amounts in Guizhou in recent years. The world's largest radio telescope is due to open in Guizhou in September 2016: at 500 m across, it has 2.5 times the area of the world's second largest radio telescope (in Puerto Rico) and will therefore be 2.5 times more sensitive. It will be in a "radio quiet zone" (so as not to interfere with the astronomical observations) stretching across 80 km^2 of countryside. Guizhou is ideal for this project. First, there are very few people living there, so the radio quiet zone is not a great inconvenience to anyone. Second, the dish is being created in a huge natural depression in the mountains, so the 4500 triangular plates that comprise the dish are basically sitting on a framework that stands on the ground (i.e. it is not one huge dish that sits on top of a stand). The radio telescope is then redirected by realigning the individual plates, not by moving a monolithic dish. There is also a massive computer data centre being built in Guizhou. The problem with computer data centres is that they create heat and are difficult to cool—especially in China, where it is very hot and humid in the summer! So you can put them in either Tibet or Guizhou, since it is cool in those places all year round. If you want privacy, then you go to Tibet: that is where the world's biggest Bitcoin mines are located (far away from government oversight). Government agencies have chosen Guizhou, and there is a $15 billion fund to subsidize private firms to go there, too (such as JD.com, which is like another Chinese Amazon and which has just signed a "strategic agreement" to relocate computing operations there).

In fact, we were looking forward to going to Guizhou partly because Lily had promised us some civilized weather. The daily high in the summer is around 21°C, which was literally a breath of fresh air after Beijing and Lianyungang. The Liupanshui locals are hoping that the new rail connection—only about six hours from Guangzhou—will lead to a steep rise in tourism as overheated, overstressed office workers escape to the cool, calm, quiet mountains. We were happy to reconnoitre the terrain for them. But getting there from Beijing is neither easy nor cheap. Liupanshui is three hours from Anshun Airport, three hours from Guiyang Airport and three hours from Kunming Airport—take your pick. In fact, owing to a combination of ticket prices, airline schedules and tour plans, we ended up flying into Anshun and out of Guiyang. There is not much traffic at all on the routes, except to Kunming, but the tickets were still fairly expensive (around $330 return). Also, the flights do not leave from Beijing Capital Airport (the big, swanky one) but from Beijing Nanyuan Airport (the small, manky one). They are equidistant from central Beijing but Nanyuan is in the south (rather than the northeast) and is accessed via local roads (rather than an expressway). So a car came to collect us around 6:30 a.m. and plough south to Nanyuan on the highways and byways. We arrived none too early for our flight, fought our way through the chaos of the check-in area and joined the long queue for security. By the time we crossed that hurdle, the children needed the loo but Lucy wouldn't let them because it was a HAZMAT 6 area, so she insisted that they wait until we boarded the plane (whose toilets are, of course, celebrated for their salubrity). This proved to be risky strategy because—having rushed and sweated to get to the gate on time—we were herded onto the plane and then told that there would be a delay. So we sat, strapped into our seats, for an hour or so—no information on our fate, and the clock ticking on a toilet time bomb. We distracted the children as best we could with books and snacks but we were extremely glad when we were eventually allowed to take off and unfasten our seat belts.

When we arrived at Anshun, Lily's father and younger brothers were there to meet us. Lily's family is rather unusual in China because it includes three children! In fact, her family is not Han Chinese, which means that they were permitted to have a second child even under the one child policy. Then the second pregnancy turned out to be twins! Her brothers are at high school—which was on summer vacation—so they had time on their hands and were kind enough to come and meet us. They had come to collect us in a minibus, so we were able to load up and head straight off to lunch (which was fortunate since we were getting hungry after the flight delay). Everything was pre-arranged and we stopped at a restaurant where a private room had been readied for us at the rear. Like many places in China—especially out in the countryside—it was a row of new, reinforced concrete structures around three storeys high. These buildings always look unfinished to a westerner: there is typically lots of bare concrete (such as on the steps or the upper walls) but the owners have moved in and started using the building. As time goes on—and money flows in—things like colourful tiles appear on the outside walls to make it look more attractive (which is obviously of some importance in businesses such as restaurants, where you are trying to attract people to come in and eat). The room where we ate was very basic (the furniture was not fancy, the room plainly decorated) and, again, you can see that in a few years' time it will become more and more elaborate. A combination of hunger, habituation with Chinese food and facility with chopsticks meant that my children managed to eat a decent lunch—an important issue, in terms of keeping your Chinese host happy. If you don't eat much then they will worry and fuss around you, and feel that they have fallen flat in their duty to welcome you. The children love to eat fish in China—it is often prepared very simply, just steamed with a little soy sauce in the serving dish—and they wolf it down as long as it does not contain too many small bones (which some of the freshwater fish do).

After lunch, we travelled a short distance to the Huanguoshu ("Yellow fruit tree") waterfall. This is claimed to be the one of the largest waterfalls in the world by area (i.e. height times breadth), being 78 m high and 101 m wide (i.e. around 8000 m^2). This does not seem to be a statistic by which waterfalls are often ranked (as I found when I tried to check its ranking!), although it makes a lot of sense: your impression of a waterfall's size is really determined by the extent of the sheet of falling water in front of you. Some falls that are very large do not fall very far—notably the Boyama Falls (a.k.a. the "Stanley Falls") on the Congo River, which is 1372 m wide and has the world's largest flow rate but never falls more than 5 m (giving a sheet around 6850 m^2). The Huanguoshu waterfall is certainly impressive (however high it ranks on the list) and it has the marvellous advantage that you can completely traverse it behind the water curtain (unlike Niagara, for example, where you have to keep a very safe distance). The waterfall is—inevitably—some distance from the park entrance and you cannot immediately see it. But you begin by walking through some glorious gardens that have been created, especially a very extensive bonsai garden. Bonsai is called "penjing" in modern Chinese; the Japanese word "bonsai" actually derives from the old Chinese word "penzai" ("pot plant") because the Chinese invented this style of horticulture in antiquity (there are written descriptions from around 300 CE and very clear pictures on tomb murals from 700 CE). The bonsai were really rather large (roughly a metre tall and a metre or more across), even though all their components (leaves and branches) were tiny: they were just very mature shrunken trees! Even an enormously reduced chestnut tree is quite big when it is full-grown. There was a nice selection—oak and chestnut and ginkgo and various varieties that I did not recognize.

As you might expect, there were lots of people in the park on a sunny Saturday in the summer. We kept a close eye on the children—aided by our most solicitous hosts—and followed the flow towards the waterfall. The approach to the waterfall is spectacular: the paved path contours the rim of the curved river valley, which is lushly vegetated; you pass across the front of the waterfall at a distance of about 200 m, glimpsing it through the trees, before winding down to a viewing area where you are confronted by its full glory at a distance of about 100 m. You can rest there as long as you like before queuing your way along a path high up on the steep river bank, maybe 50 m above the water. This section is swathed in shrubs—rather than trees—and as you round each shoulder you get increasingly close-up views of the cascade, until you finally reach the falls themselves. The path then winds its way behind the waterfall itself, sometimes in a passageway in the rock and sometimes alongside the water curtain itself—almost close enough to touch—and you can see the mosses and small plants thriving on the rocks that are soaked by the constant spray thrown up by the torrent. The pressure of people means that you have to keep moving (albeit slowly) and it is a shame to have to reach the far side. There is space enough there to pause and admire the crossing you have just made, which is really unique. Then a well-made path takes you back down the other riverbank, wending its way through the trees into the river valley and across a footbridge to the lower viewing platform. The whole affair is well managed and I think that they do a good job of coping with the crush of people. Of course, we would all like to have a natural wonder of the world to ourselves but we are no longer living in the nineteenth century and that is not a realistic aspiration. (I am also not entirely convinced that being the first white man to view the Stanley Falls was really worth the risk and discomfort that Stanley had to go through in order to do it. Half his party died en route—114 people—including the other three white men, who were less resistant to disease than the natives. So I think that the Huanguoshu Falls are a good compromise.)

From the viewing platform in the river valley you need to ascend back up to the valley rim. Either you can walk or you can pay to take a monstrous escalator (a bit like the Mid-Levels Escalator in Hong Kong). We took the escalator—partly from laziness and partly because it seemed like it would be a hassle to walk back up the outdoor path against the flow of people (obviously, everyone else was taking the escalator so there was effectively a one-way system in operation). At the top we passed through the obligatory labyrinth of tourist traps, pausing only to buy ice creams, and then headed for the exit. We had a heart-stopping few minutes when Catherine disappeared—she just cannot resist rushing on ahead—but Lily's family fanned out and managed to locate her before we reached the exit. There is a definite tipping-point in family size: when the children outnumber the adults, then you have trouble! It is physically difficult for two adults to manage three children, especially in a crowd situation; and if a child goes missing, then you suddenly discover that you are drastically short-staffed for a search and rescue operation. So we were very happy to have so many adults on hand to resolve the situation. Then it was back to our minibus to drive a couple of hours to Lily's hometown of Liupanshui.

The scenery was nice—mountainous and green—but we were unable to enjoy much of it because the afternoon sun was lulling us off to sleep (it had been a very busy few weeks!).

Liupanshui is a new city. It lies at the intersection of three counties, Liuzhi, Pan and Shuicheng, from which it derives its name (i.e. Liu-Pan-Shui). In the last ten years, it has grown from essentially nothing to a conurbation housing three million people. Such is the speed of rural–urban migration in China that enough new dwellings must be built in urban areas *every month* to house 1.5 million migrants. For reference, Norway has a population of five million—so China has to rehouse the entire population of Norway approximately every three months. Liupanshui has not grown randomly, but rather as part of a Government plan to relocate people there from the surrounding countryside. The Government view is that if it provides infrastructure and some Government jobs, then this will be enough to start an agglomeration process and private firms and individuals will follow the signal to move there. We arrived as night was falling. Our hotel was located next to the new sports stadium—which is entirely unused, but very well lit. As a municipality in China, you prove that you have made it by having lots of bright lights. Hence you have multicoloured illumination of any bridge in town (such as the cable-stay bridge at the entry to Liupanshui) and you floodlight the stadium (full or empty). In fact, the local Communist Party officials are well aware that people are using nighttime light emissions as an index of economic activity. This is a very common approach employed by economists to gauge the level of development in parts of the world—such as Africa or Asia—that have less reliable standard statistics, such as wages or GDP. The Chinese Government also uses this metric to assess the effectiveness of its economic policy. The local officials therefore respond to pressure from their Beijing bosses by switching on all the lights all the time (such as in stadia that are not hosting any sports) because this makes them seem more successful at promoting local economic development. Chinese local officials are obviously smarter than economists.

We checked into the hotel—which was very spacious and well appointed, and entirely arranged by our hosts—and were then whisked off to dinner with Lily and her family. Lamb is a local speciality, presumably because the mountains provide good fodder for sheep, and we were treated to a hot pot at their favourite restaurant. We had a private room (dining area, really) at the back of the restaurant, looking out over the illuminated bridge. The children were inevitably a cause of some curiosity, especially amongst the local children, who came to stare at them. It was a very relaxed affair, which was good because the children were starting to wilt by the end of the evening: it had been a long day, and they had yet to recover from their prior trip to Huaguoshan! Happily, the hotel was just around the corner, so we could walk back, and the children gave us no trouble about going to bed.

The next morning, our driver arrived to take us on a tour of some of the local sights. We headed high into the hills to a village that was being transformed into a conference centre. It was due to host a major Asian development conference in September—which seemed very close, since they had not even started constructing the buildings in July! Our hosts seemed confident that everything would be ready, although to us it seemed unbelievable. They were still levelling the land and installing the basic infrastructure (drains and so on). We had not come to see the conference centre *per se*; rather, we had come to see the village before it was transformed. It was a traditional mountain village distinguished by its venerable ginkgo biloba trees, some of them 800 years old. In fact, that is not so old for a ginkgo biloba—it is believed that they can live for up to 2500 years—but 800-year-old specimens are still rare. Ginkgo is an important ingredient in Chinese medicine and in Chinese cooking. It produces slightly furry fruits that look like fat green berries (indeed, the Japanese term "gin kyo" means "silver apricot") that are about the size of the tip of your little finger (if you are an adult male). It is the seeds inside the berries that are the sought-after part, being used in famous dishes such as "Buddha's delight". The local villagers happily pulled little clusters of berries off the ginkgo trees to give to our children, which seemed a terrible waste of such a noble fruit. We wandered down through the scattered dwellings of the village, beneath the tall ginkgos that shaded the path, and the highlight for the children was petting a shaggy white horse who was grazing placidly beside the stream. Happily, Catherine's motion sickness had gone off (all those twisty mountain roads get her every time!) because Lily's father had arranged for us to take lunch in the village. So we sat out on a patio, as the chickens "pocked" around us, and ate one of their brethren. It was nice to witness the "real" China—and strange to think that that village will already have been totally transformed in the few months since we sat there. Now it hosts a massive conference centre and life there will never be the same again. Outsiders will flood in (to run the conference centre) and villages will flow out (young people heading off to the city for education and jobs). What happened to the little old man who made our lunch? Is he now overwhelmed with customers from the conference workforce, or sidelined by the arrival of superior eating establishments?

After lunch we headed for Panxian, which is the old town where Lily was actually born and where her father still works in the maintenance department of the local hospital. There were many fine mountain vistas en route, but the most extraordinary sight was the power station—built atop a mighty mountain and dominating the valley like a medieval castle. In Europe, you would obviously need to hide the power station by putting it behind a mountain, so as not to offend local sensibilities; but in China it is a matter of pride to have a local power station, a sign of progress and modernity, so you would obviously want to make a feature of it. The only other power station that I can think of that is equally out of place is the one in Switzerland, at the end of Lake Geneva, which sits high up on a mountainside and blights one of the world's most beautiful views. It makes an interesting contrast with the Château de Chillon, and perhaps that was the architect's ambition.

The minibus turned off the main road just outside Panxian and climbed a concrete switchback road to a little village where Lily's father likes to walk. He led us up a track between the smallholdings that scattered the hillside and after a few hundred metres we arrived at a pear orchard. Lily's family love pears and her father knew of a place where we could take the girls to pick them; he had brought a bundle of plastic bags and the girls immediately set to with gusto, plucking the fruit and passing it to us to bag up. For some reason, the pears high up in the trees were much more desirable and the girls shimmied up as far as they could go. The trees were taller than the ones you typically see in England or the US: those trees are bred to be short because the pears are then easier to harvest, whereas traditional pear trees are actually much taller. The prime pear was christened Paul by the children: he was probably the fattest pear that I have ever seen, and easily fed all of us when he was finally sliced up. We soon had more pears than we could possibly eat: it was a good job that a large meal was planned for the evening, with the extended family invited, so that none of them would go to waste. Trying to get the children to stop picking was rather like trying to charm the birds from the trees, but we eventually managed it by pointing out that the sky had gone very dark and rain was certainly on the way (typical mountain weather—very changeable!). We scooted back to the minibus and headed back down into the valley and on to the town.

Panxian is a bustling old town in a mountain valley and we honked our way through the crowds on (what turned out to be) market day. We hopped out the minibus and Lily's father led us through the narrow backstreets—too narrow for a vehicle—to an ancient section of the city wall, dating from Ming dynasty, from which we had a wonderful view over the city centre ravelled below us. Most city centres no longer look like this in China because they have been bulldozed and reconstructed with wide boulevards and modern apartment blocks, or they are entirely new like Liupanshui. A few of them have become sanitized tourist attractions, like Lijiang. We skipped back down to the main thoroughfare and dodged the traffic as we squeezed through the old city gate—a narrow stone structure, such as you would find in many European cities. The market was in full swing and Lily's father bought some biscuits from one of the stalls on the way past. Our driver was waiting in the town square, which had a nice stone bridge across the river, and we boarded the bus just as it started raining. Then we wove our way out of town through the crowds and crazy traffic on the constricted carriageway.

Our next stopover was Lily's original family home, just outside Panxian, where they lived until they moved to a new apartment in Liupanshui two years ago. It was a very simple dwelling: the water came from a well in the garden and there was no heating except for the stove (the big brick type that they have been using in China since ancient times, and which we had seen in operation in my friend Yang Yang's house). The floor was earthen and the walls were papered with old newspapers to increase the insulation; the windows had shutters but no glass. Of course, the climate in Guizhou is temperate—it rarely snows and never gets really hot—so neither heating nor air conditioning has been a great priority for the local populace. The family shrine was on the back wall, opposite the front door, and everyone paid their respects in the traditional way as we entered. Lily's father still goes by the house from time to time but the garden was impressively overgrown because the region is very verdant.

We bundled back into the bus and happily butchered the biscuits on the way back to Liupanshui. We were expected at Lily's parents' new apartment for dinner with the extended family, where we would meet numerous brothers and sisters and nephews and nieces. This was a big show of respect to us—about which I felt rather guilty, as usual, as if I had been masquerading as someone far more important than I really am. Their new apartment is very nice inside—big windows (almost an entire wall) looking out over the city from the seventh floor, hardwood floors, all mod cons. You can see why the Chinese are leaving the countryside in droves to move into modern dwellings. There are several risks in so doing, though. One is the problem of insecure property rights. Land law is not clearly laid out in China, so it is not clear who has the right to do (or demand) something. Just as a simple example, Lily's family were happy because when we arrived the lift was working. Apparently, it has had an intermittent fault and is sometimes out of operation for weeks on end (or longer). Generally, owners of individual apartments in the US or UK would also be shareholders in the management company of the apartment building; this management company would then usually hold a reserve—financed by a levy on all the apartment owners, made by common agreement—and then they would democratically determine how the money would be spent to keep up the building. Hence they would typically pay out of the reserve to get the lift fixed, for example. But the ownership of the apartment building in Liupanshui was simply undefined and it was unclear whose responsibility it was to get the lift fixed and how it should be financed. Imagine this situation being replicated all over China (given the millions of new apartment buildings): as things start to go wrong with the buildings as they age, you can imagine that they will fall to rack and ruin rather than be repaired.

A second problem is the value of housing in China, which has fallen sharply (maybe 40 per cent) in the last couple of years. Chinese homeowners just have to grin and bear it, holding onto their property and continuing to make their mortgage payments even though they may be underwater on their investment (i.e. the outstanding mortgage is worth more than the market value of the property). Why? Well, many of them are just happy to have a (new, swanky) roof over their heads. But also the penalties for default are draconian. You basically have two types of system in the world. In the US, it is relatively easy to declare personal bankruptcy, which means that borrowers can effectively hand the house keys back to the lender and walk away while having their outstanding debt (i.e. the part of the mortgage that is not covered by the resale value of the house) cancelled. By contrast, a borrower in the UK would still be liable for the outstanding debt. China is like the UK—but with big bells and whistles. First, defaulters are put on a blacklist by their mortgage lender, so that no financial institution will do business with them. Second, their identity card is frozen. This means that they cannot do anything that requires their identity card—such as buy a train or airline ticket. In fact, borrowers who work for State Owned Enterprises (which is a high percentage of homeowners) get their loans through the pension fund of the enterprise. This must make it difficult to default, since they can presumably garnish your wages to make sure that the repayments are made and they can certainly make your life very unpleasant in various ways if you fail to comply. Third, the borrower's children are barred from school—so they not only become homeless but are also deprived of their education. Fourth, restrictions are placed on the sale of the borrower's parents' house—so, basically, your entire family is cursed. Not allowing the borrower to default in any way is good for the bank's balance sheet (something that is desperately needed because Chinese banks are notorious for the volume of non-performing loans that they are carrying on their balance sheets, for which they are periodically bailed out by the central government).

The downside of this strategy is that that property market stops working in a downturn. Why? Well, when the value of the mortgage exceeds the value of the house, then the homeowner cannot afford to sell (he will end up owing the bank money that he typically does not have in reserve). So instead he must wait until house prices rise again and the market value of the house exceeds the value of the mortgage. If the market has fallen a lot—and if there is not much economic growth—then this may take a decade because the real value of the loan is eroded only at the rate of inflation. The UK had this problem in the 1990s. In the meantime, the homeowner cannot move—so he cannot go to find work in another town, for example, and the labour market does not function properly. Also, while homeowners cannot afford to sell houses at the market price (they are determined to hold out for a higher price that will enable them to pay back their mortgage), purchasers know that houses are overvalued and refuse to buy (they are determined to wait for the price to drop). So the property market ceases to function (i.e. there are simply no trades). This depresses activity in the whole housing sector and associated sectors (household appliances, furnishing and so on). In fact, Lily's parents were still happy that they had moved to the new city—despite the fall in prices—because it gave their sons the opportunity to move to a new and better middle school, thus boosting their chances of getting into university. So their mortgage was not purely an investment in housing but also in education. Still, this is not a happy moment for the housing market in China and bodes ill for the future.

Lily's mother had had the stressful task of preparing a very large family meal in our absence. I am not sure how she coped, given that there were at least 20 people present. Her father and brothers helped with the final arrangements, when we got back, but most of the work must have been done by then. Naturally, there was a fish because this brings good luck at any Chinese feast, and it was served on a porcelain fish platter that we had previously sent Lily's family as a New Year's gift. (Since fish is central to celebratory occasions, I was confident that it would get a lot of use!) But there were also many other dishes, such as a special mushroom dish that is a local delicacy and supposed to be very healthful. These mushroom dishes tend to contain a wide variety of mushrooms—from very large ones (similar to the standard white ones that you get in US or UK supermarkets) to small and rather hard black flake ones (looking like they have been harvested from a rotting log lying on the forest floor). Some of the mushrooms are perfectly good and others are hard to eat (I mean some are physically difficult to chew up and others are simply unappetizing); obviously, one always does one's best to appreciate the food that the host had carefully prepared. There was also a great deal of toasting—as at every important Chinese meal—and I took a few mouthfuls of alcohol to show my solidarity (despite being typically teetotal). In fact, Chinese has a special verb ("quàn jiǔ") that roughly translates as "to pressurize someone into drinking alcohol" because consuming copious quantities is such an integral part of the social milieu of any celebration or business meeting.

There was a notable absence of children (except ours, of course). This was partly due to the one child policy (i.e. there are just not many children in Chinese families) but also due to chance: Lily and her cousins were just at the age of starting a family, so there was a baby in attendance but no one between babyhood and adulthood. I spectacularly failed to make friends with the baby—even though I consider myself a seasoned campaigner in this domain these days—and she dissolved into tears when I held her, much to everyone's amusement. I also endeared myself by admitting that I had been admiring the indoor tree that Lily's father cultivated by the big picture windows. (Lily's father is a keen indoor gardener—more on which later.) It looked a bit like a weeping fig but had the most beautiful little fruits—some still green, others yellow and yet others red. Only after he flipped a switch had I realized that, although the tree was real, the "fruits" were actually decorative light bulbs—which is how the "fruits" managed to be quite so perfect! It was a natural mistake, in the sense that Guizhou is a long way south and you could imagine that it is possible to cultivate some kind of miniature orange tree in a south-facing window, but the locals obviously found my mistake very funny. One or two of Lily's younger relatives spoke some English, which helped the conversation to flow a little more easily, but otherwise Lily had to translate. We were curious about their lives and they were obviously curious about ours: I don't think that many foreigners make it to Luipanshui. It was frustrating not to be able to talk freely to them and find out more about their lives: if only I spoke Mandarin! One benefit of our trip was that it has encouraged Lily's brothers to improve their English. Although they learn English at school, they could not really see the point of it because they could not imagine being able to afford to visit an English-speaking country (and certainly not going to live there). Of course, unmotivated students don't learn very well so their English was extremely basic—even though Lily really encourages their education (especially maths and English) a lot. But now they were suddenly presented with some Anglophones with whom they might be interested to talk and they could finally see the point. Hopefully it will inspire them to master the language better for the future. (In fact, mastering English is not really necessary. Being able to understand, and be understood, is good enough. Any English speaker is used to speaking to other people who speak English very imperfectly and it is no problem. I am told that this is not the case in other languages—such as German—where native speakers assume that you must be an idiot if you don't speak it properly.)

The next day, we had to leave for Guiyang Airport immediately after lunch. So we were scheduled for a morning stroll and then an early lunch before getting in the car. Lily's father is quite interested in kung fu, and turns out to be quite a supple and dynamic little man. (He is a similar age to me and, while I might be able to match him on the dynamism index, I am certainly lagging in the suppleness stakes.) He had arranged for us to meet a friend of his who is a kung fu master, and who does tai chi every morning in the park. The new city was carefully designed with an enormous public park on its edge, centred on a very large lake. The lake is encircled by a broad, paved path—almost a boulevard—so that the locals can make the most of its tranquil setting. The far side of the lake is backed by a steep, green hillside; this is considered the most desirable area of town—obviously, it is leafy and has nice views out over the park—and it is dotted with expensive villas. Mining in Guizhou (coal, iron, lead and zinc) has been very profitable in recent years, so there are a surprising number of well-heeled residents in such a remote town. We found the shifu waiting for us on a large paved terrace at the end of the lake. He was a short, slight and sun-bronzed man in his late sixties. But he gave us an amazing exhibition of tai chi—starting unarmed and then moving on to swords. This involved several spinning moves (such as suddenly switching from a standing position to sitting cross-legged and vice versa) and doing the splits (something that I shall aspire to achieve when I am 66). After a while, we were invited to muck in and mimic his moves. The children were surprisingly reticent about this—even gym-crazy Catherine—and were only persuaded by the precedent of their parents. It was surprisingly hot work, despite being "sweater weather", and my inflexibility was fully in evidence; it was a relief to finish without injury. After scooting back to the apartment for a quick lunch, we were collected by an SUV and took the two-and-half hour drive to Guiyang Airport, along the new and empty motorway.

I was sorry to have to leave Guizhou after such a short time because there are many amazing things to see there. Even in Panxian, we did not have time to visit the Panxian Dadong ("Big Cave") that was discovered in 1990: it contains human remains dating back 300,000 years and the remains of megafauna (such as stegadons and rhinoceroses) from the Pleistocene—all 1600 m above sea level, which is very surprising. Since Guizhou is largely karst (like Guilin), there is also an underground river, on which you can take a boat trip, and the world's largest cavern. There are several important minorities—the Miao and the Dong—that have remarkable architecture, dress and customs; and there are beautiful rice terraces scattered across the mountains. We could easily have spent another week or more in Guizhou.

We returned from Guiyang on Monday evening and were due to depart Beijing on Wednesday morning, leaving only Tuesday to pack the rest of our stuff and empty the apartment (working on the basis that it should be left in the same state that we had found it, with only large items of furniture *in situ*). I had always planned to give away as much stuff as possible. For example, we had a high tech air monitor and four purifiers (which cost us about $150 each) which I was very happy to leave to someone who needed them—which, let's face it, is basically anyone living in Beijing in the winter. A few calls to friends and acquaintances soon left us with only our personal possessions to pack (which was a mere dozen suitcases—ahem) and we somehow managed to stuff in everything that we had accumulated in seven months of weird and wonderful adventures.

All right, well I will soon be seeing you in person—no more need for letters!

Looking forward to it,

Liam.

Letter 17

The Art of the Steal
3 August 2016

Dear Edmund,

Disclaimer: the title of this letter has absolutely nothing to do with Donald Trump's book, *The Art of the Deal*. In fact, any resemblance to anyone, living or dead, is entirely coincidental. Great—now that we have got that sorted, let's talk money.

You should bargain for almost everything in China. When we first arrived in January, we discovered that we had accidentally left the children's ski salopettes in Boston—which was worse than unfortunate, since our first stopover was the Harbin Ice Festival. The average daily high in Harbin is −13°C in January, and the average nighttime low is −24°C (which is key because you visit the Ice Festival at night, when it is beautifully lit). So it was imperative that we buy some replacement salopettes, if we wanted our offspring to survive. You would think that this would be easy in Harbin—surely every man, woman and child must live and die in them? They should be available in every shop selling outdoor clothes. Sadly, not a bit of it. Lucy ventured out of the hotel—which was fairly centrally located—and reconnoitred the nearby clothing stores. There were no salopettes at all to be found. The best that she could find was some quilted (duvet-type) trousers in a Chinese department store called Parkson. Trousers are not as warm as salopettes because the hot air can escape more easily, and the quality wasn't good, but needs must when the devil drives and so Lucy bought them; they were about the same price as you would pay in the US, which therefore seemed quite expensive. Lily's first question was: "Did you bargain for them?" Er, no. It was a department store, with price tickets on all the items. But that doesn't mean that you are not required to bargain, apparently. Lucy had commented on the fact that she found it difficult to find someone to pay in Parkson (there was no clear cluster of cash registers, as you typically see in a Western store). In fact, Parkson is not so much a "department store" as an "apartment store": it is so compartmentalized that each department is almost an autonomous entity under the Parkson roof. So you have to negotiate the price with the vendor in that particular department and pay them directly. This would explain why everything seemed expensive: the market price was probably only about half what we had paid. We'll put that one down to experience.

We were living a steep learning curve when it came to bargaining in China. The next evening, we called a cab to take us to the Ice Festival. As we headed off from the hotel, the driver said that he could take us to his friend to get cheap entry tickets to the festival. We assured him that it was not necessary—we intended to buy full price tickets on the door and wanted to go straight there. He said that he was taking us straight there, via his friend's place to buy tickets. We said that we did not want to go to his friend's place, only to the festival. He said that if we would not go via his friend's place, then he would not take us. So I said (via Lily) OK—then just drop us here because we are not going to see your friend. Playing hardball in Harbin is a risky strategy: he did exactly as he was bid and stopped the car in the middle of a busy dual carriageway, in the dark, where we stepped out into −20°C with three small children to find our own way back to town. In fact, we were still fairly near the city centre and I knew our rough location. So we backtracked on foot via a park that also had snow sculptures, and which we had planned to visit on the following night, so we did not waste our evening (in fact, we had a nice time and the children were pretty tired by the end of it). It is very difficult to avoid being gouged by taxi drivers in China unless you are willing to press the nuclear button. But if you press the nuclear button, then you should be aware that it is highly likely to result in Armageddon—so don't do it unless you are ready to take on that responsibility. I should say that taxis in Beijing work pretty well. Like most Western cities, you can hail a cab on the street—which is usually not too difficult—and the driver takes you where you want to go; the drivers use the metre and you get charged a fair price. But outside Beijing it is every man for himself. The solution to our problem was to hire a car and driver for a whole day, through the app on the phone: he was then happy to take us wherever we wanted, whenever we wanted. Hence, we were able to complete our Ice Festival mission the following night.

Anyway, back to bargaining. I have come to realize that Chinese people have a fundamentally different understanding of bargaining to westerners. (When I say "Westerners" here, I am particularly thinking of Anglo-Saxons and northern Europeans; there some cultural contrasts with southern Europeans to which I shall return at length later.) Although the process of bargaining is superficially the same—and so you think you know what is going on when you bargain with someone in China—it is actually a very different process and you are probably in for a shock a short distance down the line. Start with the simplest case. You want to buy something at a market stall. The stallholder says that the price is 100 RMB; you offer 50 RMB; there is a counteroffer of 75 RMB; and so it continues until you settle on a price, say 65 RMB. You pay the money, you take the object and you walk away. No problem. This is what we understand by "bargaining" in the West. Chinese people also understand this to be "bargaining". But few transactions are that trivial, and it is here that cultural norms diverge sharply and create inconsistent expectations on the part of the parties to the agreement.

When you bargain over many things, the precise detail of the object or transaction is not specified. For example, when you book a hotel room, I bet you take it for granted that they will provide towels. We stayed in a resort hotel in Baoting in central Hainan—the Hawaii of China, a tourist paradise. We booked a big family room that we could share with the three girls but they provided the five of us with only two towels and four pillows. Obviously, you would expect to be issued with five pillows and at least five towels. (In fact, I would expect any decent hotel to issue us with ten towels because there was a pool—it was aspiring to be a swanky resort hotel, remember—and you typically want one towel for the chlorinated pool and another one for the shower.) When we asked for eight more towels, they happily obliged—and then charged us 10 RMB each! This didn't break the bank, but it did not leave a very good impression of the hotel, either. And it demonstrates a Golden Rule of doing business in China: you will frequently get less than you bargained for (quite literally). Now, the hotel did nothing explicitly wrong: when I booked online, there was no undertaking to provide one towel per person (and certainly not two towels per person). I just took it for granted, in the same way that I took it for granted that there would be a door in the doorframe and glass in the windows and water in the bathroom taps. Happily, those other conditions were met, so I suppose that I really had very little to complain about. But it leaves a bad taste because I feel that they deliberately withheld something that would normally be provided (without comment) and which they knew I would be forced to buy, since my children were desperate to swim in the pool.

But the lesson is this: striking a bargain with someone in China is only the beginning of the process, not the end. An Anglo-Saxon agrees a price on the basis that he will fulfil the contract to the best of his ability *under normal conditions*—where that means providing a typical quality in a typical timescale, for example. Generally, he will not agree a bargain at a painfully low price with the expectation and *intention* of then screwing some extra money out of the deal *ex post*—by either diluting the quality or requiring some kind of additional payment to complete delivery. Of course, it does happen in the West. I have agreed to lease a house—for a given rent and term and so on—and then suddenly been landed with hundreds of pounds of extra "contract fees" and "arrangement fees" by the letting agent at the time of signing (i.e. the week before my family was due to move in, when it would have been impossible to find alternative accommodation at such short notice). Again, the agent did not state that there would be no such fees and I did not ask because it never occurred to me that the agent had not disclosed all the costs upfront. But if someone does this in the West, then we consider them to be a schmuck. Let's face it, letting agent is spelt S-C-H-M-U-C-K, so their behaviour is not as shocking as it ought to be.

But this kind of behaviour is completely normal in China. In reality, it is impossible (or too costly) to specify every detail of how an agreement will be implemented. Your Chinese bargaining partner may then default if he feels that he can get away with it; this usually entails a partial default, on the basis that it will not then be worth your while to complain. Examples of this include our experience with the driver who took us to Inner Mongolia but refused to take us all the way home—dumping us instead on the outskirts of Beijing; and the boatman in Bing Ling Si who increased the price and took us only part way down the lake. Or your interlocutor may implement the bargain in a way that he knows will destroy value for you (either literally, or through imposing extra costs on you) in order that you will agree to pay more than specified in the original agreement (i.e. you will be forced to renegotiate).

An example of deliberately poor implementation comes from our trip in Wuyishan (where they produce Da Hong Pao tea) when we rafted down the river (as I recounted in an earlier letter). There are five seats on each raft, so we travelled together on one raft, while Lily made up a fivesome on another raft. As we got near the front of the line to load up, Lily pushed over to us and told us that we must be sure to tip the boatmen before we started the trip; otherwise they don't give you any narration, or even point out the sights that you pass on the river (such as the location of the ancient tombs in the cliff face, and the rock carvings); instead, they just go down as fast as possible, keeping to the mainstream in the middle of the river. The going rate for a tip was 20 RMB per person (i.e. $15 for the five of us), on top of 120 RMB for the ticket. Again, this didn't break the bank. But I have never been told in any other country that the guides will "work to rule" and guide you round in silence unless you pay them extra upfront (and, to cap it all, you are told this only after you have bought the entry ticket). Some of my previous letters provide examples of essential extra inputs that you find you have to buy—without warning—after you think you have made a bargain. In Gaochang (on our Journey to the West), we found that we had to pay extra to take the electric bus around the ruined site; this was also true in the Shilin Stone Forest Park near Kunming. In Shilin, in particular, the park entrance was so far from the rocks that walking was not really an option; in Shilin, you also had to pay extra to visit the geology museum. By contrast, I recently went to Stonehenge, for the first time in a decade. Each time I go, the visitor centre seems to have been wrested progressively further from the henge (nominally to preserve the location); it is now sufficiently far that there is an electric bus to take you from the visitor centre to the henge. The Chinese tourists (of which there were many) must have been pleasantly surprised that both the bus and museum entry are included in the entry ticket to the park.

It would be invidious to advance extra examples here, or to revisit previous vignettes (the tour agency in Zhongwei and so on). A more interesting issue is, why? Why do we see this kind of openly opportunistic behaviour so commonly in China? I think that one key component is that it is more than socially acceptable—indeed, it is actually admired. I am strongly reminded of the Italian concept of *furbo*. Now, *furbo* might be translated as astute, clever, crafty, cunning, sly, smart, sharp and probably numerous other words. The striking thing is that some of these words have clearly positive connotations in English (astute, smart), others are notably negative (crafty, sly) and yet others could be either (cunning, sharp), depending on the context. Lots of things in Italy can be *furbo*—everything from cutting to the front of the queue, to tax evasion, to avoiding prosecution for a major crime (a speciality of the former Prime Minister Berlusconi). In fact, I teach my students about corruption—that is, how to avoid it, rather than how to get away with it—as part of their "ethics in business" component, and I take Berlusconi as an interesting example. You should know that America imposes the US Foreign Corrupt Practices Act (FCPA) on everyone in the world—including you. If anything that the Americans deem to be corrupt impacts American individuals or firms, then US courts claim jurisdiction; "impacting" American individuals or firms includes making corrupt transactions anywhere in the world using the US dollar, or using an internet connection that goes via the US, or anything affecting the price or market access conditions for a US firm. (So if a US firm complains to the Department of Justice that it never got an export contract to Mars because a company on Venus paid a bribe to the Martians, then the US claims the right to fine the Venutian firm and imprison its staff, even though the Venutians may not know that the US even exists. Venutians, beware!) So if you are in business, then you had better understand the FCPA.

There is an important distinction in the FCPA between paying money for things that are "rightfully yours" and paying money in order to get things that are not necessarily "rightfully yours". Suppose that all your business accounts are in order and it is the duty of the local government official to sign off on them—but he refuses to do so without some kind of "accommodation" to cover his administrative expenses (ink for his pen and so on). In English, this could be called "blackmail". Then it is OK under the FCPA to pay him. But if you cannot be bothered to do your business accounts and you pay the local government official to sign off on them anyway, then this is not OK—this is corruption. I always refer to this as the "Berlusconi Defence". The Italian prosecutors gathered overwhelming evidence that Berlusconi authorized bribes to be paid to gain advantages for his Fininvest media empire. Whereupon, Berlusconi said: "No! No! No! You don't understand. I was not being corrupt—I was being blackmailed! I am a victim! Help!" And he got away with it—because Berlusconi is *furbo*. In fact, he is turbo *furbo*. He is Ferrari *furbo*. At this point, I cannot admit to a sneaking admiration for Berlusconi—because that would not be British. Or, indeed, American or German or Scandinavian. When people cleverly break or circumvent the rules in those societies, it is definitely not something to brag about or to be admired—we must treat those people with contempt, and denounce them publicly as sociopaths. Anyone who fails to do so will himself be treated with contempt and denounced as a sociopath.

I remember talking to an eminent political science professor at a cocktail party in Oxford; he was New Left (when that was still socially acceptable and seen as progressive, before Blair blew it up). We were debating the burden of government regulation on the economy and he said: "Well, does your father pay taxes?" To which I answered automatically: "Oh yes, whenever he can't avoid it." (My father is a small businessman and not exactly queuing up to hand over his hard-earned cash.) A stunned and embarrassed silence descended on the Senior Common Room—as if I had just dropped my trousers and people were pretending not to notice by politely finding somewhere else to look. I was rescued by a fellow student—a rustic lad, from out in the provinces, whose father was also a small businessman—who recommended that: "Your father should talk to mine!" Of course, tax *avoidance* is perfectly legal, and is in fact a fiduciary duty of management to shareholders. But tax *evasion* is illegal and punishable by imprisonment. Remember that avoidance begins with A—as in apple. But evasion begins with E—as in enron.

So what I find striking is that in China, as in Italy, it is socially acceptable to be *furbo* and—even more—it is OK to admit to admiring people who are *furbo*. It does not automatically make you a schmuck (in that society). Quite the contrary, many people in those societies would consider you a schmuck if you were NOT *furbo*. You would be an idiot not to take advantage of someone who was foolish enough to put themselves in a situation in which you could take advantage of them. People would lose respect for you. Again, the interesting question is, Why? And again I see some striking similarities between Italy and China. Italy is said to have "a thousand laws but no rules". In order to make progress, you need to be able to work around those laws (where "working around a law" does not necessarily imply breaking it). China also seems to have a lot of regulations (I avoid the word "law" here because I am never entirely clear what is laid down in law in China and what is simply a protocol imposed by a bureaucrat). So, again, in order to make progress you need to able to work around those regulations. You need to be *furbo*. But what elevates this from something requisite to something admirable? In the Italian case, there is a lot of resentment towards people in positions of power who seem to benefit personally from the imposition of these laws (such as politicians who somehow afford luxury apartments in central Rome on the basis of small salaries as Members of Parliament—best exemplified by Prime Minister Craxi, who fled to Tunisia to avoid imprisonment, and the other figures convicted during the "Clean Hands" campaign of the early 1990s). If the rules are being used to extract income from people who produce things—and feather the nests of politicians who produce nothing—then you can understand that people would come to view it as admirable (not immoral) to circumvent those rules. The next logical step is that people who are not *furbo* are dullards or holier-than-thou types who deserve to be ripped off.

Interestingly, in the Anglo-Saxon world it is admirable for a businessman to be "sharp" but it is reprehensible for him to engage in "sharp practices". This is a subtlety of the English language that is difficult to explain to a non-native speaker! But I think that it gets to the heart of the problem. In a situation where roadblocks and red tape are being thrown in your path, you need to be "sharp" to get around them and make progress: this is admirable (a David versus Goliath struggle between the businessman and the government, or perhaps between the businessman and

God—who casts misfortune upon us). But using that sharpness to get one over on other people (i.e. using "sharp practices" to take advantage of people who are less informed or less intelligent) is reprehensible. I believe that British people—and northern Europeans more generally—feel this distinction within themselves and many of them try to abide by it. But my impression is that this distinction is either not made or considered less important in Italy and in China. Hence, if you can find a way to reset the bargain *ex post*, then you are simply being *furbo*, which is an admirable quality. (I have heard that in Italy it is even considered *furbo* to systematically short-change customers, especially tourists, as a way of pocketing some extra cash; if the customer notices, then you can always smile and claim that it was an honest mistake. I have never experienced this in China. This is a level of low cunning that is really beneath contempt.) It is very difficult to translate these ideas—both because the vocabulary may not be precise and because the concepts themselves do not map exactly from one culture to another—but an acceptable attempt might be "xiaocongming" (小聪明). This translates directly as "little smart", or figuratively as "clever-clever"—which is certainly a term that people use in my hometown in England and which can have positive or negative connotations, depending on the context.

Of course, once you realize this, you are constantly trying to anticipate it in all your dealings. So you might do things such as take a taxi from the rank—even if it involves queuing and paying a higher nominal price—rather than taking a black cab. Or you might stay in an expensive Western-owned hotel (the Hilton, or whatever) rather than a Chinese chain hotel. But there is often very little that you can do to insure yourself *ex ante*. If the cabbie kidnaps you, then it may be that your only effective response is to get out and walk, which can be very costly. In most situations—taxis, hotels, food delivery—you can complain but this is very difficult unless you are totally fluent in Chinese. One of the things that I felt most guilty about in our time in China was the number of occasions on which I had to ask Lily to complain on our behalf. She is very good at complaining—I think that it is an essential life skill that you learn in China—and she often resolved the problem (sometimes perfectly, sometimes imperfectly). But I am sure that it was not the way she wanted to spend her time travelling around China.

The word on the street is that China needs to "rebalance" its economy, relying less on investment and more on consumption. At least, this is what economists and policy wonks (did I spell that right?) keep repeating like a mantra. Chinese consumption is around 45 per cent of GDP (i.e. out of every 100 RMB of national expenditure, 45 RMB is spent on the consumption goods and services, such as computers and cuisine). For comparison, consumption in Western economies is 55–70 per cent of GDP, depending on whether you are France or the US. I must confess that I am not entirely convinced by this rebalancing act because I do not have the impression that China is overloaded with infrastructure. Greater capacity on city roads and intercity rail would be great; more Metro capacity; fewer flight delays…. But suppose that you were really concerned about increasing consumption: how would you do it? Major items of consumption expenditure in most economies include housing (with its associated consumer durables, such as TVs and washing machines), automobiles and services (such as travel). Well, Chinese people would like to increase their consumption of housing but it runs contrary to government regulations and policies. For example, migrants to cities are commonly unable to bring their families because they do not have a *hukou* (a kind of residence card that permits access to local education and healthcare, which I will explain elsewhere in more detail). So, instead of buying an apartment for the family and furnishing it—which would crank up consumption—the migrant bunks in a barracks and the family continues to live in a ramshackle residence in the countryside, vaguely hoping that one day the rules will change and people will be permitted to move to the cities freely. And Chinese people would clearly like to increase their consumption of cars—which is exactly why the number of license plates available in Beijing must be strictly limited and allocated by lottery, to prevent the roads being swamped with vehicles that would bring the city to a standstill.

This brings us to the consumption of travel and its concomitant components (shelter, sustenance, shows, souvenirs…). Tourism is a major industry in Europe, worth billions of dollars per year, accounting for around 9 per cent of employment and 6 per cent of GDP. And it could be in China, too: they have an amazing variation in their natural environment, plus 7000 years of observable human history (going back to ancient pots and so on that seemingly crop up in any provincial museum). But travelling in China is work, not pleasure. We travelled to many places with Lily—all of them outstanding sites of scientific or cultural interest—and she had never been to any of them before. I expressed surprise that she had toured in China so sparingly, even as a student. She replied that she didn't like travelling in China: it was too much trouble. And it's true. You really have to harbour a burning ambition to go, to find something that can be seen or experienced nowhere else. This has a lot to do with the constant conflict over the conditions for everything—the price, the time, the quality. Throughout the day, anything can be renegotiated at any time (generally to your detriment, obviously). It is hard to see how domestic tourism will take off in China under these conditions: it will always be less stressful to go abroad. And it is not easy to see how this problem can be fixed because it is such an ingrained ethos.

One way in which the power imbalance between service providers and customers is rectified in the West is through internet reviews. If a company—such as a tour agent—defaults on their obligations, then you can post a negative review and this will hurt their business. Of course, they have this also in China, although it is not much use as a discipline device unless you can read and write Chinese! It seems to work well for restaurants: there are hundreds of reviews for every restaurant and it seems straightforward to find good ones. However, I have also seen it used against consumers. Later on our Hainan trip we were in Yalong Bay, a tropical beach resort on the south coast much favoured by Russians and rich Chinese. Lily called a car on the app to take us to the Li and Miao Village (a fascinating tourist destination that I have described elsewhere). We got into the car and departed the hotel, whereupon the driver told us that he was not interested in taking us to the Li and Miao Village but would be happy to be hired the whole day. Since we were planning on spending the whole day in the village, this obviously made no sense for us and we declined. He then said that he was not going to take us unless we hired him for the whole day. So I said (via Lily)—OK, then we'll get out here. So he stopped the car and we got out, about a kilometre from the hotel. He then demanded that Lily pay him (electronically) for the pick-up and the distance that he had taken us (totalling about 20 RMB)—which was obviously outrageous, since he was refusing to complete the agreed journey and had dropped us at some random location. Lily told him that she wouldn't pay. But as well as passengers posting reviews of the drivers on the app, the drivers can post reviews of the passengers. So the driver said that if she didn't pay, then he would post a review stating that she had not paid for her journey—at which point she would be blacklisted by the app and we would be unable to contact any more drivers. Obviously, Lily can object to this and take it up with the app provider, and she may eventually get some satisfaction. But by the time you have done all that, the rest of your holiday is ruined because you have had no transport for a week. You just can't curb a *furbo*: no matter what mechanism you dream up, they will come up a way of corrupting it. In this case, they are not just circumventing the system but actually using it as a weapon against you—such a bunch of cunning stunts (if you will forgive the Spoonerism).

Given the tendency to renegotiate bargains in China, I wonder how Western businesses cope. I can see that selling consumer goods would be relatively straightforward: if you want a Mercedes, then you put the money on the counter and drive away the car. This is just back to basic transactions at the market stall (albeit for larger sums of money). But if you are having goods manufactured in China for export, then quality control and delivery must be a nightmare. Margins for foreign firms must be very high—so that there is room to renegotiate and still turn a profit, and so as to compensate for the risk. I was telling a friend about some of our adventures in China and remarked that you couldn't call it a holiday—more of an educational experience. He replied that one of his favourite T-shirts bore the legend: "Experience is what you get when you didn't get what you wanted". I frequently find myself gaining experience, following my business transactions in China. It is lucky that my livelihood does not depend on them!

Here endeth today's lesson. And, although it started out like Trump, I certainly don't want it to end like Trump—I couldn't possibly afford the litigation.

Very best wishes,

Liam.

Letter 18

Hukou's There?
8 August 2016

Dear Tim,

Another weekend, another letter from Liam! Thanks for entertaining my wife and children, by the way. I used the time to finish this report....

The hukou (approximately pronounced "who-co") is the most important thing that a Chinese person possesses. It can be the difference between life and death. It is a kind of hereditary residence permit. It does not specify that you have to live in a certain place (although it was used that way until the 1960s). But it specifies that you can access social services—notably health and education—only in a certain place. In that sense, you are tied to a certain place. It is possible to change the registration location of your hukou, but it is rare to manage to do so: you have to get a job as a university professor, or high Party official, or senior management in a big company in Beijing or Shanghai. So you are basically tied to the place in which you were born. Moreover, your parents were permitted to register your birth only in the place in which their hukou was registered: in that sense, you inherit the hukou of your parents.

This is very similar to the feudal system that characterized mediaeval Europe. Until the collapse of the feudal system, around the late 1400s, peasants held land from their local lord. These peasants were *not* slaves:

they were *not* owned, like a piece of property, and they were free to make contracts (e.g. they could buy and sell animals and plots of land). These peasants were called serfs. And, under the law, they had both rights and obligations. In order to hold land from their local lord, they were obliged to render various services to the lord—in particular, working on his land for a certain number of days per year. If they fulfilled their obligations, then the serfs had the right to cultivate the land that they held from the lord and keep the produce; and they had the right to pass the land to their heirs (who could then continue to farm it, as long as they continued to fulfil the obligations to the lord). These serfs were also obliged to attend the local church on Sundays and Saints' days (failure to attend—recusancy—was a serious offense and serfs could be subject to severe punishments). In return, the serfs might receive care from the church—such as alms if they fell into poverty or medical treatment if they fell sick. It was generally illegal for a serf to leave his land (although the legality varied across Europe and changed over time). But if a serf did leave the land, then he both threw off his obligations (he no longer had to work for the lord) and he forfeited his benefits (his right to access land and social services, such as alms).

And so it is in China today. If your hukou is registered to a village in the countryside, then you have the right to cultivate the land that is owned collectively by that village. In fact, until recently the land *had* to be cultivated owing to the "household responsibility system": each village had to produce a quota of food for the Government, being allowed to keep any surplus over the quota. (The Government quota was abolished in 2005, but many places still require a contribution to the "collective" for the right to farm land; more on this later.) You also have the right to education and healthcare provided in that village. But if you leave that village—say, you migrate to the Shenzhen Development Zone to earn money assembling electronic gadgets in a factory—then you throw off your obligation to cultivate land (you do not labour to help fulfil your village quota or collective contribution) but you are also unable to exercise your right to education or healthcare (since you hold this right only in your home village, not in your new place of residence).

You can see immediately that the hukou system creates many problems. What happens when migrant workers get sick, or have accidents?

Either they have to pay for private medical treatment in their new place of residence, or return to the village where their hukou is registered (where there is anyway little in the way of medical facilities available, in truth). Anyone who is seriously injured—such as being maimed in an industrial accident—has to return to their hometown because they cannot afford medical care in the city and there will be no one to look after them there. What happens to the children of migrants? After all, they have no right to education in their new place of residence. Most migrant workers leave their children back in their village—either with the mother or, if the mother is also a migrant worker, then with the grandparents. Many men see their families for only two weeks per year, at Chinese New Year. This is why the Chinese New Year holiday is the greatest human migration on earth. Hundreds of millions of people—the majority of them men—travel home for their one chance in the year to see their families. But there are also tens of millions of Chinese children who don't know their parents—literally—because they have been raised entirely by their grandparents after both parents migrated to find work. Better off migrant workers take their children with them to the cities and pay for them to attend private schools, since they have no right to access state schools. So—in the reverse of what we see in the West—it tends to be less well-off families who send their children to private school in China, rather than the richest.

Of course, most Chinese—especially those doing migrant jobs—have to work six or seven days per week, often 12 hours per day. So it would not be practical for them to take their children with them because they would not have time to look after them. We saw this even in the more privileged circles in which we lived in Beijing: many of the children's classmates lived in households containing a child, parents and grandparents; the grandparents did a large proportion of the childcare because the parents spent long hours at work (and had many fewer days off work than the children had off school). In fact, Chinese migrants mostly work the longest possible hours. When they sign an employment contract, firms typically have to promise a *minimum* number of hours per week (where that minimum may be something like 72!) in order to recruit enough workers. The migrants have left their families behind, often live in barracks, and have nothing better to do with their time (especially if they are working at a chemical factory or a mine that is out in the sticks)—so they just want to make the most money possible in the months or years that they spend with their employer. Hence they demand minimum hours contracts. The contrast with Europe is stark: where Western workers are demanding a 35-hour maximum, the Chinese workers are demanding a 72-hour minimum.

If China were a very equal society, then the hukou system would not matter. I mean, if wages were the same in the countryside and the cities, then hundreds of millions of people would not want to migrate and the problem of registration would be rather minor. And if schools and medical care were equally good everywhere, then people's life chances would be unaffected by their place of birth. But, of course, China has Communism: so, in the same way that you have to pay to use public parks (whereas the self-seeking capitalist system provides public parks for free for everyone), so the distribution of education and healthcare is extremely unequal between cities and countryside. People are well aware of these inequities and naturally try to circumvent them. A friend of mine was born in a town and he has a hukou from that town. His father was born in a village outside the town, so this is where the father's hukou was registered. But the father knew that health and education services were superior in the city, so he sought to secure his son a city hukou. Again, it is a modern mirror of medieval Europe: if you wanted to become a "burgher" or "freeman" of a town 500 years ago, then you had to have money so that they would allow you to set up shop inside the city walls and join the social set. In the same way, my friend's father borrowed money from his family, bought a shop in the town and set up a small business. In the smaller provincial towns, this could be enough to get you a town hukou in the 1990s (especially if you had friends in the Party—such as people with whom you had gone to school who had subsequently risen through the ranks). When his son was born, the father was therefore able to register him in the town and get him a town hukou. (Obviously, this tactic is practically impossible in a city like Shanghai or Shenzhen, where there are millions of migrants.) The son then went to live with his mother in the village, while the father sold the business and moved elsewhere for work. Later, the mother also moved for work and, *at aged six*, the son was sent to a boarding school for his education. Why was this feasible and desirable? I believe that the school fees were paid by the father's employer because he was moving frequently for work, so this made the boarding school strategy feasible. At the same time, the grandparents could not speak Mandarin and having them raise the child would therefore put the child at a significant disadvantage—leaving aside the questionable quality of the village primary school—so this made the boarding school strategy desirable.

When the time came to move to middle school, the son was able to attend middle school in the town—which was the best in the area—because he had a hukou for that town. Otherwise, he would have had to attend middle school out in the village, which would have put him back on track to be a migrant worker. Since his family was still not living in the town, they got him an apartment near the school and he set up house there—on his own. Obviously, he has been trained in self-sufficiency—emotional, organizational and physical—from the age of six. So he was able to effectively send himself through secondary school and get top grades. Having got excellent scores in the Gaokao, my friend went to a top Beijing business university. Once there, he enrolled to take two degrees simultaneously—one in business and one in Spanish (and I can tell you that his English and his Spanish are both pretty fluent). After graduation, he won a scholarship to study abroad and get a Master's degree and is now in the management cadre of a State Owned Enterprise (SOE)—one of the huge, Government—owned entities that form the cornerstones of the Chinese economy. He will now be able to get a Beijing hukou—which his children will inherit, and so circumvent the barriers that my friend and his parents faced. This is Chinese-style social mobility.

I ask myself at this point how many Western children could be relied upon to do this? I suspect that the answer is approximately zero. While the Chinese system is harsh—and I would not necessarily want such a harsh system imposed on my own children—it does force the children grow up fast and focus on how they are going to make a living in the world, which I regard as a benefit. In that sense, Chinese students score highly not only on mathematics and science (as all the international comparisons show) but also on organization and work ethic. If the Chinese are indeed going to "eat our lunch" (in an economic sense) in the next generation, then this is why: not only are many of them highly skilled, but they are also driven to succeed by the sacrifices that they have made throughout their life to get themselves on a competitive footing with their Western peers. European youths have it handed to them on a plate, by comparison, and they don't even realize it (and therefore don't appreciate it). An English friend of mine was telling me how his colleagues complain about the juvenile behaviour of the undergraduates in his university (which is a pretty good one, in fact). As he commented, what else can you expect? British adolescents basically don't interact with adults, and have no responsibilities, so why would you expect them to act in an adult way? They are now kept in school until they are 18 years old (whereas the limit was 16 years for most adolescents only a few years ago). We then send over half of them to university, where they hang out in halls of residence with other juveniles until the age of 21 or 22. Many then stay on to do a Master's degree for another couple of years. So they do not even enter the adult world—experiencing adult levels of work discipline, financial discipline, and social norms—until they are 23 years old. At that point, they start to grow up and some of them manage it by the time they are 30. This is at totally the other extreme to the Chinese model.

Of course, it hasn't always been this way. I am reminded of Frederick Russell Burnham, the great American outdoorsman who taught bush craft to Baden-Powell in South Africa. Burnham's family was living in California in 1872 when his father died and his mother decided to return to Iowa with her three-year-old son. Frederick (who was then 12) decided to stay in California and make his way in the world, first as a mounted messenger and then (at age 14) as a tracker and scout in the Apache Wars. While not everyone enjoyed such a successful and lengthy life as him, it was normal to grow up fast in that era. My father left school at age 15, as was standard in England at that time, and went to work in a coal yard. He assures me that if you upset someone—the foreman or one of the drivers—then you were likely to get a slap: there was no process of reporting to line managers and official warnings. (I should say, of course, that coal yards were not the most genteel working establishments, even by the standards of the 1950s.) You pretty soon conformed to adult norms and learned how to take care of yourself. Is it really necessary for us to wait until people are 30 years old for them to grow up? I rather wonder if we have lost the plot in the West.

The linking of social benefits to the immovable hukou creates a lot of inefficiency and a lot of stress. I have a friend who had her child while living in the US. The child needs a hukou—so that it can get a passport, for example, in order to travel back to China. But where will the child's hukou be registered? Not in the US, obviously. Rather, in the wife's hometown because the hukou is hereditary. Now the wife (and husband) leave the US and get jobs in Beijing. They have sufficiently elevated positions that they can each get a Beijing hukou. But the child cannot. If the parents were divorced, then the child could take the hukou of one of the parents, and they get to choose which one, in order that the child can go and live legally with one of the parents. But if the parents are not divorced, then the child does not have the right to change its hukou registration. So the parents live in Beijing and want their child to live with them and attend the local school. But the child has no right to attend the local school because it does not have a local hukou. They were told that this was not a problem: the child could go and live back in the wife's home village with the grandparents (one of whom had cancer) and attend school there. (The home village was an awfully long way from Beijing, needless to say.) This is the kind of logical response that you get if you talk to someone in authority in China. It is entirely possible for this family to conform to the rules set out by Beijing—by exiling their child to their provinces until the grandparents die—but it is self-evidently inhumane and makes no sense for society, either. (Breaking up a family to move one pawn from this area of the board to that other area seems likely to result in a disaffected and less educated adult in 15 years' time—which is hardly what China needs.) Obviously, my advice was for them to get divorced—they could always remarry after changing the child's hukou, and then they could live together like a proper family. But they were upstanding citizens and refused to resort to such subterfuge.

The wife spent months trying to sort out this problem, going from one government office to the next and growing visibly older in the process. Intensive investigation revealed a resolution to this impasse. They would be sending their offspring to a school linked to a university, rather than a regular government-run school. The school leadership had a little latitude relating to entry requirements, so their child could be enrolled despite the status of the hukou. Apparently, they were not the first parents to face this problem. Another father had recently experienced a similar situation and became sufficiently upset that he went out into a public place and set fire to himself. This is a standard way of protesting in China. There was recently a case in which a disabled man tried to blow himself up in his wheelchair in an airport because he had been crippled in an industrial accident and no one was willing to fulfil their commitment to compensate him or assist with his disability. You cannot fight the Government in China (in fact, you cannot even think about fighting the Government in China because that would be a crime—more on this later). So if local Government officials refuse to listen, then people propel the higher echelons to act by publicly shaming them—usually through self-immolation, to show that they are seriously upset. Such signs of dissatisfaction are deemed dangerous for social stability and the government responds by finding sufficient flexibility to palliate the problem.

The hukou registration system has been an integral part of the "One Child Policy". Just in case you are not up with Chinese Government regulations, I should say that Han Chinese—the ethnic group that constitutes 92 per cent of the population—were prohibited from having more than one child between 1978 and 2016. The law has just been relaxed so that families are now allowed have two children. The one child policy was enforced on the back of the hukou system. Without a hukou, you do not officially exist in China: you cannot claim health or education services, travel documents and so on. So once a parent registered their child for a hukou, they were monitored to ensure that they did not have another child. Enforcement of the one child policy could be brutal, involving forced abortions and compulsory sterilization. It could also lead to economic sanctions, such as losing your job at an SOE. (Jobs at SOEs typically come with housing and health benefits, so you were then effectively thrown out onto the street.) If you were well off, then you could usually extract yourself from this difficulty by paying a fine instead, which then secured a hukou for your second child. Now, suppose that you were poor but you desperately wanted a second child. If your first child were a girl, then she would go off and marry into another family and not stay around to work the land like a son, who would then be able to support you in your old age. (Remember that there is no pension in China, so having a son to support you in old age is highly sought after.) Suppose also that you had not managed to have a backstreet abortion. (It is well known that there are substantially more males than females in the Chinese population—as in the Indian population—which is generally believed to arise because pregnant women abort girls, if they can.) Well, if you were smart, and you really wanted a second child, then you would avoid registering your first child. If you don't want to kill the baby girl, then send her off into the countryside to be raised by a relative and save your hukou for the next child—which will hopefully be a boy. How often does this happen? We cannot know—it would never appear in the official statistics. What is the true population of China? We cannot know—because we do not know how widespread any cheating on birth registrations might be.

A similar problem arises with migration data. When migrants move in Western countries, they have a reason to register themselves in their new location. For example, they may have to get a new driver's licence (when they change state in the US, or country in Europe); but Chinese migrants do not have cars, so this is no use. Or you may have to register for social benefits (child benefit, medical coverage); but Chinese migrants do not get these, so this is no use. You may have to pay taxes, but the vast majority of tax revenue in China comes from indirect taxes (i.e. sales tax), rather than income tax, and you do not have to file an individual return unless you earn more than 120,000 RMB; this is a lot by local standards, and many people work for cash anyway, so this is no use. The hukou—and all associated benefits—are immovable in China, so there are few reasons to report your location and few reliable ways of systematically mapping people's location. How many people live in Beijing? We do not know: some say 20 million people, some say 40 million people. One way that they estimate the urban population is through the number of Beijing subway transport cards in use. But it takes only a second to see the shortcomings of this strategy (people may have several cards on the go at once, some may be used for a while but then get lost, some people—such as poor people—may systematically dodge paying the fare…). If you have a portion of the population living in shipping containers on the outskirts of the city (as I mentioned in a previous missive), then you are going to have trouble correctly counting them all. So we simply do not have reliable data on the size of the Chinese population or the size of Chinese cities.

Now, let me go back to agriculture for a moment. Since China is a Communist state, all farmland is owned collectively; this was imposed by Mao through the 1950s, as individual rights to hold land were eradicated in several steps. (I say "hold" here rather than "own" because land in China had always technically been owned by the Emperor—as in Russia under the Tsars—but people gained the right to use the land and the possibility to trade that right. So the occupants were *de facto* owners of land but *de jure* merely holders of land.) Full collectivization was imposed in 1958 and the agricultural sector became a massive arena for crazy experimentation (based on unscientific agricultural practices that simply did not work) and cruel exploitation (to produce the maximum possible amount of grain to permit the fastest possible rate of industrialization). This "Great Leap Forward" led to the Great Famine of 1959–61, in which 30–40 million people died. Mao was sidelined in 1962 and his policies ended because the it was feared that the army was becoming unreliable as officers heard about the starvation and atrocities being visited on their families in the countryside: the Defence Minister, General Peng Dehuai, had already been sacked and a military purge undertaken to try to maintain order. Mao responded to his 1962 removal with the 1966 Cultural Revolution, which was another opportunity for him to have his opponents in the Communist Party killed or silenced and thereby halt reform until his death in 1976. Deng Xiaoping finally introduced the Household Responsibility System in 1978, under which one slice of the agricultural rice cake went to the Government, one went to the collective and one went to the household who cultivated each particular field. With human nature being what it is, this reform encouraged the peasants to work harder and smarter, so that they could keep the surplus, and output rose dramatically. Although the Government take has been abolished, and the collective contribution is being phased out, China is currently still stuck with collective landownership. This matters, for a lot of reasons.

As the Chinese economy grows, land is being transferred from agricultural to industrial or urban use. This involves the thorny issue of compensation for the farmers, and often their physical relocation to another area (especially when massive areas are flooded for new dams and so on). There has been a lot of anger and many demonstrations, often violent, against the seizure agricultural land—especially since it is not clear that this occurs in a fair or legal fashion. (Basically, a lot of agriculturalists believe that their land is gifted away illegally by local Government officials in return for bribes by big business.) It is not entirely clear who represents the collective in this situation—if anyone—and this has led to villages electing their own representatives to put their case and deal with local Government officials. The most famous example is Wukan, where there has been an ongoing land dispute since 2011. Direct democracy is anathema to Beijing, and they finally responded this summer by sending in the paramilitary police to arrest the elected representative, Lin Zuluan, and "restore order" with rubber bullets. (I think that we are back to entropy here, as I discussed in my letter from Xi'an: judging from the photos, restoring order seemed to involve the creation of a lot of disorder.) The basic fact is, in China the Communist Party knows best: thus democracy is a dangerous foreign import that cannot be tolerated. If I wanted to get all cultural and historical here, then I would go back to Confucianism, which constituted the official guiding concept of the Chinese Empire for over a thousand years (from the Tang dynasty—which ruled 600–900 CE—until the abolition of the Imperial Examination system in 1905 during the Qing dynasty). Confucianism outlines the rights and responsibilities of each sector of society: the obligations of the ruler to ruled, and the duties of the people to the prince (or the Party, as the case may be). The relationship is essentially filial, so the potentate is a father to his people. The people should trust in the wisdom of the prince, and therefore show obedience to him; and in return he owes them love and fair treatment. Of course, it is often "tough love"—traditionally, the father has to beat his son often in order to make him a better person. And so it is today: no one knows better than the Party what is best for China (such egotistical arrogance for an individual!) and if the child gets ahead of himself with whinging and demanding, then he has to be punished—for his own good, as well as everyone else's. That is why you cannot even think about fighting the government in China: it is as disrespectful and misguided and unreasonable as a child defying instructions from its father.

Another reason that collective landownership matters is that people in China are expecting some kind of land reform. The agricultural sector is dying—quite literally, since it is overwhelmingly old people who work the land and keep things going. Young people who have education and gumption have already migrated to the cities to raise their incomes and improve the life chances of their children. So the rural sector is denuded of labour. An obvious way forward would be to privatize the land. You would imagine that this would encourage massive investment, mechanization and modernization. Of course, it would also entail the concentration of landholdings in the hands of a much smaller number of people—just as the Enclosure Movement did in England in the eighteenth century. There is a key difference, though. The Enclosure Movement raised efficiency by throwing surplus workers off the land: that is why it was controversial. The problem in China is that the workers have already left the land: privatizing land would bring them back (because they could be as productive in the countryside as they are in the city). But this would be concrete confirmation that Communism had been cast aside in China—an unpalatable policy position for the Party. This is why nothing has been done. If you were going to privatize land, then how would you do it? An obvious approach is to divide it up between the people who are currently cultivating it, or perhaps between those who have the right to cultivate it. This is something that makes Chinese migrant workers reluctant to give up their hukou. They have a dream that the land in their hometown will be privatized one day and that they will receive a share of it. In the meantime, they live in limbo: they are not accepted into urban society, but they cannot make a living in rural society. An entire generation of people—hundreds of millions of them—is marking time (as their lives tick away and they are separated from their loved ones) until someone comes up with a bold plan to reform landownership and residency rules.

My friend's experience with Government offices when trying to resolve her hukou issue is standard in China, especially at the moment. I am old enough to remember the 1970s in England (only just, mind you—I am really not that old, honest). China reminds me of England in the 1970s in so many ways: people smoking all the time and spitting in the streets, no one wearing seatbelts or using child car seats, beaten up old trucks driving around full of scrap. I am almost nostalgic for the grittiness of it all. But some of my most vivid memories involve the "nationalized industries". Until Mrs Thatcher privatized everything in the 1980s, all the "commanding heights" of the British economy were SOEs: there was the state electricity monopoly, the gas monopoly, the telephone monopoly, the railway monopoly and so on. And when I was a child, they were constantly on strike. I remember my mother walking me home from school one day and saying: "We need to buy some candles on the way home because there is going to be a power cut later". You see, the coal miners were on strike and there were rolling blackouts to reduce electricity consumption. It took around six months to get a telephone connected when you moved house. In fact, it was quicker if you accepted a "party line", which was a line that was shared between two neighbouring houses! (If you moved into a new housing development, then this was about the only way that you could get a phone connected before you moved out again, the waiting list was so long. If you picked up the phone and heard someone talking already, that meant that your neighbour was on the phone and you had to wait until they had finished before you could make a call.) Obviously, there was no customer service. The telephone company, for example, was not the slightest bit interested in hearing any of your complaints. They did not pretend to be interested: there was just no one to whom you could complain, and if you did try to complain, then you were told to go and procreate.

This is basically the situation in China today. Anything important that needs to be done—hukous, hospitals, schools, passports, rail tickets, travel permits—has to be arranged through a government office. But what happens if the government office won't cooperate? Non-cooperation can take many forms. The simplest shortcoming may be that the office is shut when it is supposed to be open. Slightly more subtle is a situation where the person who serves you has "run out of forms", or needs to refer you to a colleague who is not there right now, and whose return time is always unknown. A higher level of obstruction is when the office claims that something is not within their remit and sends you to another office— invariably a long way away—and that office gives you the opposite order. And so it goes on. And, just like England in the 1970s, there is no conduit for complaints. They do not even make a pretence of wanting to hear your problems—they just want you to be grateful for what you got and go away. It is often hard to tell if the government official is doing their job or not (how should I know whether or not this request is within their remit?). But, even if you know that they are being off-hand or obstructive, what can you do about it? Unless you have "guanxi" (or "pull", as we would say in English), there is no point complaining to the boss of the official who is obstructing you: even if you could speak to him, he would just tell you to take a hike.

This is the importance of gift giving in China. Basically, bureaucrats have no incentive to do anything for you, including things that they are supposed to do. If you bring them a form to be processed, then they can simply refuse to do it and there is no sanction against them—there is no complaints hotline and you cannot holler to their boss. Since processing forms is work for them—and not processing forms goes unpunished—why would a bureaucrat bother to process your form? Only because you give them a gift. In return for this token of esteem, they may deign to help you. In China, these gifts are typically non-monetary, which is in contrast to the West. Sometimes Western politicians accept lavish holidays, and so on, as a sweetener but most motivation to get things done seems to involve the transfer of cold, hard cash. This can be done in a documented way (e.g. in the form of a "consultancy fee") or an undocumented way. The classic case is George Graham's "bung" when he was the manager of Arsenal Football Club: people gave him big brown envelopes full of used notes to make transfer deals happen. It is the same in Russia today. You have to give administrators "napkins" to get them to sign forms; but the napkins have to have banknotes folded into them. In many ways, this makes life straightforward. Giving gifts in China is a more subtle business because it requires more local knowledge, and preferably personal knowledge. If you know that the bureaucrat is a wine connoisseur, then you obviously bring wine; if you see that they smoke, then you bring expensive cigars and so on.

The problem is that Xi Jinping's anti-corruption drive has made everyone too frightened to accept gifts. They are aware that they could be denounced at any moment and end up disciplined—where "disciplined" can involve a long jail term and reeducation, if you are far enough up the food chain. Perhaps ironically, this type of gift giving would not even be considered corrupt under the US Foreign Corrupt Practices Act—it would just be a "speed payment" because you are paying for something that is already rightfully yours. Xi Jinping promises to catch both "tigers and flies" in his anti-corruption campaign (i.e. the big bosses as well as the petty public servants). But a more useful distinction would be between people who are corrupt (such as those secretly selling land rights that do not belong to them) and those who are abusive (such as those using their position to extract payments for services that they are already supposed to be providing). While none of us likes to be abused by bureaucrats, it is not the end of the world (you could consider it a cost of doing business—like entertaining potential purchasers of your product). But corruption is qualitatively different because it leads to a materially different allocation of resources (such as taking land from farmers and giving it to factory owners, who really have no right to exploit it in that way). Fighting both these forms of graft at the same time may not actually make much sense. Suppose that you are a basically honest bureaucrat. What do you do in this situation? Nothing. Nothing at all. You don't really want to do anything anyway because it involves effort. But—worse than that—if you do something, however innocent, then you might be accused of having done it in return for taking a bribe. So it is definitely best to do nothing. You are very unlikely to be fired for doing nothing—you can always excuse yourself by saying that you were not sure of the rules, or you were waiting for higher authority, or you were overworked, or whatever. But you can potentially be fired for doing *something*, so it is best to do nothing. This means that it is impossible to get anything done in China right now. BNP Paribas has estimated that GDP growth in China was 1.5 per cent lower in 2015 as a result of the anti-corruption campaign, and the same in 2014. Frankly, I would be surprised if the reduction were really so small.

In principle, I had a small research budget available to me as a visiting professor in China. This is part of the Government's plan to encourage more international exchange and raise the profile of Chinese universities abroad: they pay the university money to subsidize visiting scholars. Unfortunately, I never managed to reclaim a single penny from the budget because there was always something wrong with the paperwork that I submitted. For example, I tried to reclaim a hotel bill. First, I was told that it exceeded the per diem limit (which is quite low—around 400 RMB—and it is not always easy to get a decent hotel for that price in a major city). OK, so maybe you can just pay me the per diem maximum for each night? Second, I needed the itemized check out bill. (I had the booking confirmation for a certain price and a bill for exactly the same price—so I could not possibly have added any extras, such as minibar or pornographic movies or any other decadence. But this was not good enough—I had to have an itemized print out from the hotel.) OK, I can get that by email. Third, to reclaim expenses via the university, you need a special receipt from the hotel recognizing that you paid in an official capacity (I don't remember the Chinese name—and I have no idea what we would call it in English because we do not have such a thing). Now, in order to be as abstemious as possible with government research funding, I booked the hotel by the cheapest means—which happened to be online via Agoda, in this instance. Agoda operates out of Singapore (although it is part of the Priceline group, which trades on the NASDAQ in the US). Unlike other hotel booking agents, it debits your payment card directly and pays the hotel itself—so my booking was not technically with the hotel, but with Agoda. If you phone up Agoda and ask for this special Chinese receipt, they obviously have no idea what you are talking about. Gotcha. Now the university administrator has found a reason why they cannot reimburse you for your hotel room. So she is happy because she does not have to process the forms, and she cannot be accused of making any mistakes or taking any illicit payments. Fortunately for me, we are not talking about a large sum of money and it didn't break the bank. Unfortunately for me, it did waste a lot of time. They don't tell you upfront that you will need all this paperwork, so you have to go back to the administrator three times before you get definitively rejected. But for the anti-corruption drive, I could probably have offered her a box of chocolates or a packet of 50 Marlboro and got the reimbursement through. Thanks, Mr President, for inspiring such fear in the secretaries and they choose not to abuse their power over me.

My airline ticket was even more of a hoot. I had to fly to Europe to attend a PhD defence, and then on to the US to a conference and then back to Beijing. The least-cost solution was to book a Beijing–Boston return with a stopover in London (travelling from London to the location of the PhD defence on a separate ticket). But this was a problem. I submitted the reclaim and heard nothing back for weeks (which is, of course, normal in any event). When I eventually enquired, I was told that they could reimburse the Beijing–London part, but not the London–Boston part because they could only reimburse travel that started and finished in

Beijing. So I needed to tell them what portion of the ticket price was allocated to the Beijing–London leg and they would refund that part only. Obviously, this does not make any sense: there is no breakdown of the price, and a Beijing–London return was basically the same price as Beijing–London–Boston (as is so often the case with airline tickets). I pointed this out to the administrator and she passed it on to the finance office. After several more weeks, I enquired again and was told that they were waiting for me to make them an offer. What? We are going to bargain over what part of the ticket pertains to the Beijing–London leg? This doesn't make any sense to me. This all took so long to sort out that I had actually left China before it was resolved, which I am sure was a big relief to the finance office, and I never got reimbursed (in whole or in part). That was more painful than the hotel bill, since it was not small change and it was entirely work-related. We say in England: "Once bitten, twice shy". Obviously, I would think hard in the future before accepting any invitation to China, even if reimbursement were promised, since I cannot afford to burn thousands of dollars on airline tickets. Other people have had similar problems. A US-based colleague of mine had been invited independently to give seminars in Shanghai and Beijing. He thought that he should schedule them in one trip and the two universities would be happy because they could share his travel expenses between them. No go. Each university would finance him to fly directly between the US and their city, but neither could countenance combining the costs lest it look like some kind of illicit payment. But he would then need to fly right across North America and the Pacific Ocean four times, instead of two, which would be a big waste of time and a lot of wear and tear on his body (there being a 12-hour time difference between China and the US East Coast). So he simply decided not to go. Pretty smart, huh?

Not only is it hard to make progress, but the anti-corruption campaign is a setback for regular business because "Struggle Sessions" seem to have been reintroduced. During the Cultural Revolution, a struggle session was a process of criticism and self-criticism used to purify the minds of wrongdoers and set them back on the path to Socialism. Someone would be accused of something—often a totally imaginary crime, or an act that was not actually a crime but was deemed un-Socialist—and they would be hauled off to a public meeting. A crowd then berated them, sometimes tortured them (e.g. by putting them in "stress positions", as the CIA would euphemistically call it) and made them "confess" their crimes. The victims then had to criticize themselves to show that they had seen the error of their ways and were back on track towards Socialist enlightenment. If they were lucky, they would then be released. If they were unlucky, they would be sent to prison for some unspecified time. If they were very unlucky, they would be immediately executed (as happened to 2 million landlords in the 1950s during the agricultural collectivization process). It is amazing how much Communism and Catholicism have in common (speaking here as a non-combatant of either camp, you understand). Only once you have confessed your sins can you hope to be accepted into Heaven (whether that be the Chinese Socialist utopia or the afterlife, depending on which C you follow).

In September 2013, Xi Jinping embarked upon his "criticism and self-criticism" roadshow in Hebei province. Since then, he has toured widely and played gigs to thousands of regional officials, exhorting them to exemplary behaviour to avoid extravagance and hedonism and corruption, while ensuring that their junior bureaucrats follow suit. A friend was telling me about a struggle session in their local hospital. Everyone sat around a big table—from the cleaners to the surgeons, since there is no hierarchy under Communism, you know—in order to profess their peccadillos. A lot of head-scratching and teeth-sucking ensued because no one could really remember anything that anyone had done wrong. Then a surgeon admitted that he had accepted a gift from the family of someone slated for surgery. (This is normal in China: families like to think that they can ensure the best treatment for their relative by giving a bottle of wine, or whatever, to the surgeon beforehand.) At this point, the others fell upon him like a pack of wild dogs—which is, of course, entirely natural because it deflects attention from any imaginary crimes that they themselves might have committed, and it gets the meeting out of the way. (They can hardly walk out of the meeting saying that it was pointless and a waste of everyone's time: they need to be able to report that the hospital management was morally cleansed by the President's wise campaign.) So the surgeon ate a big slice of humble pie, regretted his actions, cried, promised that he would not do it in future and then they all adjourned for a well-earned cup of tea. Imagine this happening all over China—it is a wonder that they find the time to do any work. Still, I am sure that it will strengthen their sinews and society will rebound with renewed vigour and raised efficiency.

Well, I am going to end this letter on that positive, purgative note. Creating it was very cathartic and I hope that my confessions will conduct me to get back onto the true path to something beginning with C (maybe "common sense"?).

Have a lovely weekend,

Liam.

Letter 19

China's "Japan Moment"
31 August 2016

Dear Erik,

The time has finally come to stop talking about the past and start talking about the future. As many have discovered—typically to their cost—talking about the future is a lot more tricky than talking about the past. That is why universities are replete with History Departments but not one has a Futurology Department. (Historian: easy life—just dig up a few long lost manuscripts in an archive and you have got the basis of a book; your biggest danger is an attack of the sneezes from all that dust. Futurologist: tough life—coming up with eye-catching and insightful predictions that are sufficiently precise that they could be falsified in finite time, but which you hope will not be.) I just think back to the days when the British economist, Richard Layard (now Lord Layard), predicted an explosion of growth in Russia and Eastern Europe after the fall of the Iron Curtain in 1990. It is lucky that he had several other *avant-garde* lines of research because if his reputation were dependent on that one, then he would have vanished into obscurity long ago. I am sure that I am a better Oracle than that, and I have evidence to prove it. When I was a graduate student, back in 1995, I went to study in Paris for a year. Since it was the 50th anniversary of the end of World War 2, the radio was wall-to-wall with praise of De Gaulle and lauding the contribution he had made to changing world history. I have to say that I think De Gaulle's role in bringing World War 2 to a successful conclusion was, at best, marginal: let's face it, he was the exiled leader of a defeated power dependent on handouts to get a few troops into battle (or not into battle, actually, for the first four years). I agree that he played a central role in resurrecting French pride after 1945—although anyone else who had found themselves in his fortuitous position in 1940 might have done an equally good job—but that hardly makes him a central figure in world history (unless you are French, of course).

The thing that struck me at that time—and which I actually wrote to friends in France to point out—was that the Chinese economy was growing at 10 per cent per annum. If that continued for 15 years—as seemed almost certain—then the Chinese economy would have grown by 420 per cent by 2010. Which it did. In 15 years, the Chinese economy went from being half the size of the French economy to twice the size of the French economy. Put that in your pipe and smoke it, De Gaulle. By 2015, China was *four* times larger. By 2020 it will be *six* times larger. At the moment, the Chinese are adding *two* French economies to their own economy every five years. This makes any possible achievement ascribed to De Gaulle look rather small (short of creating two French economies from zero, which I don't think anyone is claiming for him). The wisdom that "you should never wage a land war in Asia" has never been more true. Of course, De Gaulle never accepted that particular wisdom anyway—which is why he committed France to a war in Vietnam in 1946 (and look how that turned out).

Jim O'Neill (then-head of Goldman Sachs Asset Management) built his reputation on BRICs—predicting in 2001 that growth in the world GDP over the next decade would be driven largely by Brazil, Russia, India and China. I definitely feel that he stole my thunder on that one: I had already pointed out in 1995 that Chinese economic growth was going to make Western democracies pale into insignificance, whatever the talents (or not) of their political leaders. Moreover, O'Neill's focus on the BRICs created a great acronym but not much predictive accuracy. Brazil's average growth rate was not remarkable up to 2010 (3.3 per cent per annum on average—barely higher than the US, and starting from a much smaller base, so its overall contribution was limited); and Brazil is currently in its worst depression since the 1930s, with no sign of recovery. Russia's growth has been spectacularly high and then spectacularly low—if you take the story through to 2015, then it also averages 3.3 per cent per annum since 2001, and will be even lower when we include 2016. Only India and China have grown consistently at 7 per cent per annum or more, and China has outperformed India by far. So I actually claim superior foresight on that score.

Sadly, I cannot see this trend for extraordinary growth continuing in China, for many reasons. First, I should be more specific about what I mean. The official figures suggest that total GDP has been growing at around 7 per cent per annum over the last five years (although the accuracy of these figures is open to question—and no one has ever suggested that they are underestimates!). I would guess that GDP growth will slow over the next decade to more like 5 per cent per annum or less, depending on whether you are looking at official figures or accurate estimates. I will return to the reasons for this in a moment. At the same time, we need to think about GDP *per head of population*. The growth in total GDP captures the raw economic importance of China in the world economy; but GDP per head captures changes in the Chinese standard of living, which will be an important influence on how things develop. Population growth has been less than 1 per cent per annum in China for the last 15 years, and most recently has been around 0.5 per cent per annum. This means that GDP growth rates were almost the same whether you think about it as total growth in the economy or growth per head of population. But with the relaxation of the One Child Policy, I expect population growth to pick up quite substantially and quite quickly. There are around 800 million people in China aged under 40 (with another 600 million being aged over 40). A lot of the under-40s have been delaying their fertility. That is, there are a lot of 30-something women out there who would like to have had a second child but have been blocked by the One Child Policy—and their biological clock is ticking. So relaxing the One Child Policy does not just affect people in their 20s, or those currently in childhood; it will also unleash this "backlog" of fertility that has been building up amongst those in their 30s. That is why I imagine that the effect of the change in the One Child Policy will be abrupt and sizable.

Of course, if total GDP growth slows to 5 per cent per annum—and population growth rises to 1.5 per cent per annum—then the growth in GDP per head will drop to 3.5 per cent per annum (rather than the 10 per cent average that we have observed since 1995). This is a massive reduction. I will draw out some implications of this in a moment.

Why do I think that the growth rate of total Chinese GDP will slow down to 5 per cent, or less? This is partly because Chinese growth depends on selling stuff abroad and I am pessimistic about the prospects for the rest of the world economy. If there is no one to buy Chinese goods, then the Chinese economy is not going to grow very fast. I think that Japan is going to stagger along for another decade (or more) growing at 1 per cent per annum, as it has done since the property price bubble burst there in 1991. I think that the EU is also going to stagger along for another decade (or more) growing at 1 per cent per annum. Back in 2008, I was driven to the airport in Norway—at very high speed—by an unemployed airline pilot who was filling in as a taxi driver. (At least, it was very high speed for me—I assume that for him it was slow motion. I guess that he is like a human fly: he has a higher heart rate than those around him, so time seems to pass more slowly and he has an age to react to everything. This young man's situation is what we call "under-employment" or "hidden unemployment": a brain surgeon may get a job as a bulldozer driver, but he is clearly not putting his skills to their most productive use and this is a real loss to the economy.) When he realized that I was a business school professor, he asked me how long I thought that the recession would last—he wanted to know when the airline market might pick up again and he could find a proper job. I said that it would last at least five years: there is a lot of debt overhang in the housing market (i.e. people whose house loans were nominally valued at more than the houses themselves) and a lot of physical excess capacity (whole towns that stand empty have been built in Spain because no one can afford to buy them). I could not see the housing market—and hence the general economy—growing enough, in terms of the quantity of houses demanded or in terms of market prices, to throw off this drag for at least five years. (In fact, this problem also afflicts China: when you travel round the country you see whole suburbs composed of skeletal, unfinished tower blocks with no one working on them—a point made in the BBC News article "China's zombie factories and unborn cities".) With hindsight, I was too generous and should have said ten years. Or maybe 20 years. There are a lot of structural problems in the European economy: government debt in Greece and Italy that is worth nothing; banks that are *de facto* bankrupt, but disguised by the face value of these wonderful government bonds that they hold; low productivity growth everywhere except Germany; dysfunctional labour markets everywhere except the UK.

Most worryingly, I cannot see anyone in the EU who has the gumption to tackle these problems. In the US and the UK, financial institutions were essentially allowed to fail in 2008. This wiped the slate clean and rejuvenated the financial sector so that it could support future economic growth. But the EU has not allowed any financial institutions to fail: instead, it has bailed them out and propped them up. This is the approach that Japan followed after their property bubble burst in 1991 and it created "zombie banks". What are zombie banks? Obviously, they are the "living dead" of the financial system. They have a lot of non-performing loans (NPLs) on their books. In the European case, this is a lot of mortgages and a lot of government bonds (such as Greek government debt). If they foreclose on these loans, then they will have to write down their value to their true market value (which is maybe 20 per cent of their face value). This will shrink the asset side of their balance sheets (since the loans are an asset for the bank) and make them *de jure* bankrupt. So the smart thing to do, if you run a bank, is to *not* foreclose on the NPLs. Then you keep them on your books at face value and you are *de jure* not bankrupt (even though you are *de facto* bankrupt). Suppose that someone cannot keep up their repayments to the bank—what should you do? You should lend them some more money so that they can make their repayments and you do not have to foreclose on them. In this way, the capital (money) that European savers deposit in the banks gets lent to firms and individuals who are not profitable and cannot repay their loans. Firms that *are* profitable and might want to get a loan to expand—such as by buying new machinery—cannot get a loan. So they have to stay small and not contribute to economic growth in the EU. This is the current situation in the EU. Interest rates are zero but no one can get a loan. It is obviously a stupid policy—just look at Japan…. But if Merkel and Hollande were to admit that German and French banks were bankrupt, then they would be revealed as incompetent. So instead they have to insist that Greece will repay its loans in full—so that German (and French and Italian) banks can keep those bonds on their books at face value and not be declared bankrupt.

In any case, back to our main story. I don't think that the Chinese economy can rely on foreign demand to drive economic growth in the next decade or so, certainly not at previous rates. But I cannot see the Chinese economy transitioning towards more consumption and thereby boosting domestic demand, either. I gave some reasons for this in a previous letter: for example, Chinese people cannot buy more cars because the number of licence plates is limited in Beijing; and they cannot buy more housing because it is forbidden (as in Beijing) or because their families cannot get urban *hukous*. But there are other reasons, too. Most Chinese workers get very little vacation (just two weeks around Chinese New Year) and often work seven days per week; so it is hard to see how the domestic tourist industry is going to take off. (In this sense, China is much more like the US than it is like Europe.) And that is leaving aside the fact that travelling in China is anyway more like work than pleasure. More fundamentally, there is no state safety net in China. There is no pension; you may have to pay for your children (or grandchildren) to go to private school if you end up as a migrant worker; you may want to pay for them to study abroad; you may need to pay private medical bills. This means that you need a heap of savings sufficient to handle any eventuality. In the simplified world of economists, there is consumption and there is saving. If Chinese people are going to continue saving 50 per cent of their income (which is what they do right now, and which is about the highest savings rate in the world), then consumption cannot rise. Unless some of these underlying issues change—such as the Government promises everyone a pension, and can persuade people that they will really pursue this policy—it is hard to see why the Chinese savings rate would fall. So consumption cannot rise.

I earlier expressed some scepticism about refocusing the Chinese economy on consumption, rather than investment. It strikes me that there is still a stack of investment that could usefully be undertaken in China to increase both GDP and the quality of life: air pollution improvements (such as installing scrubbers in power station chimneys), sanitation systems (improving water and waste management to increase hygiene), transport improvements (more subway capacity) and so on. In theory, this is the perfect complement to a high savings ratio. Again, in the simplified world of economists, whatever is saved is also invested (banks just recycle purchasing power from savers to borrowers). So the high savings rate (low consumption) is not a problem if there are useful things in which to invest. The economy just ends up with more bridges and fewer burgers, which could be a good thing (as anyone who drives around America can agree—if waistlines were thinner and thoroughfares were wider, then the USA would be a healthier and happier place). The problem is that Chinese banks are even worse than Japanese and European banks. They are stacked high with NPLs. They were bailed out about ten years ago (i.e. the Government exchanged billions of dollars of NPLs for government bonds), since which time they have accumulated another mountain of NPLs. The State-Owned Enterprises are particularly deeply in hock to the banks. Obviously, the banks cannot foreclose on them—that would be politically totally unacceptable.

Restructuring the state sector would be extremely painful, certainly on the scale that they need to secure it in China. I remember England in the 1980s, when police cavalry charged striking coalminers to keep them in check; the social and political dislocation was so great that Mrs Thatcher only survived the 1983 General Election because the Argentines kindly invaded the Falkland Islands and made everyone feel patriotic. The Chinese State-Owned Enterprises are reputed to be particularly inefficient; if this is true, then, judging by the inefficiency that I see in the private sector, they must be very inefficient indeed. But raising efficiency requires millions of workers to lose their jobs at the State-Owned Enterprises and be absorbed into the private sector. Remember that this is especially traumatic for Chinese workers: many of their social benefits (housing, healthcare, childcare) are tied to their jobs, so they are in danger of becoming destitute if they lose their jobs; they will probably have to retrain, since many of them are skilled in heavy industrial jobs (such as steelmaking) that are in decline; and they may well have to migrate thousands of miles across the country. This reallocation might have been possible when the Chinese economy was growing fast. It is always easier to persuade (or make) people switch career when there are lots of job opportunities and wages are rising. But that ship has sailed: the Chinese economy has been slowing in the last few years and is surely set to slow further. Xi Jinping is not going to throw millions of workers out of a job at this point, as it would spawn severe social unrest—which is absolutely the last thing that he wants. Instead, China will stagger along without structural reforms, just like the EU and Japan. And this will continue to suck up the savings that people put into Chinese banks as they continue to fund the State-Owned Enterprises to run at a loss. This will restrict growth in the rest of the economy.

What about productivity growth? This is the magic bullet beloved of politicians and economists because it is a "free lunch". If we all produce 10 per cent more this year, using the same quantity of resources as last year, then productivity has gone up by 10 per cent. And we can all consume 10 per cent more, without anyone else consuming less, so everyone is happy. As far as I can see, there is still a lot of room for productivity growth in the Chinese economy and this is why I think that the Chinese economy will manage to continue growing (albeit at a much more modest pace). One way in which labour productivity can rise is by workers achieving more work in a given time. For example, if it took four hotel staff only 15 minutes to complete your checkout, rather than 30 minutes, then their output per hour would obviously double. I see plenty of potential for this kind of improvement in China. Another way in which labour productivity can rise is by workers producing the same amount of physical output but raising its value. For example, instead of the supermarket staff selling me raw peas, they could sell me frozen peas for a higher price (a bigger profit margin). Again, I certainly see scope for raising Chinese value-added in this way.

A key question, though, is whether—or to what extent—this kind of productivity increase can be realized. It is not that Chinese businessmen lack entrepreneurial skills—far from it. But a lack of trust is an important potential problem. For example, one reason that the hotel checkout takes so long is that a member of staff physically goes to the room to ensure that the TV is still on the wall. In Europe and the US, we do not feel that this is necessary—we simply trust the guest to leave the TV *in situ*, and we are usually right. In terms of food distribution, you need to be able to trust that the suppliers at each link in the food chain have kept the peas properly frozen—all the way from the field to the checkout. Just one person failing in their duty can be catastrophic. We saw this in the US listeria outbreak of 2011, when the fact that a farmer had not properly washed the melons that he sent to market killed 33 people. This was big news precisely because it is so rare in the US. I should say that it is not all about trust; it is also about monitoring and enforcement. For example, my Chinese friend was amazed that every cow born in England is immediately tagged and then has its movements logged (from one farm to another, from the farm to the abattoir, from the abattoir to the supermarket and so on). Not only that, but every cow also has a record kept of its diet for every day of its life, and any medical treatment received. This is how we ensure food safety. You just cannot imagine such a system being instituted in China, or not being widely circumvented if it were imposed. So how are Chinese food producers supposed to raise their value-added if they cannot commit to high quality? So, while I see many ways to raise productivity enormously in China, I do not think that it is so easy to actually implement them.

What about the "One Belt, One Road" initiative? Can it save the day by lowering the cost of securing raw materials and boosting foreign demand for Chinese products? I am afraid that I am deeply sceptical about the economics of this project—even though it may be good politics for the current President—and I think that it will make the situation worse, rather than better. First, I don't see that this is going to generate enough trade (and therefore profit) to justify the expenditure. For example, a new railway line is just opening in Kenya, linking Nairobi (the capital) to Mombassa (the biggest port). The line was built by Chinese engineering firms using Chinese track-laying technology; it is 90 per cent financed by loans from China to Kenya (which just increased its national debt to pay for the project by a massive 6 per cent of GDP!). This is the first new line in Kenya since the British opened one on the same route in 1905. Why? Because the trade volumes nowhere near justify the expenditure (BBC News, "Will Kenya get value for money from its new railway?"). A World Bank report points out that in order to break even the railway will need to transport 20–55 million tonnes of freight per annum (although I am not sure if those figures incorporate the fact that the project came in four times over budget—see Harriet

Constable's article "The rising cost of Kenya's railway"). By contrast, total freight in the whole of the East Africa Community rail network is projected to reach only 14.4 million tonnes by 2030. Currently, the total volume of freight passing through Mombassa—by train or truck—is only 26 million tonnes. And the railway is anyway designed to carry only 22 million tonnes of freight. So, in order to stand a chance of breaking even, the new railway will basically need to capture the whole traffic of the port of Mombassa and operate continuously at full capacity. It would be interesting to know the details of the contract. For example, who pays for the cost overruns (the engineering firm or the Kenyan government?) and what is the repayment plan for the loans? If Kenya defaults on the repayments—which seems very likely—then what action can the Chinese take? This whole situation sounds very like the overly exuberant lending that Western banks made to developing countries in the 1970s, in which they got financially badly burnt. To me, China seems to be making the same mistake on a grand scale.

There is actually a more general point here about the profitability of Chinese railways. Since they do not produce public accounts, we cannot know if they make a profit. One strongly suspects not. Some 2015 financial figures were released recently for the Beijing-Shanghai high-speed route to support a public bond offering, as reported in the Wall Street Journal article "China's Busiest High-Speed Rail Line". It is claimed that the line made a profit for the first time in 2015 (although this is essentially unverifiable, since the accounting data are incomplete, and the issuer has an obvious incentive to paint the figures in a favourable light). It seems certain that the Beijing-Shanghai line is the most profitable in China, given the importance of those two cities. If that line first declared a profit in 2015, then the accumulated losses across the whole of the rail network over the last decade must be horrifying. There is a silver lining in this for China. The trains do not make a profit because ticket prices are artificially low. So the headline figures for profitability do not necessarily reflect the true economic benefit of the railways—the Government is effectively giving away the surplus to passengers by giving them cheaper tickets. Fundamentally, China still gets the benefit of any unprofitable (or uneconomic) railway line built in China because Chinese passengers and shippers get to use it. Crucially, this is not true of Chinese railways built in Kenya. Any losses made on those lines are effectively a gift from Chinese citizens to Kenyan citizens. This is not going to increase economic growth or the standard of living in China in the long run. Of course, it does pump up demand for infrastructure investment—and the associated engineering jobs—in the short run. In that sense, the "One Belt, One Road" initiative is an extension of the previous policy focusing on infrastructure investment. But it is worse than before because China will get less economic benefit from it.

For these reasons, I feel that this is China's "Japan moment". It has grown at extraordinary rates for almost 40 years (albeit from a very, very low base)—just like Japan between 1950 and 1990. In the 1980s, people thought that Japan would take over the world, in an economic sense. They had the best products, the best research and development (R&D), the lowest costs, the most dedicated workers, the strongest financial system—was there anything that they could not do better than the West? The US and UK responded by reorganizing their financial systems purely in an effort to compete: most notably, they permitted "universal banking"—along Japanese lines—whereby banks could undertake all kinds of financial transactions (not just banking) and thereby grow to enormous sizes to match the Japanese banks. Labour markets were liberalized (the right to strike was reduced, for example) precisely to promote a workforce as compliant as the Japanese one. (If you have never listened to "Industrial Disease" by Dire Straits, then check it out on YouTube—it exactly captures the zeitgeist.) And then it all came tumbling down. Their financial system collapsed and people began to outcompete their products (either making like-for-like products more cheaply elsewhere, or focusing more on the social aspects of the products—such as the social network element of playing videogames, rather than the hardware element, which is why Microsoft's Xbox beat up Sony's PlayStation). Also, practices that had seemed so socially advanced and economically beneficial came back to haunt the Japanese. For example, many Japanese factory workers were promised jobs for life. All the time that the company is growing, this promise costs the company nothing and raises worker morale. But when the company needs to start shrinking, this is very burdensome and slows adjustment within the economy. Does this sound like another East Asian economy, just across the Yellow Sea…?

19 China's "Japan Moment"

It has seemed for the last 40 years that China is going to take over the world. Indeed, I have been concerned myself about how we, in the West, are going to be able to compete in the future. They seem to have so many able and well-trained students (certainly in the sciences), together with low wages and a strong work ethic. Now that I have been to China, I am considerably less worried! The first issue that I see is a whole host of institutional problems that will have to be resolved if they are going to continue growing at the same rate as the last 40 years. My own experience of England in the 1970s suggests to me that these institutional constraints are unlikely to be shifted—certainly not in the next decade or two, and probably not in my lifetime. Thatcher's UK Cultural Revolution was a truly remarkable and rare event that was enabled by an extraordinary constellation of coincidences, such as the Winter of Discontent (when a wide array of workers went on strike) and the Falklands War. Her legacy was not merely to remould the UK economy in the 1980s but to move the mentality of the masses from support of state ownership to a belief in free enterprise. It is difficult to imagine a comparable conversion occurring in China anytime soon. The second issue that I see is that the skilled, smart and motivated students coming to the West from China—although numerous—still constitute only a tiny proportion of the Chinese population (even though they may constitute a large proportion of the Western population!). There may be millions of such people in China, but I don't think that there are hundreds of millions of such people. Millions of highly skilled and educated people are not that many in a population of 1.4 billion. It is a lot of weight on those people to take the Chinese economy forward and raise productivity—inventing innovative products, organizing efficient production and so on.

Moreover, the challenge of raising productivity is becoming increasingly difficult in China. For one thing, they are getting ever closer to the "technological frontier". Catching up with Apple is one challenge; surpassing Apple and generating products that are even better is much more difficult. The Japanese seemed super-inventive as they closed on Western levels of technology in the 1980s, but I don't see that they have pushed the frontier very far forward since then. In fact, I can't think of a single category in which Japan is a world-beater (they don't produce the best phones, or computers, or cars, or aircraft, or medicine, or software). For another thing, the research situation in China is difficult, and becoming increasingly so. Google is blocked, so how are you supposed to find information on the internet? Even if you locate a research paper that might be useful, it often takes an entire morning to download it—something that would take five minutes in a US university department can take five hours. (You never know whether the wisest choice is to give up or persevere as the blue bar creeps across the page—is it your internet connection that is slow, or the VPN, or the fact that the site is blocked, or…?) The internet has become significantly less functional in the last couple of years as the Great Firewall has been reinforced. A new rule requires all VPN providers to register with the government, so access to sites such as Google will become even more difficult. At the moment, every Chinese scientist at a good university has an army of able research assistants helping to run experiments and churn out papers. Since the Chinese university system is expanding, there will be jobs for these research assistants in the future (as professors) and therefore they are willing to work like slaves to establish their careers. But what happens when the university system stops expanding? Will gifted postgraduate students still want to work in the labs, or will they go somewhere else, such as overseas? Or choose some other career entirely, such as finance?

To the extent that China will be able to make technological advances, I think that it will stem from the fact that they are still a long way behind in many areas. Huawei and Xiaomi produce good phones: I happily used a Xiaomi myself in China. But they are not exactly cutting edge. What about in other areas? Well, consider the case of the Jade Rabbit—the probe that the Chinese Government sent to the moon in 2013. Essentially, it broke down after two days. It continued to send back information for many months; but the ground-penetrating radar could send back only the same information everyday because the rover was totally unable to move, owing to… an electrical fault (technically, a control circuit malfunction). Remember that the US put a man on the moon in 1969 and successfully recovered him. So one could reasonably argue that Chinese technology is still 50 years behind, at least in space exploration. It is not clear to me that their ability to manufacture cars or computers or ships or planes or military hardware is really much more advanced. True, some of the world's biggest "Bitcoin mines" are in China. To mine Bitcoins requires powerful computers to find a mathematical solution to a puzzle. But this is not really high-tech: it just requires a lot of computers and a small number of competent people to run them. Both of these inputs are relatively cheap in China, which is why it is a good place to set up a Bitcoin mine. Just how close to the cutting edge is the Chinese computer industry? Supposedly, Chinese hackers are omnipresent. But, again, is this a question of sophistication or just a question of the amount of manpower and computer power devoted to the problem? China has the world's fastest computer, and the world's second fastest computer. But the Soviet Union also had a lot of hi-tech vanity projects: that did not mean that it was able to remain at the technological frontier, or harness its technology to generate economic growth.

To heap further misgivings onto the Chinese economy, we have to think about the replacement of capital goods in the coming decades. China has urbanized very fast. But urbanization is easy: you take a green site, install services (sewers, water and electricity supply and so on) and you build blocks of flats on it. But urban *regeneration* is difficult. In a decade or two, those urban areas will be falling into disrepair. So either the standard of living will fall—as people continue to live in housing that becomes unfit for habitation—or it will have to be renovated. This will raise a lot of organizational problems. For example, the law on real estate is very incomplete in China, so how will you coordinate every owner of an apartment block and force any reluctant ones to pay their share of remedial work to benefit everyone in the building? There are clear mechanisms and legal remedies for this in the West; but is it going to work straightforwardly in China? Note also that renovation is much more expensive than construction. Putting sewers in the ground is easy when you are dealing with a farmer's field; it is expensive when you are digging up city streets. Building bright new apartment blocks in the future will involve blowing up the old ones and removing the rubble. Creating so much infrastructure in such a short period compresses the subsequent process of renewal—most of China is going to have to be rebuilt at the same time.

This would be less of an issue in Switzerland, where everything is over-engineered and conceived to last forever. But a lot of Chinese construction is very poor quality. I have talked about housing in a previous letter, so I shall say no more about that. But I was frankly shocked to find that the water in China is undrinkable. The reason that I was shocked is twofold. First, their water system is essentially new. In England, we have water and sewage pipes that are 150 years old; you might expect these to be inefficient (a lot of leakage) and potentially open to contamination (although contamination is rare). But the Chinese water system has basically been created in the last 15 years: it should be perfect, with no leakage or contamination. Second, water is a local product. That is, a local water purification plant pumps water into local pipes and it is consumed by local residents. So it is within the power of local mayors to make their supplies drinkable: it is not rocket science, and it does not depend on a national grid (unlike electricity, for example). I would have thought that this would be an easy way for an ambitious and enterprising mayor to make himself popular with local residents—men such as Bo Xilai, who was mayor of the important city of Dalian (formerly Port Arthur) for 17 years before his wife later murdered someone and he was convicted of corruption. But it seems not. Given the low quality of construction, it seems likely that Chinese infrastructure and urban construction will need to be replaced much sooner than we might expect in the West. This is going to suck up a lot of capital, which then cannot be invested in R&D or education or some other productive use. China is going to have to run increasingly fast just to stay in the same place. It is also going to prevent this fabled "rebalancing" of the Chinese economy towards consumption.

China is still going to be massively important in the world economy. Its size alone will ensure that. Depending on how you measure it, GDP per head in China is about 60 per cent of the level of Russia (15,000 "international dollars" per head in China compared to 25,000 "international dollars" per head in Russia, according to the World Bank). But China has been growing at 7 per cent per annum and Russia has been growing at an average of 0 per cent over the last four years (in fact, Russia has seen substantial *negative* growth since the invasion of Ukraine a couple years ago). Even if Chinese growth slows dramatically, a persistent disparity with Russia of (say) 3.5 per cent per annum would see Chinese GDP per head equal Russia by 2030. But Russia has a population of 140 million, whereas China has a population of 1.4 billion! So China will be approximately ten times more important—economically—than Russia.

Since Russia's population has also been falling over the last two decades, the difference in absolute economic clout is likely to widen even faster than suggested by the figures on GDP per head. Naturally, China will become more politically and militarily important, too. (Frankly, unless you have the misfortune to live next door to Russia—like Georgia and Ukraine—Russia is really a minor inconvenience these days. It has shrunk from being a superpower to a regional power. And all the posturing and poking of Putin will not change that fact. The Russian economy has stalled since 1990 and unless Putin can revive it—which is not something that he seems very concerned with—the country will simply continue to fade into military and diplomatic insignificance.) This is one important difference between China and Japan. When Japan stopped growing around 1990, its population was only 124 million—and it is expected to start shrinking any time now, so that it will have only 95 million by 2050. At that point, the populations of Germany and the UK will be both larger (assuming that that UK still exists, of course—ahem). So what happens in Japan is of decreasing importance. But not so of China, where the population is set to rise faster as a result of the new "Two Child Policy".

My Chinese friends have seen their country's transformation over the last 30 years—which has admittedly been drastic—and say things like: "Yes, but think where China will be in 30 years' time". They seem to be expecting the standard of living to continue to rise at breakneck speed, even to surpass the US in 30 years. My reaction is: "Don't worry—China will look much the same in 30 years' time as it does now". I believe that Chinese development is going to largely stall from hereon. There will continue to be some growth, but the positive impact of this will be eroded by the increasing population, the rising costs of replacing worn out capital, the difficulty of making fast progress as you get closer to the technological frontier and the immutable constraints of Chinese politics and society (the Communist Party and corruption). We are already living in "the new normal". China is important, and will continue to be, but it is not going to take over the world. There, I said it. I nailed my colours to the mast. Now you have something to ridicule in years to come (if you can still lay hands on a copy of this missive).

Being a rather downbeat character, with a sharp tongue, much of what I have written about China may come across as a bit harsh. Transitioning to life in China was indeed tough. But I must also say that going to China for seven months was a life-changing experience for me (and I do not use the epithet "life-changing" lightly). I learnt a huge amount—partly through my own efforts, partly through the efforts of my children, partly through the kindness of the many Chinese people who welcomed us (treated us like royalty, really) into their homes. I am extremely grateful that we had the opportunity and seized it. And I will happily return, if I remain *persona grata* after these letters appear in public. I have been keeping up my kung fu, just in case I get to study under the shifu again….

Well, I hope that you enjoyed the ride and that you haven't been gritting your teeth all the way through, like I did on that Mongolian horse.

Very best wishes,

Liam.

References

Constable, Harriet, "The Rising Cost of Kenya's New Railway", *African Business Magazine*, 10 January 2017.
Gray, Richard, "China's Zombie Factories and Unborn Cities", BBC News, 23 February 2017.
Kacungira, Nancy, "Will Kenya Get Value for Money from its New Railway?", BBC News, 8 June 2017.
Yu, Rose, "China's Busiest High-Speed Rail Line Makes a Fast Buck", Wall Street Journal, 20 July 2016.

Index

A

Afternoon nap, 112, 127, 128, 131
Agent, 75, 144, 152, 156, 162, 188, 231, 235, 266, 273, 290
Agriculture, 63, 88, 91–93, 200, 204, 213, 214, 226, 284
Army, 6, 38–40, 81, 91, 123–138, 145–147, 171, 189, 191, 193, 212, 229, 235, 247, 284, 307
Ayding Lake, 226, 227, 232, 233

B

Bai Juyi, 41, 42
Bank, 2, 36, 42, 71–73, 85, 102, 110, 118, 191, 225, 235, 251, 252, 258, 266, 267, 290, 299–305, 309
Bargaining, 264, 265, 267
Beijing, 1, 4, 6, 10–13, 16–18, 20, 21, 28, 29, 33, 34, 36, 40, 42, 47–49, 51, 60, 61, 64–69, 71, 75, 76, 81, 82, 85, 88, 89, 101, 114, 118, 120, 124, 133–135, 137, 140, 141–144, 153, 156, 159, 160, 162, 170, 172, 173, 176–178, 196, 197, 201, 204, 205, 210, 215, 225, 227, 229, 230, 235, 236, 239, 241–243, 245, 247–249, 253, 262, 265, 267, 272, 275, 277, 279, 281, 283, 285, 290, 291, 300, 304
Bezeklik, 224, 230, 231
Big Goose Pagoda, 45
Bing Ling Si, 197–200, 203, 224, 267
Boat, 36, 43, 47, 87, 104, 109, 110, 155, 179, 200, 203, 262

BRICs, 296
Buddha, 15, 20, 45, 94, 99, 101, 118, 181, 182, 185, 188, 197, 200–203, 210, 222–224, 230, 231, 247, 254
Budget, 23, 40, 130, 169, 239, 289, 303

C

Camel, 46, 149, 158, 179, 187–189, 192, 214, 217, 219
Canal, 156, 157
Carving, 24, 36, 62, 78, 98, 101, 181, 182, 202, 267
Censorship, 49
Chang'an, *see* Xi'an
Chengde, 141, 143
Cixi, empress dowager, 47
Concubine, 41, 42
Consumption, 137, 176, 272, 287, 300, 301, 309
Corruption, 21, 91, 268, 269, 289, 292, 309, 310. *See also* Gift
Crescent Moon Lake, 219, 220

D

Dali Lake, 153, 154, 157
Default, 10, 258, 267, 273, 304
Desert, 14, 77, 111, 139, 141, 154, 158, 179, 183, 185, 187–193, 211, 213–217, 219, 225, 226, 230, 232, 246
Desertification, 139, 153, 156, 178
Drugs, *see* Opium
Dunhuang, 217–221, 230, 235

E

Economic growth, 91, 179, 258, 296, 299, 300, 305, 308
Efficiency, 8, 286, 293, 301
Elevator, 125, 245, 270, 281
Entrepreneur, 70, 147, 302
Exams, 162–166, 202. *See also* Gaokao
Exports, *see* Foreign demand

F

Flaming Mountains, 224, 230, 232
Foreign demand, 300, 303

G

Gansu, 225
Gaokao, 60. *See also* Exams
Gaozong, emperor, 45
Genghis Khan, 149, 156
Gift, 28, 39, 47, 62, 100, 126, 137, 140, 148, 168, 170, 171, 237, 259, 285, 288, 292, 305, 307. *See also* Corruption
Grapes, 225, 228–232
Great Firewall, 6, 49, 307
Great Wall, 18, 20, 179, 211, 212, 215, 225
Guizhou, 63, 229, 230, 241–262

H

Hainan, 62, 63, 74, 154, 265, 273
Hami, 231
Han, 38, 50
Han Chinese, 40, 59, 60, 209, 231, 236, 250, 282
Harbin, 14–16, 76, 134, 135, 263, 264
Hexigten Geopark, 141, 143

Holiday, 1, 7, 34, 37, 55, 70, 77, 85, 87, 98, 100, 105, 119, 143, 193, 274, 277, 288
Homework, 3, 4, 18, 29, 51, 64, 165, 166, 173
Hong Kong, 12–14, 74, 76, 101, 136, 163, 235, 238, 243, 252
Horse, 14, 35, 38, 46, 67, 101, 103, 140, 147, 149–151, 154, 156–158, 180, 184, 187, 192, 216, 254, 311
Hospital, 11, 85, 120–122, 255, 287, 292
Hotpot, 134
Housing, 19, 112, 159, 253, 257, 259, 272, 282, 287, 298, 300, 301, 308
Huaguoshan, 241–262
Huangguoshu, see Waterfall
Huawei, 307
Hukou, 272, 275–293, 300

I

Impressions shows, 42, 79, 102, 170, 184
Infrastructure, 98, 153, 176, 177, 197, 253, 254, 272, 305, 308, 309
Innovation, see New technology
Internet, 12, 32, 40, 48, 49, 89, 177, 184, 268, 273, 307
Investment, 98, 129, 228, 258, 259, 272, 286, 300, 305

J

Jade Dragon Snow Mountain, 78
Jiayuguan, 211–215, 219, 223, 225
Jingdi, emperor, 50
The Journey to the West, 41, 207–241, 247

K

Karaoke, 190, 191
Khitan, 153
Kublai Khan, 143, 185
Kunming, 19, 73, 74, 76, 79, 80, 82, 125, 134–136, 196, 201, 249, 267

L

Lanzhou, 176, 196–198, 200, 203, 204, 207
Liao, 143, 153
Lijiang, 42, 75, 76, 78, 79, 196, 256
Liupanshui, 248, 249, 252, 253, 256, 257

M

Ming, 20, 32, 44, 49, 60, 146, 178–183, 188, 200, 209, 216, 256
Minorities, 19, 48, 59–63, 169, 170, 178, 242, 262
Mogao grottoes, 219, 220, 224
Mongol, 60, 61, 133, 143, 146, 149, 150, 156, 177, 179–181, 185, 192, 225
Mongolia, Inner, 139–160, 171, 179, 192, 267
Monkey King, 25, 244–247
Mountains, 3, 19, 20, 61, 63, 76, 78, 79, 83, 88, 93, 95–100, 109–111, 114, 115, 124, 141, 157, 177, 179, 181, 182, 186, 191, 199, 205, 212, 216, 220, 224, 226, 227, 230, 232, 235, 236, 241, 243, 244, 246, 248, 249, 253–256, 266, 301

316 Index

Museum, 33, 36, 46, 62, 78, 107, 114–117, 124–126, 131, 132, 140, 155, 177, 178, 181–183, 185, 186, 202, 208, 209, 214, 224, 227, 230, 234, 237, 267, 268, 273

N

National Park, 19, 83, 98, 99, 105, 110
New technology, 31, 96, 170
Ningxia, 176, 179, 194, 195

O

Oasis, 5, 78, 139, 158, 159, 190, 219, 220
One Belt, One Road, 48, 303, 305
One Child Policy, 60, 109, 250, 260, 282, 297
Opium, 91, 163, 164
Opium War, 92
Oven, *see* Stove

P

Parking, 35, 66, 67, 70, 81
People's Liberation Army (PLA), *see* Army
Plumbing, 31, 32, 129, 156
Police, 2, 12, 21, 73, 82, 84, 110, 199, 234, 235, 238, 285, 301
Pollution, 2, 3, 17, 18, 23, 33, 35, 43, 61, 66, 98, 242, 300
Porcelain, 113–117, 259
Productivity, 120, 156, 168, 299, 302, 303, 306
Profit, 130, 261, 274, 299, 302–304
Propaganda, 57, 240

Q

Qin, 38
Qing, 41, 47–49, 60, 92, 143, 146, 164, 183, 184, 209, 212, 285
Qin Shi Huang, emperor, 38–40, 50, 58, 61

R

Rafting, 105, 187, 194, 267
Railways, *see* Train
Rain, 44, 66, 67, 85, 114, 116, 118, 148, 160, 182, 185, 186, 218–220, 227, 256
Residence permit, *see* Hukou

S

School, 1, 3, 4, 6, 7, 17, 18, 21, 22, 29, 34, 37, 41, 51, 52, 56–60, 64, 66, 67, 69, 80, 87, 89, 90, 107–109, 114, 119, 120–122, 124, 127, 133, 137, 140, 146, 161–176, 216, 233, 234, 243, 250, 258–260, 277–281, 287, 298, 300
Security, 9, 21, 71–85, 97, 105, 117, 186, 187, 213, 231, 233–235, 237, 243, 249
Shanghai, 62, 140, 163, 242, 275, 278, 291
Shangrao, 88, 89, 98, 113, 114
Shilin, 267
Shuidonggou, 177–179
Siesta, *see* Afternoon nap
Silk Road, The, 14, 40, 43, 48, 175, 212–214, 221, 224, 225, 230
Soviet, 125, 131, 308
Stomach bug, 20, 136, 196, 208

Stone Age, 177, 178, 209
Stone forest, *see* Shilin
Stove, 50, 62, 107, 112, 126, 127, 133, 134, 256
Summer Palace, 36, 47, 141, 142
Sun Wukong, *see* Monkey King
Supermarket, 27, 28, 119, 137, 259, 302, 303

T

Taiping Rebellion, 92, 164
Tang, 40–42, 45–48, 185, 209, 212, 223, 225, 285
Tang Seng, 41, 45, 140, 175, 230
Tea, 28, 32, 78, 87–122, 135, 148, 267, 292
Temple of Heaven, 23–25, 85
Tengger, 187, 188
Terracotta warriors, 38, 40, 41, 58, 126
Tiananmen Square, 73, 75, 82, 129, 147
Tibet, 60, 62, 149, 248
Tomb, 20, 38–40, 50, 107, 126, 185, 188, 202, 213, 214, 234, 251, 267
Traffic, 21, 50, 66–68, 74, 81, 99, 100, 153, 154, 159, 187, 197–199, 213, 237, 239, 249, 256, 304
Train
  bullet, 88, 89, 114, 176, 212, 234, 242
  sleeper, 79, 176
  station, 73, 85, 176, 187, 196, 213, 217, 234, 237
  ticket, 82, 84, 176, 204, 205
Trust, 8, 9, 43, 285, 302, 303
Turpan, 224–227, 229–232, 235
Tuyoq, 231–233

U

Unemployment, 80, 298
Urbanization, 308
Urumqi, 226, 234, 236–238

V

Virtual Private Network (VPN), 6, 307
Visa, 1, 5, 7, 9–14, 16, 63, 74, 84, 88, 140
VPN, *see* Virtual Private Network

W

Water, 2, 14, 24, 27, 31–33, 43–44, 47, 91, 95, 96, 105, 112–115, 117–119, 126, 135, 145, 152–154, 156–159, 169, 177, 178, 182, 188–190, 197, 199, 203, 204, 214, 215, 219, 220, 225–227, 229–233, 239–246, 250–252, 256, 258, 266, 301, 308, 309
Waterfall, 43, 104, 182, 241, 242, 245, 250, 251
Watermelon, 189, 190, 214
Western Xia, 177, 181, 182, 185
Work permit, 7, 10
Wuyi, 88, 93, 98, 99, 102, 122, 148, 201

X

Xi'an, 37–53, 55, 58, 71, 104, 107, 143, 185, 285
Xining, 176, 204, 205, 207, 210, 212, 218, 237
Xinjiang, 134, 135, 169, 211, 212, 225, 234, 236, 239
Xuanzong, Emperor, 41

Y

Yang Guifei, 41
Yinchuan, 61, 176–178, 181, 183, 185, 187
Yuan, 60, 133, 143, 186

Z

Zhang Yimou, 42, 78, 184